# MAKING THE WORLD
# LIKE US

# MAKING THE WORLD LIKE US

EDUCATION, CULTURAL EXPANSION,
AND THE AMERICAN CENTURY

Liping Bu

Perspectives on the Twentieth Century
*Edward R. Beauchamp, Series Adviser*

 PRAEGER

Westport, Connecticut
London

**Library of Congress Cataloging-in-Publication Data**

Bu, Liping, 1960–
   Making the world like us : education, cultural expansion, and the American century /
Liping Bu.
     p. cm—(Perspectives on the twentieth century, ISSN 1538-9626)
   Includes bibliographical references and index.
   ISBN 0-275-97694-7 (alk. paper)
1. Educational exchanges—United States—History—20th century. 2. United States—Foreign
relations—20th century. I. Title. II. Series.
  LB2376.B8 2003
  370.116'0973—dc21    2002072819

British Library Cataloguing in Publication Data is available.

Library of Congress Catalog Card Number: 2002072819
ISBN: 0–275–97694–7
ISSN: 1538–9626

First published in 2003

Praeger Publishers, 88 Post Road West, Westport, CT 06881
An imprint of Greenwood Publishing Group, Inc.
www.praeger.com

Printed in the United States of America

The paper used in this book complies with the
Permanent Paper Standard issued by the National
Information Standards Organization (Z39.48-1984).

10  9  8  7  6  5  4  3  2  1

In memory of Ruth L. Farkas
and
to my parents

# Contents

# Illustrations

# Series Foreword

Whoever first coined the phrase, "When the siècle hit the fin," described the twentieth century perfectly! The past century was arguably a century of intellectual, physical, and emotional violence unparalleled in world history. As Haynes Johnson of the *Washington Post* has pointed out in his *The Best of Times* (2001), "since the first century, 149 million people have died in major wars; 111 million of those deaths occurred in the twentieth century. War deaths per population soared from 3.2 deaths per 1,000 in the sixteenth century to 44.4 per 1,000 in the twentieth."[1] Giving parameters to the twentieth century, however, is no easy task. Did it begin in 1900 or 1901? Was it, as in historian Eric Hobsbawm's words, a "short twentieth century" that did not begin until 1917 and end in 1991?[2] Or was it more accurately the "long twentieth century," as Giovanni Arrighi argued in *The Long Twentieth Century: Money, Power, and the Origins of Our Times*?[3] Strong cases can be made for all of these constructs and it is each reader's prerogative to come to his or her own conclusion.

Whatever the conclusion, however, there is a short list of people, events, and intellectual currents found in the period between the nineteenth and twenty-first centuries that is, indeed, impressive in scope. There is little doubt that the hopes represented by the Paris Exhibition of 1900 represented the mood of the time—a time of optimism, even utopian expectations, in much of the so-called civilized world (which was the only world that counted in those days). Many saw the fruits of the Industrial Revolution, the application of science and technology to everyday life, as having the potential to greatly enhance life, at least in the West.

In addition to the theme of progress, the power of nationalism in conflicts—not only over territory, but also economic advantage and intellectual dominance—came to characterize the last century. It was truly a century of war, from the "little" wars of the Balkans and colonial conflicts of the early 1900s to the "Great" War of 1914–1918 that resulted in unprecedented conflict over the remainder of the century.

Every century has its "great" as well as "infamous" individuals, most often men, although that too would begin to change as the century drew to a close. Great political figures such as Lenin, Trotsky, Stalin, Hitler, Mussolini, Churchill, the two Roosevelts, de Gaulle, Adenauer, Mahatma Gandhi, Mao Tse-tung, Ho Chi Minh, and others were joined in the last part of the century by tough competent women like Golda Meir, Indira Gandhi, Margaret Thatcher, and scores of others who took the reigns of power for the first time.

A quick listing of some major events of the century includes World War I, the Russian Revolution, the Rise of Fascism, the Great Depression of the 1930s, the abdication of Edward VIII, Pearl Harbor and World War II, the unleashing of atomic bombs on Hiroshima and Nagasaki, the long Indochina War, the Cold War, the rise of nationalism (with an increase in nation states from about fifty to almost two hundred), the establishment of Israel, the triumph of the free market, and increasingly strident battle between religious fanaticism and secular preferences, and on and on. At the same time that these events occurred, there was a great creative flourishing of mass entertainment (especially television and the Internet), no to mention important literary, dramatic, cinematic, and musical contributions of all kinds.

These elements incorporate some of the subject matter of this new series focusing on "Perspectives on the Twentieth Century," which strives to illuminate the last century. The editor actively seeks out manuscripts that deal with virtually any subject and with any part of our planet, bringing a better understanding of the twentieth century to readers. He is especially interested in subjects on "small" as well as "large" events and trends, including the role of sports in various societies, the impact of popular music on the social fabric, the contribution of film studies to our understanding of the twentieth century, and so on. The success of this series is largely dependent on the creativity and imagination of its authors.

*Edward R. Beauchamp*

## NOTES

1. Haynes Johnson, *The Best of Times: The Boom and Bust Years of America Before and After Everything Changed* (New York: A James H. Silberman Book, Harcourt, Inc., 2001), p. 3.

2. Eric Hobsbawm, *The Age of Extremes: A History of the World, 1917–1991* (New York: Pantheon, 1994).

3. Giovanni Arrighi, *The Long Twentieth Century: Money, Power, and the Origins of Our Times* (London: Verso, 1994).

# Preface

No matter where you travel today, either in Africa, Asia, or Europe, you are bound to see the symbolic dominance of American global influence—McDonalds fast food, Coca-Cola drinks, Levi jeans, Hollywood movies, and American military bases. Moreover, American ascendance as the world economic, military, and political power is also manifested in its role in shaping the international orders of the 20th century. But all of these subjects are not the focus of this book, because scholars have done an abundance of research in these areas. Instead, this study offers an in-depth look at the not-so-obvious but fundamentally vital aspect of American global expansion—the spread of American values and way of life via educational and cultural activities—that contributes to the making of the American century. It intends to help us understand how international cultural expansion adds, as a significant and inevitable element, to the American century.

This book does not argue that the world is like the United States, because the world is not. Rather, this book examines the efforts to spread American values, ideals, and practices in the world in the hope of making the world like the United States. The study concentrates on the roles played by religious organizations, philanthropies, professional associations, educational institutions, and the government in the promotion of the expansion of American culture via international educational and cultural activities in the 20th century. It shows the progression from private efforts to government commitment in spreading American cultural influence worldwide in three major phases: the pioneering missionary thrust, the cultural internationalists' outreach for world peace in the interwar years, and the state's promotion of cultural expansion for international power politics in the Cold War.

The subject of culture in U.S. international history is a less-researched area, although it is gaining increasing attention among scholars. Emily Rosenberg's *Spreading the American Dream* and Frank Ninkovich's *The Diplomacy of Ideas* are pioneering works that laid the foundation for scholars to further pursue the cultural theme in their studies. Recently, we have seen more scholarship on the cultural aspect of U.S. international relations, including Richard Pells' *Not Like Us,* Walter L. Hixson's *Parting the Curtain,* and Volker R. Berghahn's *America and the Intellectual Cold Wars in Europe.* In addition, a group of historians have contributed their latest works on cultural international relations to a collection entitled *The Cultural Turn* (edited by Frank Ninkovich and Liping Bu). From a different research angle, this study attempts a systemic interpretation of American cultural expansion in the course of American ascendance as an international power and superpower. Although the study mentions many American overseas programs, the primary focus of my research is not on activities abroad but on what was happening within the United States, especially the educational endeavors to train the "future leaders of the world." In undertaking this study, I was inspired by the concept of cultural internationalism put forward by historian Akira Iriye and the relation of power and culture (power/knowledge) interpreted by Michel Foucault. I am indebted to their works that informed my interpretation of the empirical data.

I choose to focus the examination on several major "institutional players" primarily for two reasons. First, all of these institutional groups served as the core driving forces for the expansion of American political and cultural values and practices. Second, it is simply impossible for a modest volume of this size to have a detailed discussion of the voluminous variety of cultural programs and activities conducted throughout those long decades. Specific programs of educational and cultural exchanges and evaluation of them, however, are discussed in detail along with foreign students' experiences in the examination of the various efforts made by each of the different institutional players. Despite such methodological approaches, this study is by no means an institutional history. Rather, it demonstrates the functions and inter-plays of state and society (mostly non-governmental organizations [NGOs] in this case) in the milieu of U.S. cultural international relations.

Some subjects such as the brain drain and the development of human capital in postwar international education are not discussed in this book for various reasons. If this study stimulates further research to enrich the subject of culture in historical studies, it will achieve its humble goals. This book would not have been possible without the generous cooperation and help of many archivists, whose kindness and hospitality made my research both productive and enjoyable. With deep gratitude and fond memories, I thank Dagmar Getz at the YMCA Archives, Thomas Rosenbaum at the Rockefeller Archive Center, Faith Coleman, Allen Divack, and Gloria Walters at the Ford

Foundation Archives, Kim Scott, Betty Austin, Michael Dabrishus, Nan Lawler, and Vera Ekechukwu at the Special Collections of the University of Arkansas Libraries, Clair McCurdy and David Ment at the Special Collections of Teachers College, Columbia University, William Massa at the Manuscripts of the Sterling Memorial Library, Yale University, and Martha Smalley at the Special Collections of the Yale Divinity School Library. Thanks also go to Hollee Haswell, Rhea Pliakas, Rebecca Abromitis, Marian Sylla, John Naughton, John Wells, Ralph W. Nicholas, Ben Mangan, Ellen Davis, Josiane Siegfried, Marianthi Zikopoulos, Edwin Battle, and Amy Yenkins.

Over the years, I have accumulated intellectual debts to various scholars and friends. I am particularly indebted to Peter Stearns, John Modell, and Steven Schlossman for their generosity of intellectual guidance and mentoring. I also benefited, as a graduate student at Carnegie Mellon University, from David Hounshell, Liz Cohen, Herrick Chapman, Kate Lynch, Mary Lindemann, and Donald Sutton. Portions of the early versions of the project were presented at the Applied History Seminar and the History Graduate Student Research Seminar at Carnegie Mellon, where faculty and fellow graduate students made constructive criticism and useful suggestions. I enjoyed the intellectual challenge and collegial warmth in the history department. Peter Rose of the American Studies Program at Smith College will be happy that my first major work is on America.

My thanks also go to Jay Chapin for fixing my computer problems, to my student assistant Scott Sawyer, and to the library staff at Alma College for their cheerful assistance.

Portions of the text were published as journal articles and book chapters. I am grateful for the generous permissions from various publishers. Heather Staines at the Greenwood Publishing Group provided patient help while I was completing the manuscript.

Many other people gave support and encouragement on different occasions. While I can't list them all, I'd like to thank Daniel Horowitz, Frank Ninkovich, Eugenia Kaledin, Marsha Wagner, Elinor Barbar, Pamela Ehrenkranz, Daniel DeWolf, Mary Mazur, Deborah Gershenowitz, and Stephen Lassonde. Former ambassador Ruth L. Farkas provided unwavering support of all kinds from the day she encouraged me to come to the United States for a Ph.D. degree to my fledgling start of a career in American academia. Although she did not live to see the book published, she would be proud of what I have done. Finally, I thank my parents with deep affection for their support. Their poems and letters across the Pacific provided the inspiring encouragement of the best kind.

# Abbreviations

| | |
|---|---|
| ACC | Association of Cosmopolitan Clubs |
| ACE | American Council on Education |
| AID | Administration of International Development |
| CEIP | Carnegie Endowment for International Peace |
| CFRFS | Committee on Friendly Relations among Foreign Students |
| CSCA | Chinese Student Christian Association |
| ECA | Economic Cooperation Administration |
| GEB | General Education Board |
| ICA | International Cooperation Administration |
| IEA | International Education Act |
| IEB | International Education Board |
| IES | International Educational Exchange Service |
| I-House | International House |
| IIA | International Information Administration |
| IIE | Institute of International Education |
| INS | Immigration and Naturalization Service |
| IRC | International Relations Club |
| KAPIS | Know America Program for International Students |
| LSRM | Laura Spelman Rockefeller Memorial Archives |
| NAFSA | National Association for Foreign Student Affairs |
| NGO | Non-governmental Organization |
| RAC | Rockefeller Archive Center |
| SVM | Student Volunteer Movement |

| | |
|---|---|
| T.C. | Teachers College |
| UNESCO | United Nations Educational, Scientific and Cultural Organization |
| USIA | United States Information Agency |
| VISIT | Ventures for International Students Interested in Travel |
| YMCA | Young Men's Christian Association |
| YWCA | Young Women's Christian Association |

# Introduction

From the Spanish-American War of 1898 to the end of World War II, the United States as an international power took a short span of fewer than 50 years to reach the zenith of a superpower, topping the world in economic, military, political, commercial, financial, technological, and cultural influences. The center of the world, accordingly, has moved to the United States, as key international organizations such as the United Nations, the World Bank, and the International Monetary Fund established their headquarters in the United States. Also, Wall Street has become the heart of the financial world.

In its short history of 200 years, the United States spent the first century making a nation of the United States in North America and the second century a superpower of the world. Scholars have tried to explain the ideological drive for the American expansion by pointing out the notion of the "City on the Hill," the belief of "Manifest Destiny," and the constant search for new frontiers to sustain economic development.[1] While the various ideological explanations help make sense of the robust outward reach of a young nation, a systemic discussion of the cultural expansion in this study further enriches the interpretation of 20th-century America and U.S. international history.

The spread of a particular culture was constantly seen in world history when a society attained the supreme position of power. The dominance of French culture in Europe during Louis XIV's France and the spread of Chinese culture in Asia during the Tang dynasty are just two examples. The spread of American cultural influence around the globe in the 20th century, however, had its unique features. Apart from the "invasion" of American pop culture—or more precisely, "pop entertainment"—in other societies, there was a conscious effort to "sell" American values and ways of life to the foreign elite, especially through educational means. From the missionary enterprises to the state-sponsored cultural relations programs, education was used as a vital channel to train the "future leaders of the world" with American values and ideals. Americans were sent abroad, and foreigners were brought to the United States for educational purposes—making America the center of both the dissemination of knowledge and the cultivation of political idealism. Knowledge—science, technology, and American know-how—empowers American prestige as a modern and advanced nation applicable as a model for other nations in their aspirations for success.

At various time periods in the 20th century, different core values of Americanism[2] were promoted throughout the world via educational and cultural programs. For instance, American missionaries emphasized Christian religious beliefs and the democratic values of American society in their evangelical missions abroad. American philanthropies and the secular cultural elite focused on modern sciences and American democracy as key ingredients for world peace and progress in their activism in international relations in the inter-war years. The U.S. government, when it assumed the leadership of promoting international educational and cultural activities after World War II, incorporated private institutions' efforts into a "total diplomacy" in the Cold War to project America as the ultimate choice of emulation for the world versus the Soviet model. These three major different forces for cultural expansion each played a leading role at different times to advocate and promote American values and practices worldwide. Each, however, had a different agenda of concerns and goals in their efforts. Religious leaders, secular cultural elite, philanthropic foundation officers, educators, and government policy makers did not always have the same emphases on their advocacy of American ways of life and American values. Conflicts of interests and tensions among them in terms of objectives and goals were inevitable to arise in the programs that aimed at expanding American cultural influence and making the world like the United States. Moreover, while American educational experiences liberalized the minds of the students from abroad who embraced the concepts of freedom, equality, and democracy, their existential experiences made them aware of the contradictions of those concepts in the daily life of American society. Interracial relations, religious freedoms, and nationalism were constant challenges in the exportation of Americanism that created tensions in the implementation of American educational and cultural exchange programs. The following chapters analyze the complexity that is inherent in this endeavor while discussing the enormous efforts made by each of these groups in spreading American political and cultural values.

The expansion of American culture into other continents started with the rise of the United States as an industrializing power. Christian organizations were the first major force that pushed American Christian values and practices abroad. In the 19th century, American churches of different denominations sent missionaries to Asia, Latin America, Africa, and the Middle East. The missionary enterprise was immensely increased and strengthened with the Student Volunteer Movement (SVM) for Foreign Missions and the globally positioned YMCA. The missionary thrust, which in a sense was a continuation of westward expansion, signified a worldwide commitment of American Protestantism to changing non-Christian societies with the gospel.

Education was one of the chief means that the missionaries used to create contact with and develop trust among native peoples in order to convert them to Christian beliefs. Missionaries built schools wherever they went, be it China, India, Brazil, South Africa, or Turkey. Moreover, missionaries sponsored promising young natives to come to the United States for Christian education so that they would become future leaders of Christianity in their homelands. Christian organizations not only introduced the students to American families and community organizations but also helped them form their own Christian associations. Christian leaders also encouraged the students to keep in constant contact with student and Christian movements back in their homelands to integrate them into the worldwide evangelical crusade.

The full participation of the United States in World War I brought the country into closer contact with other nations (especially the European nations) than ever before. As one of the winning powers, the United States attempted, for the first time in its history, to give the world a new order of self-determination and democracy with President Woodrow Wilson's Fourteen Points. Old European empires of France and Great Britain, however, though terribly wounded in the war, were still strong enough to block America's plan for a new world. Disappointed and disillusioned, the United States decided to go back to the tradition of non-entanglement, or in other words, to "return to normalcy." But segments of American society were not ready to beat a quick retreat from the international arena. The country had obviously emerged from the war as an economic powerhouse and political leader. With the unprecedented postwar prosperity and exuberance of American life, there was a growing confidence in American success as the model for the world. The educated elite (especially those on the East Coast), big businesses, and the powerful philanthropies were anxious to play an active role in international affairs to promote American trade and ideas for a new world order, although Congress and the U.S. government was determined to stay "un-entangled."

The educated elite were especially interested in promoting international cultural understanding via educational exchange as ways to shape people's world outlook and international goodwill. They believed that American democratic values and practices were crucial for the maintenance of world peace.[3] Historian Akira Iriye described the emphasis on the cultural approach to international relations as "cultural internationalism."[4] The international outreach of the cultural internationalists in the 1920s–1930s thus formed the second major force that pushed American cultural influence abroad.

New York City became the center of America's cultural internationalism while Washington was bent on isolationist policy in the 1920s. Lawyers, professors, magazine editors, and former statesmen of international minds usually met at the Columbia University Club to discuss their concerns of international relations and efforts to maintain world peace. A luncheon group of these people eventually evolved into the Foreign Policy Association. Moreover, the IIE (Institute of International Education) was created with the initiatives of three key figures—former Secretary of State Elihu Root, Columbia University President Nicholas M. Butler, and City College of New York Professor Stephen Duggan—to advance the flow of knowledge and to develop international cultural understanding. Ethnic groups of European origins were also active in helping develop cultural and educational exchanges between the United States and their motherlands. In the midst of this enthusiastic pursuit of cultural internationalism, faculty at Teachers College, Columbia University established an International Institute to offer educational assistance to many non-western countries in an effort to generate social progress in the world through democratic education.

All of these international educational and cultural programs were not possible without the financial support of American philanthropies. In fact, the American philanthropic endeavor for the advancement of humankind was first demonstrated by the medical and scientific emphases of the Rockefeller philanthropy and the peace emphasis of the Carnegie philanthropy. It should be noted that both of these philanthropic giants had intimate working relations with Christian groups. John D. Rockefeller (Sr. and Jr.) and Andrew Carnegie had close personal relations with Christian leaders, some serving as their advisors. Similarly, the philanthropies supplied financial support to Christian programs and projects.

American philanthropies were a unique private institution whose power of wealth has exerted unusual impact on the social and cultural developments in both the United States and the world. Their financial sponsorship of educational and cultural exchanges significantly facilitated the international flow of ideas and knowledge, intellectual cooperation and interaction, and the spread of American ideals and values. The Rockefeller philanthropy, which was keen on making direct links between scientific knowledge and human progress, created a large number of fellowships to facilitate the flow of scientific knowledge and human talent in the 1920s–1930s. As a private organization, or NGO, the Rockefeller philanthropy also worked with the League of Nations to cooperate with the league's health work, despite the U.S. government's official rejection of the League of Nations.

The Rockefeller philanthropy was the sole sponsor of the International Institute at Teachers College, Columbia University. The institute, which demonstrated a new effort at using American educational resources to influence foreign educational systems and social progress, performed the dual task of rendering direct educational assistance to foreign countries and providing professional training for selected foreign students as world educational leaders. Committed to spreading American democratic ideals and fostering international understanding and goodwill, the institute served as an intellectual base to extend American educational and cultural practices to the world. The international activism of American educators substantially influenced the educational reforms and developments in Asia, the Middle East, Latin America, and Africa.

The Carnegie and Rockefeller philanthropies were fundamental to the creation and operation of the IIE. Originally established as a department of the Carnegie Endowment for International Peace in 1919, the IIE gained independent status in the mid-1920s and administered various exchange programs primarily with European countries during the interwar years. With financial support from the Carnegie Corporation and the Laura Spelman Rockefeller Memorial, the IIE became the single most important private agency representing the United States in international educational exchange before World War II.

Unique about American philanthropies' roles in U.S. international relations was John D. Rockefeller, Jr.'s effort to sponsor an International House Movement in the 1920s–1930s to promote world peace and American diplomacy. Andrew Carnegie had previously supported the creation of the Committee on Friendly Relations Among Foreign Students to help expose the best of American civilization to foreign students and to stimulate Western ideals for world peace. Now, John D. Rockefeller, Jr. was strongly motivated by the belief that students were future leaders of the world who could do what guns and battleships could not in creating friendly relations among nations, especially friendly relations toward the United States. He donated nearly $10 million to build four major international houses in New York, Berkeley, Chicago, and Paris, respectively, with the aim to cultivate "brotherhood" among all races and nations. The International House Movement, which emphasized the spread of American ideals of democracy and American social and business practices, embodied a particular vision of international relations with American leadership. The liberal cultural internationalism of the International House Movement reflected the optimistic views of the 1920s that world peace and harmony could be maintained if people appreciated other cultures and if leaders of nations were friends who understood each other.

The active leadership of the big philanthropies and the intellectual elite in international cultural relations made a sharp contrast to the conspicuous absence of the state in this realm in the 1920s. Instead of playing the role of a cooperative state, as Emily Rosenberg discussed in regard to American commercial operations abroad,[5] the U.S. government was almost invisible in the international educational and cultural activities. Furthermore, the discriminative immigration laws of the 1920s actually hindered the development of international educational exchange. Private groups, however, tried to enlist the support of the state through personal friendship with government officials. For instance, John D. Rockefeller, Jr. invited Secretary of State Charles Evans Hughes as his friend to give a speech at the cornerstone ceremony of the International House New York in an attempt to inform the public of the supportive association of the government. Leaders of big philanthropies clearly believed that non-government institutions should serve an important purpose to stimulate and guide governmental effort through their initiatives and experiments when the government could not (or would not).

International cultural and educational operations remained an activity of the private sector until the U.S. government gradually became involved under President Franklin D. Roosevelt's "Good Neighbor Policy." In the 1930s, European governments—British, French, Italian, and German—carried on extensive cultural exchanges with Latin American countries.[6] Germany was especially active in expanding its cultural influence in Latin America by means of establishing German schools, libraries, and the exchange of students and scholars. The European expansion of influence in the Western Hemisphere seriously encroached upon "America's sphere of influence" and posed a challenge to the privileges of the United States and the Monroe Doctrine. The United States conducted very limited educational exchange with Latin American countries through private efforts. European cultural penetration in Latin America brought home to Washington the inadequacy of the traditional "dollar diplomacy" in expanding American influence and prestige. The U.S. government began to realize that a new set of cultural diplomacy was needed to counter European expansion and to retain U.S. dominance in the Western Hemisphere.

In 1936, when President Franklin Roosevelt called for a special "Inter-American Conference for the Maintenance of Peace" to discuss urgent matters among American republics, Secretary of State Cordell Hull headed a delegation to the conference in Buenos Aires and proposed "the facilitation by government action of the exchange of students and teachers."[7] Subsequently, Congress approved an agreement of educational exchange with Latin America. In a radical departure from its tradition, the United States government began to sponsor with federal grants cultural relations programs with Latin America via educational exchange.

It proved that the educational exchange with Latin America was a prelude to the U.S. government's commitment to worldwide cultural activities after World War II. During the war, the government increasingly expanded educational exchange programs with countries in East Asia and the Middle East. After the war, the government's cultural and educational programs accelerated with the Fulbright Act and the Smith-Mundt Act (the United States Information and Educational Exchange Act), which marked the total commitment to worldwide cultural exchange as an irrevocable component of American foreign policy. The Smith-Mundt Act initiated the unilateral emphasis of making the world understand the United States, instead of the traditional approach of a two-way street in educational exchange. The Fulbright Programs and the Smith-Mundt Act not only changed the pre-war situation where private-funding and advocacy were the primary sources for international educational and cultural operations, but they also pushed international educational activities on American campuses to a full-scale expansion. With the government taking the lead in promoting educational exchange came the third major force—the state—that pushed American cultural expansion worldwide.

The United States also asserted its world leadership through the Marshall Plan and the Truman Doctrine, whereby various economic and technical aid programs were established to help rebuild war-devastated Europe and to assist developing countries. These programs brought new meanings to educational exchange, which now covered a wide range of cultural, economic, technological, and military education activities. The term "educational exchange" became so inclusive that it was a synonym for cultural relations in Cold War America.[8] In order to win the hearts and minds of "future foreign leaders," the state (the federal government, especially via the State Department) urged universities to accept more foreign students although American campuses were already swamped with returned GIs. Large numbers of foreign students (broadly defined) were brought to the United States for training and study,[9] but they were expected to learn the American way of life and act as leaders, upon returning home, to shape public opinion and re-orient it toward favoring American policies. Whether a military alliance or a student exchange, it was all an important component in the "total diplomacy" of the Cold War.

In the competition with the Soviet propaganda, "educational exchange" became an important instrument to project favorable images of the United States—symbolized by its material affluence, consumerist culture, technological know-how, individual freedom, and political democracy. A unilateral approach to emphasize the exportation of American culture, values, technology, and products was increasingly employed, because the purpose of exchange was to make the world understand the United States. Since technical assistance, economic aid, and military defense were integrated in educational exchanges, the international operations of these programs helped spread not only American cultural influence but also its political and military power in the world. In the Cold War, educational exchanges were quickly incorporated into the state apparatus to boost American leadership of the "free world" against the Soviet-led "Communist world." Culture finally began to play an indispensable role of importance in American power politics of international relations. Philip Coombs, former Assistant Secretary of State for Education and Cultural Affairs, pointed out that educational exchange had become the "fourth dimension" of foreign policy—cultural, interwoven with the more traditional aspects, namely, political, economic, and military. Coombs characterized educational and cultural relations as "the human side" of foreign relations, because they focused on peoples, ideas, and values.[10]

The immediate political objectives of the Cold War shaped the government's interest in and policy of international educational exchange.[11] The U.S. government, which designed exchange programs with strategic goals in mind, would weigh each undertaking in view of its political impact on foreign policy. These considerations greatly affected the function of private institutions in educational exchange. The government not only relied on private institutions (universities included) for the implementation of exchange programs, but also desired a specialization of key national professional organizations in the field of educational exchange. As a result, the IIE was restructured while a new professional organization—the National Association for Foreign Student Affairs (NAFSA)—was established in order to effectively handle the expanding international cultural relations programs through student exchange. NAFSA played a crucial role in bringing about two related campus developments in the administration of educational exchange and foreign student affairs. One was the professionalization of foreign student advisors, and the other was the establishment of the office of international education on campuses. The movement to professionalize foreign student advising and to establish the office of international education was carried out with the support of the IIE, the State Department, and the Ford Foundation.

Philanthropic foundations began to play new roles in the postwar national thrust of worldwide educational exchanges. While the Rockefeller and Carnegie philanthropies continued to offer financial resources for new international programs at universities and to sponsor social science research on educational exchange and international relations, the Ford Foundation, as a newcomer, established a unique position of cooperation with the State Department to conduct international exchange operations. The Ford Foundation made sure that its programs fit well with government foreign policy objectives and supplemented, in various cases, government programs. The fact that many chief officers of the Ford Foundation had, at one point or another, worked for government programs or agencies helped facilitate such cooperation and collaboration. The Ford Foundation's exchange programs targeted foreign community leaders and public opinion shapers— journalists, businessmen, scientists, artists, and religious leaders—in bringing them over to the United States for training. As a private organization, the Ford Foundation could create programs and grants in areas where political sensitivity might hinder the potential candidates to come to the United States on the U.S. government ones.

In the Cold War, the government incorporated private efforts into a collaborative system where state imperatives commanded the private sector's planning, programming, and practice of cultural exchange. As one program officer mentioned, "Government program exercises a controlling influence over the exchange field and in a sense determines its character as well as its size and scope."[12] The guideline of government policy was "even if the government had the necessary resources it would still be desirable that private groups do the bulk of the work in this field."[13] Private institutions were urged to do what the government wanted. In such circumstances, some non-governmental organizations assumed more than the role of liaison between the public and the private sectors and functioned virtually as an extension or subsidiary of the state machinery. The integration of private institutions and professional organizations into the state scheme of cultural diplomacy and the emphasis on political returns of the exchange programs clearly demonstrated a corporate state in action.[14] Legislative mandate, state ideology, and the flow of leadership personnel among the government, big businesses, philanthropic foundations, think tanks, and even universities facilitated the function of a corporate state.

Different views of educational exchange existed among government policy makers, however, and so did the tensions between the government and various private groups. A variety of educators and old champions of cultural internationalism attempted to separate educational exchange from political propaganda in the early days of the Cold War, although their efforts resulted in a minimal impact on government policies. Still, something was changing. In the late 1950s, there was an increasing voice in the educational exchange field to urge a two-way street of exchange to make Americans understand the world while making other nations know about the United States. The 1961 Fulbright-Hays Act signified this shift from unilateral to mutual approaches of cultural exchange and understanding between the United States and the world. President Lyndon Johnson's attempt to extend "the Great Society" to the world through education brought international education in America to its peak. However, Congress was more interested in seeing the political results of educational exchange than the educational objectives of the programs— which was manifested by the frequent reduction of government funds for educational exchange and the significant increase of budget for information programs (propaganda). In the end, Congress failed to appropriate the funds as mandated by the 1966 International Educational Act, triggering an anti-climax in international education in the late 1960s. To most Congressional leaders, educational exchange was not an effective (or at least, not a fast) propaganda weapon in the war of images against the Soviet Union. Educational exchange for *educational* purposes hardly ever gained the committed support of the government.

In retrospect, international educational and cultural operations were closely intertwined with major concerns of American society at different times: ecumenical evangelism, international peace, foreign policy, and new definitions of the "national interest" in the Cold War. The programs fluctuated with changing international situations and domestic policy concerns. When these concerns (or any of them) corresponded with the overriding

American political priorities, domestically and internationally, the operations enjoyed support from both the private and public sectors. All those various players might be categorized as cultural internationalists in their approach, but their motivations and purposes differentiated them to such an extent that any one particular label seems inadequate to convey their true nature.

Looking at the private championship and the state leadership in promoting the spread of American culture in those decades, we see an inherent continuity of cultural expansion and the demonstration of manifest destiny throughout the 20th century.[15] The zeal to push American democracy in other parts of the world after World War II resembles such an intense similarity with the missionaries' evangelical passion that American educators abroad called themselves "educationaries." The Cold War created an environment where cultural expansion became a vital weapon to fight the propaganda war with the Soviet Union. Educational exchange facilitated the exportation of American ideas, values, ideology, technology, commerce, military defense, and our way of life. Moreover, with the perception of the Soviet danger to the American system, the American state justified itself in utilizing the expertise and resources of the private sector for political purposes and national security interests. The concerns of national security during the Cold War helped forge the cooperative relationship between the public and private sectors in building American power and influence in the world, although tensions existed among major groups because of their contention for different emphases and conflicting views of policy objectives.

## NOTES

1. Donald W. White, *The American Century: The Rise and Decline of the United States as a World Power* (New Haven, CT and London: Yale University Press, 1996).

2. Key components of Americanism include Christian religion, democracy, free enterprise, consumerism, and individualism.

3. Liping Bu, "Cultural Understanding and World Peace: The Roles of Private Institutions in the Interwar Years," *Peace & Change* 24, (April 1999): 148–171.

4. Akira Iriye, *The Cambridge History of American Foreign Relations* 3, ch. 7 (Cambridge University Press, 1993); *Cultural Internationalism and World Order* (Baltimore: The Johns Hopkins University Press, 1997).

5. Emily S. Rosenberg, *Spreading the American Dream* (New York: Hill and Wang, 1982).

6. For the educational and cultural exchange programs conducted by other governments, see Ruth E. McMurry and Muna Lee, *The Cultural Approach—Another Way in International Relations* (Chapel Hill, NC: University of North Carolina Press, 1947).

7. For more information about Inter-American Conferences, see J. Manuel Espinosa, *The Inter-American Beginnings of U.S. Cultural Diplomacy, 1936–1948* (Washington, D.C.: State Department, Bureau of Educational and Cultural Affairs, History Studies, U.S. Government Printing Office, 1976); Francis J. Colligan, "Twenty Years After: Two Decades of Government-Sponsored Cultural Relations," *The U. S. Department of State Bulletin* 39, (1958).

8. "Educational exchange" was long regarded as a synonym of cultural relations. According to Walter Johnson and Francis J. Colligan, it was first formally used in the Information and Educational Act of 1948 (the Smith-Mundt Act). It included all elements of cultural relation activities. Walter Johnson and Francis J. Colligan, *The Fulbright Program: A History* (Chicago: The University of Chicago Press, 1965), 19, 21*f.*

9. The term "foreign student" is broadly defined here to refer to any foreign national studying in the United States either as a regular student, a trainee, or as a short-term visitor.

10. Philip Coombs, *The Fourth Dimension of Foreign Policy: Educational and Cultural Affairs* (New York: Harper and Row, 1964), 6–7, 17.

11. Liping Bu, "Educational Exchange and Cultural Diplomacy in the Cold War," *Journal of American Studies* 33, no. 3 (December 1999), 393–415.

12. Melvin Fox, "Report on Exchange of Persons Activities of the Ford Foundation," (January 1953, Ford Foundation Archives Report 001567, 6).

13. U.S. Advisory Commission on Educational Exchange, "Report to Congress" (December 9, 1949).

14. For more information about corporatism as a useful device for interpretation, see Michael J. Hogan, "Corporatism: A Positive Appraisal," *Diplomatic History* 10, (Fall 1986), 363–372.

15. For more information about manifest destiny, see Anders Stephanson, *Manifest Destiny: American Expansionism and the Empire of Right* (New York: Hill and Wang, 1995).

# Part I

Before World War II

# Chapter 1

## Cultural Expansion: Missionary Thrust of an Ecumenical World

The American missionary movement beginning in the 19th century was the first major thrust of the expansion of American culture. As cultural agents, missionaries pushed American evangelical Protestantism and social gospel to countries in Asia, Latin America, and Africa. They assumed that by spreading the message of Christianity they were bringing social progress to those various societies, where they emphasized their moral leadership and Christian reform mission in their evangelical drive to conquer. This self-righteous sense of moral and reform leadership might very well have been strengthened by the racially and culturally degrading representation of the backward non-white "others" versus the advanced white "self" in post-Reconstruction America.[1]

Missionaries built schools, provided rudimentary medical care, and offered vocational training in foreign lands through which they introduced the native peoples to Christian beliefs and western concepts such as individualism and democracy. Education was one of the important means that missionaries effectively used to spread Christian beliefs in non-western countries. They believed that education would not only civilize the "backward natives" but also imbue them with Christian values and ideas. Moreover, missionaries sent young natives to the United States for a Christian education so that they would become indigenous leaders of

A different version of this chapter was published in the *Journal of American Studies* 35, no. 2 (2001), 217–237, with the title "The Challenge of Race Relations: American Ecumenism and Foreign Student Nationalism." Reprinted with the permission of Cambridge University Press.

Christianity in their homelands. Missionaries of different denominations tended to recommend students to the educational institutions with which they were affiliated. For instance, Methodist missionaries directed the students to educational institutions of the Methodist Church; the Presbyterians, Episcopalians, Catholics, and other denominations did likewise.[2] They hoped that the students, upon their completion of studies, would go back to their homelands to assume leadership in spreading Christianity. To the missionaries, a Christian education in the United States was a vital process for the training of indigenous Christian leaders.

The most widely cited examples of Christian-educated foreign students in the 19th century were Yung Wing from China and Joseph Hardy Neesima from Japan. In 1847, Yung Wing came to study in the United States with the support of the missionary he had worked with in China.[3] He first enrolled at Monson Academy, then entered Yale College in 1850, and graduated in 1854 with honor. Yung Wing returned to China in 1859 to spread Christianity while trying to persuade the Chinese government to send students to the United States. The Imperial Court of China finally approved his proposal in 1870 and sent a total of 120 young Chinese boys to America for their entire education from grade school to college. Many of them stayed in New England, where they quickly picked up the American way of life and became Christians.[4] Their assimilation into American culture shocked some Chinese officials, and in 1881 the Chinese government called all of the students home. But Jonathan Spence pointed out that the decision of the Chinese government to cut short the program was also triggered by the fact that the American government would not allow some of the Chinese students to enroll in West Point and the naval academy at Annapolis, as the Chinese government wished.[5] Although those students did not finish their education as planned and went back to China in disgrace, they nevertheless became the first engineers, technicians, railway builders, and mining experts in their homeland.[6]

Joseph Hardy Neesima was one of the first Japanese students educated in the United States. He came to America by working his passage on an American ship. The Boston ship owner sponsored him to study at Phillips Academy and Amherst College. He graduated from Amherst in 1870 and continued his final studies at Andover Theological Seminary. After that, Neesima went back to Japan and began teaching Christianity. Within a year, he founded the Doshisha University. Like Yung Wing in China, Neesima not only taught Christianity in his native country but also promoted the sending of Japanese students to the United States.[7]

By the early 20th century, thousands of foreign students—many of whom came from areas where American missionary activity was strong—were studying in the United States. But those young natives of other lands, especially the non-white ones, encountered racial prejudices and discrimination at public places such as restaurants, hotels, barber shops, and even on college campuses. They had difficulty in renting a room or freely mingling with ordinary Americans. They found that many Christian Americans did not practice the Christian love that American missionaries preached in their lands. Because two-thirds of foreign students came from regions where America sent missionaries, the experiences of these students in the United States became crucial for missionary undertakings abroad.

In an endeavor to improve the experiences of foreign students in this country, religious organizations, especially the YMCA-affiliated Committee on Friendly Relations Among Foreign Students (CFRFS), developed service programs and social activities to help foreign students. Programs such as the port-of-entry service, personal visits, group meetings, faculty advising, summer conferences, home hospitality, and the emergency fund not only helped students with many personal and financial problems but also created opportunities to increase the contact and communication between Americans and foreign students. These activities, although inspired by the vision of creating an ecumenical world, greatly influenced the lives of the students and later shaped the scope of services to educational and cultural exchanges in post-World War II America.

CFRFS also helped foreign students organize Christian associations according to their national origins, which included the Chinese Student Christian Association, the Japanese Student Christian Association, the Filipino Student Christian Movement, the Korean Student Federation, the Indian Student Organization, the Russian Student Christian Association, and the Latin American Student Organization. These student organizations, together with the CFRFS' service programs, were developed to help students adjust to American society and to foster ecumenical fellowship.

The educational experience of foreign students, therefore, had a direct impact on the work of the American missionary movement not only because the students were expected to become Christian leaders of their own countries, but also because it shaped their opinions of the United States with personal experience and firsthand observation of American society. Hence, the students presented both an opportunity and a challenge to American Christian organizations in the missionary endeavor. Despite the remarkable success of American Christian groups with the students, there were tensions between the YMCA's drive for ecumenical fellowship and the students' assertion of nationalism. The students' existential experience of racial discrimination generated their strong criticism of American racist practices both at home and abroad. Demand for equal relations among races appeared to be the focal point of their contention. The following section examines how American Christian groups, especially the Committee on Friendly Relations Among Foreign Students, influenced the social, intellectual, and spiritual lives of foreign students before World War II. It also discusses how western education and the existential experience of the students in American society led to the students' political liberalism and nationalism and their challenge of American racism.

## CHRISTIANITY, FOREIGN STUDENTS, AND WORLD PEACE

The migration of foreign students to the United States was intertwined with American missionaries abroad. Since the mid-19th century, American missionaries had been sponsoring young natives to the United States for Christian education. Information from the U.S. Bureau of Education indicated that in 1904, American universities enrolled 2,673 foreign students from 74 countries, excluding those studying at women's colleges.[8] The number of foreign students almost doubled by 1913.[9] Many of the non-white students, however, encountered racial discrimination and social alienation. Asian students, due to anti-Asian sentiments and the Chinese Exclusion Act, endured unpleasant experiences that began at the immigration stations even before they were allowed to enter America. There were numerous cases where Chinese students were detained for days or even weeks by immigration officials for investigation. Ailing Soong (who later became one of the powerful Soong sisters in China) came to the United States for education in 1904 but was prevented from entering the country in San Francisco because she was Chinese. Even though she was accompanied by an American missionary friend and her family had extensive connections in the United States, it did not help.[10] She was transferred from ship to ship for three weeks before missionaries helped solve the problem. Asian students generally found Americans indifferent to them, not to mention speaking to them. Their social alienation was reinforced by the denial of services at public places such as restaurants, hotels, barbershops, and theaters.[11] Many students who had been inspired to come to America by missionaries became quickly disillusioned. They wrote their missionary teachers and friends, and their families and relatives, complaining that they were discriminated against in America and that they had a limited opportunity for social contact with Americans. They even warned incoming fellow students to keep aloof in the United States.[12]

The students' description of their unpleasant experiences contradicted what missionaries had said about the United States. Their unfavorable opinions of America threatened to undo the work of missionaries and posed a new challenge to American missions abroad. It appeared that the missionaries' endeavor to train indigenous leaders via American Christian education was turning into a disservice to American missions. In addition to racial prejudice and discrimination, the students also had difficulties in social, psychological, and academic adjustments as well as financial problems. These problems required the special attention of university administrators, who lacked the incentives and facilities to meet the needs of foreign students at the time. A survey conducted in 1910–1911 by the Association for the International Interchange of Students indicated that a large number of universities in the United States, Canada, and Great Britain expressed only mild interest in foreign students although the flow of students to these countries was increasing. Universities were most reluctant to grant fellowships and scholarships to students from abroad.[13]

Under such circumstances, Christian leaders began to hammer out programs to meet the needs of foreign students. Their efforts, which were motivated by the need to tackle the unforeseen student challenge to Christian missions abroad, aimed to improve the students' experiences in the United States. John R. Mott, General Secretary of the World Student Christian Federation and the YMCA International Committee, attempted to sensitize American college students to the problems of their fellow students from abroad. He appealed to them "to follow and service those in loneliness." Mott was a long-time leader of the international student Christian movement. He began his prominent career as a visionary leader of the student Christian movement when he was a student at Cornell University.[14] At the 1886 Mount Hermon Meeting, the first international Christian student conference held in the United States, he was chosen to be part of a delegation to travel across the country making appeals to college students for volunteering in foreign missions. Thousands of students responded to the appeal, and leaders of the Intercollegiate YMCA immediately directed the enthusiasm into a Student Volunteer Movement (SVM) for Foreign Missions. Representatives of the Intercollegiate YMCA and YWCA and the Interseminary Missionary Alliance formed an executive committee of the SVM, and Mott was made chairman of the committee in 1888. From then on, Mott undertook the task of integrating student Christian movement into the life of the YMCA as a whole.[15]

In the 1890s, Mott made various world tours to promote the international student Christian movement. During his visits, he noticed the increasing migration of students from country to country and realized their potential for world Christianity. At the same time, he became aware of the plight of these students in foreign lands and their urgent need for help. Deeply concerned with the special problems that the Chinese students had in the face of racial discrimination and social alienation, Mott mobilized campus and local YMCAs to contact and help the Chinese students. Local YMCAs began to enlist every Chinese student in Bible study. The State Committee of the YMCA of Michigan, for example, planned a Bible institute during summer holidays with the hope of getting a large number of Chinese students to attend. Later, when the political upheavals in China in 1911–1912 made financial support uncertain from their home government, Chinese students became very anxious. Some even quietly left universities when their funding was cut off. Local YMCAs extended help to prevent the Chinese students from leaving universities. University campuses also made special efforts to help the students. At Cornell, a fund of student loans was used to solve the temporary financial difficulties of Chinese students; at Wisconsin and Michigan, the matter was even brought to the attention of the Board of Regents.[16]

In the years before the outbreak of World War I, the Peace Movement became popular in American society. Businessmen who were enthusiastic about the cause of peace spearheaded the movement by providing strong financial support. Edward Ginn, the Boston textbook publisher, endowed the World Peace Foundation with a third of his wealth. Andrew Carnegie endowed and helped organize the Carnegie Endowment for International Peace in 1910. Moreover, in an effort to recruit churches to the Peace Movement, Carnegie supported the organization of the World Alliance for Promoting International Friendships through the Churches. In 1914, he endowed $2 million for the Church Peace Union, which included Protestants, Catholics, and Jews.[17] The Peace Movement greatly impacted student life, making American college students increasingly aware of international events. College branches of the YMCA emphasized the goal of international brotherhood and friendship on campuses. They "urged representatives of Christianity in heathen lands to pay special attention to their role as international interpreters and as mediators between Orient and Occident, between the tropics and the North."[18]

Inspired by the ideals of international peace, a movement of Cosmopolitan Clubs began to spread on American campuses in the early 20th century. With the help of the American Peace Society, Louis Lockner, a journalist by profession but a peace advocate by choice, played a leading role in organizing the Cosmopolitan Clubs Movement.[19] The first Cosmopolitan Club was formed at the University of Wisconsin in 1903 with both American and foreign students as active participants. In a few years, it developed at various campuses and was then federated into a national organization in 1907 called the Association of Cosmopolitan Clubs (ACC) of the United States of America. The ACC was also affiliated with the European student organization, Confédération Internationale des Étudiants. Holding up to the motto, "Above all nations is humanity," the Cosmopolitan Clubs aimed at developing in the world "the spirit of human justice, cooperation, and brotherhood, and the desire to serve humanity unlimited by color, race, nationality, caste, or creed, by arousing and fostering this spirit in college and university students of all nationalities."[20] Encouraged and supported by peace activists such as Edwin D. Mead and Edward Ginn, who believed that educational work for peace was most effective among youth, student leaders of the Cosmopolitan Clubs set up international forums, and as one scholar acknowledged, "welded the Cosmopolitan Clubs into an explicit instrument for promoting international understanding and world peace."[21]

The Cosmopolitan Clubs, which were popular among both foreign and American students, were recognized and encouraged by campus authorities. Each individual campus, however, ran its own programs for the clubs. Popular topics of the clubs included international relations, U.S. government and political parties, governments and economic conditions of other countries, youth movements of different countries, and habits and customs of different peoples. Those discussion forums mutually broadened the vision of American and foreign students. Americans came to respect the views of foreign students and the citizenship of other lands while foreign students increased their understanding of American ways of political campaigns and the legislative functions of the U.S. government.[22] Through the activities of the Cosmopolitan Clubs, foreign students not only kept in constant contact with American students but also became participants in the American Peace Movement to promote the spirit of internationalism.

Although the ACC was not a religious organization, it had close interactions with the YMCA and YWCA on campuses. In 1924, the National Association of the Cosmopolitan Clubs had about 1,500 foreign student members from Europe, Asia, South America, Africa, and Canada—many of whom were also members of the YMCA and YWCA. The clubs also had men's, women's, and co-ed chapters in 31 educational centers and institutions, which encouraged alumni memberships to further the friendships forged at colleges.[23] This student organization contributed to promoting international cultural understanding and friendship, although its influence was limited to several dozen campuses. In the years immediately after World War I, the clubs enjoyed the greatest success—having about 50 chapters across the country.

But ACC had its problems as a national organization. Different views of world conflict engendered tensions within the organization and aggravated its internal politics. Various groups vied with one another for control of the national association to assert their own agenda. One critic pointed out, "nothing common held them fast to the national association."[24] In the eventful 1910s, national conventions of the ACC were often scenes of political riots. It was little wonder that by the 1940s, memberships of the ACC had shrunk drastically and practically had little influence on foreign students.[25] Cosmopolitan Clubs on individual campuses, however, continued to be active after the national association ceased to function. One important outgrowth of the Cosmopolitan Clubs movement was the International House movement, which we will discuss in Chapter 3.

Peace and missionary movements greatly stimulated Americans' interest in foreign students and foreign countries. In the summer of 1911, the Committee to Promote Friendly Relations Among Foreign Students (later changed to the Committee on Friendly Relations Among Foreign Students) was organized in New York City under the auspices of the YMCA with John Mott as its general secretary. For years, Mott had been contemplating a plan to "wage a campaign" among thousands of Chinese students in Japan, the United States, and Europe as "part of his vision of winning all of China for Christ through its future leaders."[26] He believed that American educational influence would shape the thinking of the youth and win their sympathy, if not loyalty, to Christianity. For Mott, the future of a nation lay in the youth, and nothing was more important than winning the young students for the

Christian cause. His vision of shaping a nation's future through its students gradually broadened from one group—Chinese students—to students from all countries who came to study at colleges and universities in North America. Mott once wrote:

My world-wide travels have shown me that in Latin-America and Asia, quite as much as in Europe and the United States the schools and universities are the strategic points. From them come a vastly disproportionate number of the statesmen, editors, teachers, professional men and others who exert the great influence upon thought and action.[27]

As part of his global plan of reaching students for Christianity, Mott tried to bring the work of foreign students under the supervision of a special organization. The founding of the Committee on Friendly Relations Among Foreign Students brought his long-range plan into a concrete form.

## JOHN R. MOTT AND THE CREATION OF CFRFS

The formation of CFRFS indicated the beginning of a unique effort of American Christian organizations to win the hearts of foreign future leaders to Christianity. The story of how the committee was created also illustrated Mott's shrewd entrepreneurship in setting up an organization for his cause. According to Basil Mathews, Mott's biographer, one day in April 1911, Mott met Cleveland H. Dodge, chairman of the International Committee of the YMCA in New York, and talked about the challenge of solving problems of the increasing number of foreign students in the United States. Mott spoke of the need to make the situation known to individuals who were in a position to help. Dodge mentioned Andrew Carnegie, whom Mott said he had never met.

"I will take you to Andy now," said Dodge. They immediately went to Carnegie's residence on Riverside Drive. Carnegie was out but soon came home in golf clothes and in an irritable mood. He had lost the game. Sitting down with a thud on the sofa, he exclaimed, "Lord, what a day!"

"I have brought you a man you ought to know," Dodge said as he began to introduce Mott. Carnegie cut in, "What has he got to say to us?" Mott went straight ahead and talked about the large and rapidly increasing numbers of foreign students, their problems, and their potentials for promoting world peace and Christianity. Mott emphasized the urgency of meeting their needs.

"You've got a charmer here," said Carnegie to Dodge. Turning to Mott, he questioned, "Why are you giving your life to such work? You are wasting your time." Then he demanded, "What is your plan?" Mott explained that he would locate capable men at universities the world over where large numbers of foreign students clustered, and through them he would provide a means to expose foreign students to the best side of Western civilization, good comradeship, and stimulating ideals. He hoped that Carnegie would make a gift of $10,000 a year for at least two or three years to implement his plan. Carnegie responded that if Dodge gave such a sum, he would too. Dodge immediately accepted the challenge. On their way back to Dodge's home, they happened to see George Perkins, a leading figure in the United States Steel Corporation. After hearing their story, Perkins joyfully offered, "That's talking some, if you have got Carnegie to come across there must be something in the proposition. You ought to let me in on it. I will give you another ten thousand."

The following night, Mott was sitting next to William Sloane at a committee meeting in the Union League Club. After he told Sloane what had happened the previous day, Sloane said, "Let me add eight thousand dollars to that."[28]

Mott had a unique way of approaching prospective donors. In his opinion, many people did not have the special gift of advocacy but could give a point of contact and create confidence for the man who could present a cause. He lost no time using the influence of those people to open the doors to wealth for a specific cause. The experience of securing in two days practically the entire fund necessary to start his organization for foreign student affairs was a typical example of his strategy.[29] With the money available, Mott began organizing the committee with Cleveland H. Dodge as the chairman and treasurer and Willard Lyon, who had just returned from a distinguished career with the YMCA in China, as the executive secretary. Gilbert A. Beaver, a long-time associate with YMCA student work, volunteered to give full time to the organizational and administrative duties of the committee until a full-time salaried director was found. Beaver and Mott served as secretaries of CFRFS for years while Mott, at the same time, was also secretary of the International Committee of YMCA and held leading positions with several other organizations such as the International Missionary Council and World Council of Churches. Other people involved in the initial stage of CFRFS' work included Elihu Root, John W. Foster, Sir Edward Grey, and Andrew D. White, who were all influential figures in international affairs.[30]

The aim of the CFRFS was "to promote sympathetic and helpful relations between Americans and the foreign students—especially those coming from the Orient, the Near East, and Latin America; to influence the character, spirit, and attitude of the future leaders of these Oriental and Latin American nations; and to bring the educated young men and young women of these different lands under the best influences of the Western Christian nations."[31] CFRFS emphasized that "in the early stages the scope of work of the Committee should be confined largely on behalf of Chinese students...who are studying in North America, Europe, Japan...and in China itself."[32]

The committee's emphasis on Chinese students, however, was not so much determined by the urgent needs of Chinese students as by the plan to evangelize China and the special opportunity to do so present in China at the

time. First of all, the Boxer Rebellion in 1900, which was put down by the
joint forces of imperialist powers,[33] had a great impact on American missions
in China. China's defeat resulted in more Western penetration and a payment to the powers of an indemnity of $334 million in gold, including $25
million to the United States.[34] This amount of the indemnity was widely
viewed as exorbitant. Some American missionaries argued that the money
could be remitted to China for better use, namely to bring Chinese students
to the United States for education. Arthur H. Smith of the American Board
of Foreign Missions conferred with Lyman Abbott and his son, Lawrence
Abbott, who was the powerful editor of *The Outlook*, an influential foreign
affairs periodical, about the idea of suggesting to the U.S. government to
return a sizable portion of the Boxer Indemnity to the Chinese government
for educational purposes. The young Abbott talked about the suggestion
with Secretary of State Elihu Root, who arranged an appointment for him
with President Theodore Roosevelt. The President was receptive to the idea,
and a bill was later passed for the return of Boxer Indemnity money in the
amount of $12,700,000 to China for educational purposes.[35] President
Theodore Roosevelt referred to the good that the fund would do: "This
nation should help in a very practicable way in the education of the Chinese
people so that the vast and populous Empire of China may gradually adapt
itself to modern conditions. One way of doing this is by promoting the coming of Chinese students to this country and making it attractive to them to
take courses at our universities."[36]

With the "Boxer Fund," the Chinese government was instructed to "send
to America 100 students a year for five years and thereafter 50 students a year
arriving over a period of 29 years."[37] The agreement between the two governments also indicated that the students were to remain in the United States
from five to nine years. The "Boxer Fund" began to flow to China in late
1908, and a Qinghua College was set up in 1909 as a preparatory school for
prospective students. American personnel from missionary groups were
selected to be in charge of the preparation of the Chinese students for their
study in the United States. Student nominees had to pass competitive imperial examinations in the English language, literature, mathematics, physics,
Latin, and ancient history. In addition, they were required to have a thorough grounding in Chinese history and literature. The program of the
"Boxer Fund" was not incompatible with the overall modernization urge in
China. Indeed, it fit well with the growing Chinese enthusiasm to learn from
the West to strengthen China. As a result, the number of Chinese students
in America increased from about 80 in 1905 to nearly 800 in 1911.[38] The
"Boxer Fellowship" students continued to come to the United States for the
next 20 years, during which thousands of Chinese studied at and graduated
from American universities.

Secondly, the 1911 Revolution suddenly turned an imperial China into a
republic. Radical changes were taking place, and China was groping for the

future. This period brought about revolution and chaos. John Mott estimated, "At present China is plastic but will soon become fixed like plaster.
Shall she set in moulds of militarism, gross materialism and racial antagonism, or of good will, idealism and helpfulness? This question will be
answered in the near and not in the distant future. But by whom?"[39]
American Christian missions assumed that they should be the agents to
shape the future of China. John Mott and his associates firmly believed that
ideas and ideals must first take hold of the students in schools, colleges, and
universities in order to influence a nation or a people. They often cited the
German proverb "What you would put into the life of a nation put into its
schools" to demonstrate their faith in education as an essential means to
change a society. Mott once told Carnegie, "If we influence on right lines the
ideas, spirit and practices of the men who are to become the legislators,
statesmen, jurists, editors, authors, teachers, doctors, engineers and other
leaders of thought and action, we determine the destiny of a nation or people." He emphasized six major points why China fit especially well into this
educational scheme for Christian evangelism. He mentioned, among other
things, the long tradition of China where scholars ruled, China's uncertainty
of its future at the moment, China's vast land and population, and the traits
of the Chinese people that were compatible with Christian values—"industry, frugality, patience, tenacity, great physical and intellectual vigor, independence, and conservatism." Mott even thought that the Chinese "are the
Anglo-Saxons of the Orient."[40]

In China, leaders of the new republican government also placed high
hopes on Chinese students abroad. Many government officials received their
own education abroad, and American influence was strong among them.
Tang Hua Lung, leader of the Lower House of the Republic of China, mentioned in his letter to Chinese students in America, "It is the supreme duty
of the Chinese students in the United States to try faithfully to give us an
accurate interpretation of the word 'republic.' They must not neglect studying the republican principles, they should pay attention to the causes of the
success and the failures of the American Republic, so that when they return
they can inject into the minds the true republican spirit."[41] Believing that the
United States was one of the best examples of a republic, Tang continued,
"The United States can do China no greater service than to furnish our students with all the possible opportunities which will enable them to see, learn
and imbibe the spirit of liberty, freedom and equality."[42]

When dozens of young Chinese came to the United States every year for
education on Boxer Fellowships, CFRFS coordinated their journeys within
the United States. For instance, 71 Boxer Fellowship students were sent to the
United States in 1912 despite the unrest in China. At the suggestion of
Willard Lyon, the "Y" leader in China, the China YMCA placed its secretaries
at the ports of Shanghai and Tianjin to assist the students en route
to the United States. The "Y" secretaries secured passports and steamer

accommodations for the students, advised them on appropriate dress and appearance, and discussed American customs with them. At the same time, on this side of the Pacific CFRFS arranged for local "Y" secretaries to welcome the students when they arrived in San Francisco. The secretaries also accompanied the students through immigration stations in order to reduce possible unpleasant delays there. CFRFS representatives then traveled with them to their destinations in the East. CFRFS organized activities and programs to provide the Chinese students with opportunities to meet Americans. The port-of-entry service was gradually extended to other foreign student groups, such as the Japanese, Koreans, Indians, and Latin Americans, as CFRFS developed working relations with these national groups of students.

Back in 1908, John Mott and W. W. Lockwood, general secretary of the YMCA of Shanghai, had helped T. C. Wang organize a Chinese Student Christian Association (CSCA) of North America. Wang was a student at Yale who later became Minister of Foreign Affairs of the Republic of China. CSCA received partial funding from the Foreign Division of the YMCA of North America. By the time CFRFS was established, CSCA had about 800 members. The two organizations established a close working relationship, with CFRFS providing CSCA with organizational guidance and financial support for activities and publications.[43] Their cooperation lasted for more than 40 years before it ended on an unpleasant note in 1953, complicated by the Cold War. Other national organizations of foreign students, such as the Japanese, Korean, and Filipino Christian Student Associations, were later formed and became affiliated with CFRFS just as CSCA did.

During the Peace Movement, CFRFS adjusted its work toward international peace. Mott planned to launch an educational campaign in colleges and universities for world peace, just as the Church Peace Union was doing among churches in the world. Andrew Carnegie was much attracted to Mott's plan and promised $25,000 as support "to advance the cause of peace and good will between the nations and races of the world through promoting right ideals and relations among students and educators."[44] The principal means to carry out the plan included the use of literature (pamphlets, books, and periodicals), intercollegiate and international lectures by qualified men in institutions and at conferences, and visits by deputation and specially appointed representatives. Mott also proposed the use of existing agencies wherever possible to save expenses and to secure the largest results.[45] The outbreak of World War I, however, prevented Mott from taking a worldwide tour of his educational peace campaign. Carnegie thought that because the conditions had changed "it would be unavailing to send forth [peace] missionaries at this time." He nonetheless sent CFRFS the final installment of the promised fund for its satisfactory performance under the contract.[46]

In order to effectively coordinate services for foreign students, CFRFS maintained correspondence with missionaries and educators abroad, faculty at colleges and universities at home, and foreign students themselves. CFRFS initially used the nationality approach to help students get connected at different educational institutions. For instance, students of Chinese nationality were put in touch with their own country fellows in other universities through publications and summer conferences. CFRFS also took the initiative to interest faculty members to counsel Chinese students and encourage professors and citizens of the college communities to invite them into their homes from time to time. CFRFS first concentrated the nationality approach on foreign students on the East Coast and then spread the strategy to students in the Midwest and on the West Coast. Moreover, foreign students were introduced to American people and American life through Bible classes and forums of Cosmopolitan Clubs and through student volunteers and missionary societies.

After a few years of experimental work with various national groups of foreign students, Willard Lyon, Charles Hurrey, and two other "Y" secretaries held a conference at Northfield, Massachusetts in the summer of 1914. They outlined a few strategies for YMCA secretaries to work with foreign students. First, American Christian students were encouraged to consider the work of winning the friendship of foreign students as a service of far-reaching results. The friendship of Americans with foreign students, however, should *not* be professional but rather natural and cordial. They suggested that in conversation with foreigners, the achievements of the race in question rather than their failures should be stressed, using welcoming topics such as their natural resources, industries, commercial enterprises, educational policies, and so on. They warned the secretaries not to make remarks or ask questions that reflected unfavorably upon the political, social, moral, or religious conditions in the countries from which the foreign students came. Secondly, they suggested that the secretaries should show the best of American life to foreigners, who often saw enough of the other side without any help. This goal could be achieved by inviting foreigners to meals, taking them on hiking trips, calling on them in an informal and friendly way, and making them feel that they were worthy friends. Classes on American etiquette—etiquette of the street, of calling, of dress, of meals, of correspondence, and so on—were suggested as one way to help foreigners better adjust to the American way of life.[47] The secretaries were also urged to mobilize commercial clubs of neighboring cities, to invite foreign students to visit their cities, and to allow them to see their industries. Thirdly, "Y" committees should be organized of (and for) foreign students everywhere to provide Bible classes and daily association for the presentation of the positive side of Christian religion while recognizing the good in other religions. Moreover, foreign students were recommended as occasional speakers for mission study classes and given opportunities to make public presentations of their own countries. Leaders of CFRFS believed that such interactive programs would both promote a better understanding on the part of American students and make good use of foreign students at the same time.[48] These strategies later became the guiding policies of CFRFS in directing "Y" secretaries' work with foreign students.

## INTEGRATING FOREIGN STUDENT ORGANIZATIONS INTO CFRFS

In 1915, the Executive Board of CFRFS appointed Charles Hurrey as general secretary when Willard Lyon had to return to China. Hurrey had been the executive secretary of the Student Department of the YMCA of North America and had been in active contact with CFRFS. He also had a distinguished missionary career in Latin America, where he had gained an acute understanding of Latin American peoples and their cultures. This experience gave him an extra edge in working with Latin American students, who had proven to be most difficult for CFRFS to organize and win over. Most Latin American students were sponsored by their governments, and they had considerable restrictions regarding their social and political responsibilities. All Latin American students were Roman Catholics and were very skeptical, if not openly antagonistic, toward the Protestant denominations.[49] Hurrey proved to be a dynamic leader when he pushed for changes in CFRFS in the 1920s–1930s.

The first major effort of Hurrey's administration was to restructure CFRFS. In early 1917, Hurrey made two fundamental suggestions to John Mott. First, CFRFS should be an organization of its own with the special task of promoting friendly relations with foreign students and visitors, rather than a subcommittee under the International Committee and the Student Department of the YMCA.[50] Second, CFRFS should include foreign women students in its programs to make a comprehensive appeal to the whole foreign student population. Hurrey argued that CFRFS should enlist the support of many more women and subsidize women's work in all cases, because "much of our service is promoted through social life and the home." In this respect, CFRFS needed female board members nominated by the YWCA and a secretary for women students.[51] Moreover, CFRFS began to appoint regional secretaries and local representatives to coordinate foreign student service programs across the country. CFRFS also reached out to seek cooperation with other organizations such as peace societies, bureaus of foreign and domestic commerce, home and foreign mission boards, and colleges and universities.

When World War I broke out, many foreign students were stranded in the United States without money from home countries while at the same time more foreign students were coming to the United States because the war prevented them from enrolling in European universities. Officials from a variety of institutions—universities and colleges, churches, The Red Cross, the Rockefeller Foundation, and CFRFS—held a series of meetings to discuss the special problems of the students "displaced" by the war. Assisting the displaced students thus became a priority of emergency for CFRFS. Hurrey traveled more than 8,000 miles in 1917 to campuses where large numbers of foreign students stayed.[52] His interviews with the students and school administrators indicated that the immediate need of the students was emergency financial assistance. Students also expressed their need for help at the port-of-entry and for more contact with American people. Making use of its wide institutional network, CFRFS skillfully mobilized other sources to provide assistance. Organizations such as the World Student Christian Federation, Pax Romana, the Cosmopolitan Clubs, and the National Council of Churches of the United States and Canada were all enlisted in this effort.

After World War I, the United States emerged as an educational center for world students. CFRFS leaders reviewed that several factors, in addition to the war devastation in Europe, motivated foreign students to come to the United States. First, "the awakening Orient" led the students of Japan, China, and Korea to come to the United States to seek scientific knowledge and Western learning in general. Secondly, the increasing ties between the North and South Americas led many Latin American governments to send students to the United States. Thirdly, the rising spirit of nationalism influenced students to seek the best possible education abroad in order to help strengthen their own countries. Fourth, growing specialization in all fields of disciplines stimulated ambitious students to excel in their chosen profession by studying with the best experts in their fields. And finally, scholarships provided by foundations, educational agencies, and governments further facilitated students from various countries to come and study in America as part of the efforts to strengthen their national industrial development and education and so on.[53]

As the numbers of foreign students in America increased to 7,000 in 1921, leaders of Christian organizations, particularly those who worked in the international field and the student department of the YMCA, were concerned with "what impression these students would have of American Christian civilization" and "how Americans could help sharpen their intellectual capacity and build up their Christian character."[54] Hurrey saw the students as a great challenge as well as a unique asset to the Christian cause. He asked, "Why should we send missionaries to their lands and neglect their students now with us? Why not win now, hundreds of these selected leaders to Christian life and service on behalf of their people?"[55] Like John Mott, Hurrey considered students an important force that should not be neglected in world evangelization, because they "soon would occupy positions of large influence and responsibility in their own countries." He argued that although a large number of them were not Christians, they were sympathetic with the Christian spirit and also "open-minded to the teachings of Christ." Some came with "exalted ideas concerning the moral and spiritual life" of American people, others with "suspicion and prejudice about the motives of our democracy."⁵⁶ The challenge, thus, was as significant as the opportunity.

CFRFS considered its responsibility to help the students adjust to American life—social, religious, industrial, and political. CFRFS leaders believed that they could make a difference if they helped the students get the best out of American society. The fundamental aim of CFRFS since its inception had been to facilitate the Christian character building of foreign students. It emphasized the importance of "promoting sympathetic and helpful relations between foreign students and Americans" and of "influencing their character and spirit" so that "when they returned to their homelands they would be truly friendly toward the American people and more useful citizens in their own lands."⁵⁷ In order to make the service more effective in light of the fast-growing foreign student population after the war, CFRFS leaders agreed that local Christian student associations must carry out the work with foreign students in colleges and universities. They also realized that foreign student leadership should be used in the work with local associations and that all the resources of goodwill and helpfulness in the college community should be utilized, particularly the homes, churches, and civic organizations.⁵⁸ Foreign students as a group generally received sporadic assistance from church organizations, particularly the foreign missionary societies, but missionary societies had no systemic program to assist foreign students.

CFRFS officials used the following working methods to build friendship between foreign students and Americans as well as bringing the non-Christian foreign students to positive Christian beliefs. First, they mobilized American students to make personal friends with foreign students, to bring them to summer conferences during vacations, and to enroll foreign students in campus discussion groups on international affairs. Second, they published comprehensive guides in English and Spanish for prospective foreign students from Asia and Latin America. Third, they increased the interest of colleges and universities in offering scholarships to capable foreign students and brought the critical financial needs of foreign students to the attention of all those who were in a position to help.⁵⁹

In the meantime, CFRFS began to integrate foreign student organizations into its own administrative system so that they could conveniently exchange information and ideas on a regular basis. CFRFS appointed foreign student leaders as student secretaries on the staff. But these student secretaries were often paired with American "Y" secretaries who had returned from particular foreign countries. For instance, CFRFS had two student secretaries specifically in charge of the Chinese Student Christian Association: one was an American "Y" secretary returned from China, and the other was a Chinese student leader of CSCA. For the Japanese students, Mr. Kato, leader of the Japanese Christian Student Organization, was appointed as the student secretary, working with the 1,000 Japanese students in the United States. The two secretaries for Latin students included one American "Y" secretary who had returned from Latin America and one Latin American student leader. Their job was to meet Latin American students at the port of entry and keep in touch with them via correspondence.[60] In the 1920s, student secretaries were also appointed for other national groups such as the Koreans, the Filipinos, and the Russians.

The creation of student secretaries as part of CFRFS staff went hand in hand with the formation of various foreign student Christian organizations. After years of work with the YMCA at summer conferences and cooperation with CFRFS, foreign students organized their own Christian associations according to national origins. These organizations included the Japanese Student Christian Association, the Filipino Student Christian Movement, the Korean Student Federation, the Russian Student Christian Association, the Indian Student Association, the Armenian Student Association, and the Latin American Student Organization. These associations served as the national organizations of their fellow students. CFRFS had provided financial support to these organizations and urged foreign students to interpret their home cultures to American people as an exchange of cultural experiences. It emphasized that good understanding between America and foreign countries should involve true friendship rather than just formal receptivity on either side.

All the foreign student Christian associations were headquartered in New York City with CFRFS and staffed with Christian students, but they had a broad platform of activity that drew a large number of non-Christian fellow students. The Chinese, the Japanese, and the Filipinos were the three largest national groups of Asian students in the United States, each of which had a full time American "Y" secretary to help them orient to American life. Moreover, the student Christian associations established local chapters at big universities where large numbers of their nationals gathered. In the 1930s, these foreign student Christian organizations were structured as national divisions of CFRFS, and their activities were integrated into CFRFS' course of action.[61]

CFRFS often sent student secretaries to visit campuses to spread the influence of CFRFS. These secretaries conducted personal visits and interviews with their fellow students to find out their needs and problems. The interviews and correspondence indicated that many foreign students lived in loneliness, faced racial and national prejudices, had inadequate finances, and were confronted with other personal problems. These findings, in some degree, helped shape the priority of CFRFS' service programs. Internationally, CFRFS pushed the student Christian movement in the United States to the native lands of those students. Leaders of Chinese, Japanese, and Filipino Christian associations traveled back and forth between the United States and their homelands in an attempt to link the Christian student movement in the United States with the student movements in their home countries. Student leaders also traveled to Europe and Russia to study student movements there.

In an effort to encourage foreign students to continue their studies and to circulate their news to American people, CFRFS urged the student secretaries to write about foreign student life for Christian journals and for their own organizational publications. Almost all the foreign student groups had their organizational publications, be it a newsletter or a bulletin. For instance, the Chinese students published a monthly journal called "Liu Mei Qing Nien" (*China Youth in U.S.A.*). The Japanese students had their publication of *News Bulletin,* and the Korean students had *The Korean Students' Review.* The Indian students had *The Indian Patrika,* Russian students had their *Bulletin,* and Armenian students simply printed an annual report and directory of the Armenian Student Association. CFRFS not only helped with the preparation and circulation of these publications but also subsidized them. In addition, CFRFS printed a monthly magazine in Spanish for Latin American students. Thousands of copies of these publications were circulated every month among foreign and American students. The journals and bulletins helped maintain the connection between the headquarters and local chapters of foreign student organizations; they also provided a forum for foreign students to express themselves and keep their fellow students informed. Furthermore, through these publications, special important messages from Christian leaders reached foreign students with the endorsement of their national organizations.[62]

CFRFS was not the only organization influencing foreign students on campuses. The Intercollegiate Student Christian Movement and the Association of Cosmopolitan Clubs were two other major organizations active with foreign students. The former emphasized evangelical Christianity as its goal, whereas the latter concentrated on promoting international relations and understanding. There was competition between the two organizations for constituencies and conflict over their different orientation with foreign students. Because the Cosmopolitan Clubs did not give preference to religious discussion in their programs, some criticized them as an anti-Christian movement. There were also attempts at introducing religious discussion at meetings of the Cosmopolitan Clubs in order to merge the clubs with the Christian Movement. CFRFS, which was affiliated with the YMCA and the World Student Christian Federation, tried to mitigate the conflict between the Christian Student Movement and the Cosmopolitan Clubs. It also sought cooperation with the Cosmopolitan Clubs in discovering and meeting the needs of foreign students. In an article calling for a united effort, Hurrey stressed the necessary cooperation between the clubs and the Christian Student Movement, although he also encouraged their independence and different prior interests.[63] While CFRFS publicly took an encouraging and cooperative attitude toward the clubs, it nonetheless urged its secretaries to secure for Christian foreign students "places of responsibility and leadership" in the clubs so as to "influence the thought of the Cosmopolitan Club movement."[64]

When the International House of New York was established in 1923,[65] CFRFS encouraged student secretaries of the Japanese, Chinese, and Filipino Christian Associations to contact Harry Edmonds, director of the International House, to offer cooperation. CFRFS leaders had hoped that the International House would become "a good phase" of the "Y" Movement and "should be part of our Association program."[66] When the International House began to adopt policies independent from the YMCA and YWCA, "Y" leaders were disappointed at this "lack of cooperation." Only when Edmonds helped secure a grant of $5,000 for the work of CFRFS in 1928 did the relation take a turn for the better. Hurrey acknowledged Edmonds' help as a gesture of cooperation and apologized that "our national secretaries should understand your work and cooperate heartily with you. They have not always felt as friendly toward you and your work as they do at present, and therefore have not given the kind of cooperation in the past which would have been most effective."[67]

## STREAMLINING SERVICE PROGRAMS

While foreign student Christian organizations were incorporated into CFRFS structure, General Secretary Charles Hurrey tried to streamline the various service activities into four major programs: the Port-of-Entry Service, Student Summer Conferences, the Hospitality Program, and the Emergency Fund Program. These programs were interrelated and aimed at the welfare and Christian character building of foreign students. The programs eventually evolved into a system that fundamentally shaped the national scope of services to educational exchange and foreign students in the United States in post-World War II America.[68]

The Emergency Fund Program proved essential for foreign students because unexpected international events often cut short the home funding of those who relied on government and family support. CFRFS first encountered such an emergency situation in 1911, when many government-sponsored Chinese students were suddenly stranded in the United States without government funds because of the revolution in China. When the First World War broke out, CFRFS extended financial assistance to war-displaced students. In the early 1920s, many Japanese students were devastated by the great earthquake in Japan and were stranded in America. CFRFS arranged about $50,000 as temporary loans to the Japanese students to enable them to complete their studies. In addition, CFRFS also participated in the administration of a separate Russian Student Fund in the 1920s. In 1924–1925 alone, a total of $62,700 was loaned to 116 Russian students; almost all of them returned the loans within the next few years.[69] In the 1920s and 1930s, hundreds of thousands of dollars were used as loans to foreign students. Some went to students who had no money temporarily because home remittance was suddenly held up by domestic events or natural disasters. Other loans went to those who were self-supporting and needed a small sum just to finish their work. CFRFS helped students from many countries with small loans to complete their education in the United States. Chinese, Japanese, Russian, and East European students had all benefited from the Emergency Fund.[70]

The Hospitality Program was an Americanization program for foreign students, although it was also intended to internationalize the minds of the hosts. The program included visits to American homes and American institutions. CFRFS emphasized the role of American Christian homes in bringing foreign students into contact with the church. American homes were considered the most congenial place for foreign students to mix with American people, to improve their knowledge of English, to pick up American customs, and to learn about American Christian values and democracy. Home hospitality was informal and easy to make the students feel at home. After making friends with foreign students, individual Americans or families were encouraged to act as "group shepherds" to foreign students by organizing Bible classes or forums on "questions of serious interest" in their homes. CFRFS wanted each student to have adequate opportunities to observe the expression of Christian life and experience in American homes, churches, and agencies. CFRFS leaders seemed to agree that "He [the student] is obliged to make first hand study of the manifestions [sic] of organized religion, the decision regarding his own attitude and relationship is up to the student as a personal matter."[71] Knowing the eagerness of foreign students to contact Americans, student secretaries arranged social events to bring foreign students to American homes. Simultaneously, some local communities formed Home Hospitality committees for foreign students and invited them as guests to churches, civic clubs, and local "Y" associations. Women's Clubs also took an active interest in foreign students by organizing discussion forums and providing assistance.

The Hospitality Program extended from homes to factories, business enterprises, settlement houses, and other social institutions for foreign students to learn about American industry and society and for Americans to promote international trade. Local businessmen often invited foreign students to visit their industrial plants. Rotary Clubs regularly invited foreign students to luncheons at which they spoke about the conditions in their countries. Moreover, Chambers of Commerce in San Francisco, Philadelphia, and other big cities usually gave an annual dinner for foreign students to promote international trade. Through these activities, many foreign students were attracted to the subjects of mass production, efficiency, expertise, advertising, and salesmanship in industries. In fact, a large percentage of the students from Asia and Latin America were interested in business techniques and industrial management. For instance, 60 percent of Chinese students in America were studying engineering and business in the 1920s–1930s. Many foreign students, when they returned home, became prominent businessmen in their own countries by applying and adapting methods and experience acquired in the United States. Naturally, they introduced American products and promoted the sale and distribution of things with which they had become familiar in the United States. CFRFS encouraged American manufacturers to be aware of the international goodwill of foreign students as a business asset and urged them to extend every possible courtesy to the students from abroad.[72]

Summer Conferences were one of the oldest programs through which the YMCA and YWCA introduced foreign students to Christian brotherhood/sisterhood through recreational and educational activities together with the "choicest American students and professors." Each year, the Student Department of the YMCA held summer conferences in different parts of the country, providing athletic competitions between different racial groups and offering discussions on religion and international affairs between American and foreign students. A special fund was created for the attendance of foreign students at these conferences. Interracial relations was one of the major topics of discussion, and students often shared different views. For instance, at the San Anselmo Conference in California, De Souza, a student from India, ardently championed mixed dancing and intermarriage, and his opinion was seconded by an American, the president of the Cosmopolitan Clubs. But Assadi, a student from Iran, maintained the opposite position. He believed that the amalgamation of races was not desirable and that the refusal of American white girls to dance with foreign students of different colors did not necessarily imply race discrimination. "He argued that the purity of race should be maintained and that the difference in race does not imply superiority, and that by maintaining that difference, each race is in a position to make its own unique contribution to the enrichment of the whole."[73] The students at the conferences, however, were made aware that only when they cooperated with internationally minded Americans to create a new attitude could they make a difference in overcoming prevalent racial prejudices and discrimination. One of the positive outcomes of these conferences was that foreign students made new friends and gained a new understanding of America while Americans opened their minds and changed their views of foreign students and their countries. The experience at the conferences appeared to be effective in shaping the Christian character of those young men and women from abroad. Many foreign students became involved in Christian service as a result of the conferences. More importantly, almost all the foreign student Christian organizations were formed at the summer conferences.

The Port-of-Entry Service was one of CFRFS' most important assistance to foreign students. It was originally set up to help Chinese students avoid unpleasant delays at immigration stations. The service was later extended to other national groups of foreign students. It became all the more necessary to the students in the early 1920s, when restrictive immigration laws adversely affected the coming of foreign students from a much broader range of nations than ever before.[74] The 1924 immigration laws led to more strenuous investigations of foreigners at the immigration stations. A student traveling third class (as many of them did) had to pass through an immigration inspection that required two or more days. A student traveling first or second class, without possessing all the necessary papers, had to go through a special inquiry. If he or she could not verify a non-quota status and was in excess of the quota allotted to his or her country, he or she would be detained on board the ship or in the immigration station, pending special inquiry and possible deportation. A sad example was an Egyptian student traveling second class who was detained for 23 days at the immigration station. He fell ill and became very much embittered about American institutions in the end.[75]

Besides the unpleasant incidents at the immigration stations, there were numerous cases where foreign students were ill-treated at the hands of taxi drivers, hotels, and restaurants. One day in 1921, two Hindu students arrived at New York's pier and paid $30 for a cab to CFRFS' headquarters in Mid-Manhattan.[76] From the missionaries, tourists, businessmen, books, newspapers, and movies, foreign students had often formed the impression that the American people were generous, just, and sympathetic. A typical foreign student would romantically think of America as a land of freedom, wealth, and kind-hearted people.[77] Hence, the impact of the initial disappointment upon entering the United States became all the more devastating.

CFRFS officials considered the Port-of-Entry Service crucial for the success of foreign student work because they believed that the first impression had an indelible impact on the students' attitude towards America. Committee leaders wanted the students to have a positive orientation as soon as they stepped on American soil. In order to carry out the program effectively, CFRFS maintained representatives/advisors at major ports where foreign students landed, namely San Francisco, Seattle, New Orleans, Boston, and New York. CFRFS also kept an information directory through correspondence with missionaries, educators, and businessmen abroad who knew of the intended departure of students for America. When notified in advance, representatives of CFRFS, who were usually "Y" secretaries, foreign students, and church volunteers, would meet the new students upon their arrival at a pier or train station and assist them with their continuing journey. For example, in New York City, students were met at Ellis Island and then directed to local institutions and placed under the care of the Intercollegiate Cosmopolitan Club of New York City. Students bound for colleges and universities elsewhere were assisted with obtaining tickets and with the transportation of their luggage. Those students were also given letters of introduction to "Y" secretaries and associates who would look after them at their destinations. Sometimes the Committee representatives would help the students with room and board and even employment occasionally.[78]

The Port-of-Entry Service, when successfully delivered, helped foreign students avoid the "embarrassment on the account of the attitude and treatment of customs officials and immigration officers" and the "mistakes and delay at railroad transportation and baggage handling."[79] During August and September 1930, for example, 360 students were received at the ports of Seattle, San Francisco, and New York. One of them was a Palestinian student en route to Chicago. He was welcomed at the pier of New York. After customs and immigration matters were cleared, he was directed to an associate of the committee in the city, and five days later a committee representative at Chicago met him at the LaSalle Street Train Station and accompanied him to his school.[80] The Port-of-Entry Service was one of the most popular services for foreign students. In the 1920s and 1930s, thousands of students benefited from the service, although the number helped was still a small percentage of the total foreign student population.

On the West Coast, CFRFS also extended the port-of-entry service to visiting Asian delegations that represented commercial, educational, missionary, and even diplomatic missions. This effort was deliberate on the part of the YMCA to ease the strained relations between the United States and Asian countries in the first two decades of the 20th century. Because immigration laws and regulations required all Asians to go through investigation and interrogation at immigration stations, unhappy incidents had led to the deterioration of U.S. relations—especially with Japan and China, which interested American missionaries and businessmen did not want to see. CFRFS and the Foreign Department of the YMCA were determined to strengthen the "foreign relations enterprise at the gateway to the Orient." George Day, the Pacific Coast Secretary of CFRFS, pointed out that "we are in a position to help formulate the first impressions our Oriental guests receive as they come to us and the last impressions they take with them as they leave our shores. God give us the grace and tact to reciprocate the spontaneous generous hospitality which we secretaries in the foreign service of the Association [YMCA] received at the hands of our Oriental friends in their homelands."[81]

The importance of coordinating foreign student work with foreign relations in general was reflected in George Day's emphasis that "we are on the front where race prejudice of provincial Americans and the rising tide of color are real factors to be reckoned with."[82] Consequently, a secretary to cultivate general friendly relations with all incoming and outgoing foreign delegations was appointed, in addition to a secretary to coordinate foreign student work at all institutions on the Pacific Coast and several local secretaries to promote campus programs. With the support of Christian businessmen who were keen on cultivating good relations with Asia, YMCA secretaries and the CFRFS secretary of friendly relations began to give formal receptions, whenever necessary, to incoming and outgoing Asian delegations and supplied them with introduction letters when they were on route to the

East Coast. Moreover, the friendly relations secretary kept a good communication with "Y" secretaries in China, Japan, India, Siberia, and the Philippines for information about incoming delegations. CFRFS called on "Y" secretaries to act not only as ambassadors of international goodwill abroad but also as champions for interracial friendship at home "to melt away all bitterness and race hatred."[83]

Besides these service programs, CFRFS served as an information clearinghouse for foreign students. It maintained correspondence with many Americans abroad, including missionaries, "Y" secretaries, and educators, to sustain a worldwide network for the dissemination of American education information and to keep in touch with prospective students who planned to come to the United States. It published a variety of brochures and pamphlets to help foreign students adjust to American society, such as *Living in the United States: A Guide for New Visitors, International Campus, Community Resources for Foreign Students, Port of Entry Services for Foreign Students,* and *Summer Opportunities.* CFRFS also conducted an annual census of foreign students in North America since 1915. Its cooperation with the IIE provided valuable statistical information on foreign students when no such information was available from any other source. In the 1940s, IIE gradually took over the census of foreign students in the United States and published the data in its annual reports.[84] Such an effort eventually evolved into a systematic data collection published in *Open Doors* by IIE.[85]

## RACE RELATIONS, FOREIGN STUDENT NATIONALISM, AND AMERICAN MISSIONS

American education not only acquainted foreign students with a knowledge of modern technology and sciences but also inspired them with modern western political ideas of democracy, equality, and liberty. The students enthusiastically embraced those political concepts and expected them to be fully practiced in America. However, racial prejudices and discrimination made them acutely aware of the contradictions between political rhetoric and social practice. In fact, racial discrimination was the major obstacle to true understanding between Americans and foreign students. As Charles Hurrey, general secretary of CFRFS, pointed out, American "racial prejudices make the foreign student subject to difficult and sometimes humiliating experiences that do not come to him elsewhere in the same degree."[86]

Some students criticized their American hosts who offered home hospitality as a charity. They pointed out that the hosts were comfortable in inviting groups of students but reluctant to make personal friends and establish any intimate relations with foreign students. There was fear on the part of Americans that intimacy might lead to interracial marriage. Other critics felt suspicious of the motives and aims of the various efforts made on behalf of foreign students by the Christian organizations. They contended that the "courtesy to foreign students is a form of propaganda for American industry and trade."[87]

In an effort to overcome the barriers of mutual understanding, CFRFS leaders increased their publicity activities to make sure that other organizations and individuals were aware of the needs of foreign students for friendship and of what the students could contribute to this country via friendship. Hurrey pointed out that the presence of foreign students offered a great opportunity for American students to learn about other countries' history, commerce, and culture. He urged American students and professors to get acquainted with foreign students with a view to overcoming prejudices and broadening their outlook.[88] He appealed to them to treat foreign students as brothers, and "by magnifying the virtues of different races and speaking frankly and sympathetically regarding national weakness, we may look forward to the establishing of true friendship among the future leaders of all the nations."[89]

Racial prejudices were culturally nurtured. As a result, it took the conscious efforts of all people in a society to work toward racial equality and tolerance. Thanks to the efforts of various organizations on behalf of foreign students, a change of attitude gradually occurred at colleges and universities in the 1920s and 1930s. Dozens of universities appointed faculty members as foreign student advisors or formed committees on foreign student affairs.[90] At the University of Michigan, for example, several foreign student advisors were appointed by the colleges of engineering, science, literature, and arts. Professor J. Raleigh Nelson, who later played an active role in the profession of foreign student advising, began to serve as the university counselor to foreign students in 1933 after he had been chairman of the Committee on Foreign Students at the College of Engineering for 20 years.[91] At the University of Pittsburgh, Ruth Crawford Mitchelle played a great role in the lives of foreign students. Although she was appointed to take charge of the nativity study of foreign-born American students on campus, her interest and concerns extended to foreign students. She sat on the Committee on Foreign Students Affairs when it was formed in 1927 and acted as the first foreign student advisor of the University.[92] To some extent, American students' attitudes toward foreign students also began to change from indifference to curiosity and appreciation, thanks to the work of the Intercollegiate YMCA and YWCA and the Cosmopolitan Clubs. In the 1920s, about 30 American universities had Cosmopolitan Club houses where students of all nationalities could mingle in international fellowship. Some foreign students were elected to sit on student bodies like the Welfare Council at Stanford University, which clearly indicated the integration of foreign students into campus life. But at colleges and universities, opposition to admitting foreign students still existed—especially Jewish, Asian, and black students—into honor societies and fraternities. Segregation also occurred on campuses in certain states. For example, several national Greek fraternities accepted foreign students as members on the East Coast, "but in California and Washington, Club houses are maintained by the Chinese, Japanese, Filipino and East Indian students, thus providing, through segregation, homelike surroundings for their fellow nationals," reported Charles Hurrey.[93] Obviously, CFRFS officials felt comfortable with the practice of segregation in those states. Even when the treatment of foreign students was improved on campus, however, "the same struggle" for equality and acceptance had to be fought in the community. The following story is a case in point. Two American "Y" students at Stanford, Tom Faucette and Don Chase, "tried successfully the experiment of living in the Chinese Club House." They made friends with many Chinese students and as a result brought the largest delegation of Chinese students to the "Y" summer conference at Asilomar in the history of Stanford. But one day Faucette brought three Chinese students to San Francisco and applied at the San Francisco YMCA for rooms for the night, but they were turned down because the students were Orientals.[94] What the Chinese students experienced with the campus "Y" and the community "Y" illustrated that the institutionalized practice of discrimination in the society was even reflected by the YMCA, although the general principle of the "Y" was to champion racial equality.

Racial discrimination not only humiliated the students personally but also frustrated their national aspirations. Such existential experiences gave rise to student nationalism in the fight against racist treatment. Student personal experience took on a national twist when the "national spirit, which has its most intense expression in some of the countries from which these students come, introduces a political factor which makes the foreign student still more restless under American conditions."[95] Misconceptions of America also occurred among foreign students due to a lack of free interaction with Americans and mutual understanding. Thus, while racial prejudices were hard for Americans to overcome, national pride and personal dignity of foreign students became intensified in the racial hierarchy of American society.

One of the manifestations of students' adoption of equality and liberty was their challenge to the racial inequality practiced by missionaries. Two-thirds of foreign students came from countries where American missionaries were stationed. Those students challenged the missionary practice that was established on the basis of racial inequality. Asian students, who were by far the largest foreign student group in America, were very vocal about their criticism of American missionaries in their homelands. As national awakening in Asian countries filled the students with a new passion for equality and freedom, they protested that missionaries only presented a one-sided picture of their countries: backward, immoral, and ignorant. They challenged the assumption of white superiority, especially "the domination of the white race and the discrimination against the Orientals by missionaries in matters of salary, housing, social practice, official status."[96]

Furthermore, the students shocked America's complacency by criticizing its discriminatory immigration policies and imperialist expansion. They expressed their criticism in their letters to CFRFS and in the articles published in their organizational journals and newsletters. Asian students denounced American racism, the injustice of immigration laws, and American cultural practices abroad, albeit their elitist views:

The United States government is inconsistent; you grant eligibility to citizenship to the most backward person from Europe but deny that privilege to the most cultured representatives of Japan, India or China; with one hand you give generously to build colleges, hospitals, churches, and Y.M.C.A.'s in Asia, while with the other you release corrupting cinema films, gunboats and commercial exploitation. Your missionaries preach brotherhood but you and they practise social snobbery and discrimination.

Latin American students condemned American economic aggression and military interference:

You are glutted with gold; your avaricious investors are not willing to take risks in our countries similar to those taken at home but they insist on commandeering your army and navy to defend their investments; the integrity of our governments is sacrificed to satisfy their greed. You built the Panama Canal but in so doing created widespread suspicion of the purity of your motives. Your efforts to promote Pan American friendship are actuated by commercial rather than cultural motives.

European students also criticized:

Americans are out to Americanize the world through refusal to enter the League of Nations, mass production in industry, trade imperialism and subtle philanthropy. Crime and corruption in public officials and disrespect for law characterize your present civilization and are results of your silly attempt to govern people by prohibitory enactments rather than by education.[97]

These critical comments of the students were derived from the distinctive experiences and interaction each of the different continents had with the United States. Documents also showed that even amidst the criticism, however, students expressed their appreciation of the genuine assistance that they received from American people.

In the face of student challenge, CFRFS officials responded that "alert American citizens are not unmindful of the significance of students in the field of international commerce, diplomacy, and religion, but our aspirations are far higher and broader than any narrow process of 'Americanization.'"[98] YMCA leaders remarked: "We recognize that many students were restless and discontented with past and present conditions; they seek a better world order; they are idealistic and will pay any price to realize their dream."[99] Nonetheless, they warned the U.S. government: "A world of cooperative nations will not be established by enforcing discriminatory legislation or otherwise putting obstacles in the pathway of student ambassadors."[100]

Taking students' protests seriously, Hurrey suggested that missionaries should "present a balanced report and not allow the pressure to obtain financial support to tempt them [into] a one-sided picture of poverty, ignorance, and distress" of other nations. He frankly admitted that the principles of Christ were not fulfilled in its full implications "even by the advocate of foreign missions." Hurrey mentioned that through contact with the students, many supporters of foreign missions came to see that the future of the missions could not continue under the old assumption of white superiority but instead had to recognize the value of mutuality and equality.[101] The average American audience, however, did not enjoy students' criticism of the missionaries. Hurrey observed, "The Oriental student who persists in such attacks soon becomes obnoxious and is alienated from church societies."[102] The consequences were often the setback of the very goals of ecumenism toward which CFRFS and other Christian organizations had so arduously worked with foreign students.

As student criticism was increasing and student nationalism was rising, some Americans began to question the function of the students' Christian orga iizations. Were they an instrument for internationalism or nationalism? Some argued that "separate racial organizations of foreign students have a tendency to stimulate and maintain narrow nationalism."[103] But CFRFS leaders maintained that students' organizations "are the means of multiplying points of contact with other groups or agencies, and of developing Christian experience amongst such groups."[104] National identity was regarded as necessary in working toward internationalism. CFRFS officials were aware, however, that the student organizations, when led by narrow-minded and cynical nationalists, tended to engender strife and therefore defeat the highest goals of ecumenical fellowship. They believed that Christian associations of the students were playing a positive role in promoting good fellowship, dispelling loneliness, interpreting other cultures to Americans, and furthering the cause of international understanding. CFRFS maintained the policy of achieving internationalism through nationalism and encouraged each foreign student Christian organization to keep in close contact with the National Student Christian Movement to work toward the goal of maximizing interracial goodwill.

In the mid-1930s, when military aggressions led to international crisis, national political strife affected the personal relationships of foreign students. Foreign students were pitted against each other along national lines when their countries were involved in wars or political conflicts. This situation was particularly evident between the Chinese and Japanese students when Japan made a full-scale military assault on China. Furthermore, Filipino students protested against the American colonization of their country. Their nationalist surge proved difficult for CFRFS to handle. Indian students demanded British withdrawal from their country and engaged in heated debate with British students. With the tension intensifying between student groups, Americans found it "extremely difficult to establish friendly relations with individual students on both sides."[105] Student nationalist movements grew even stronger following the outbreak of World War II. In the late 1930s, foreign students literally lived in a zone of conflict. CFRFS found it hard to adhere to the program of international fellowship through national groups. Administrative difficulties made CFRFS' work less effective in the turbulent war years. In 1947, CFRFS decided to stop sponsoring foreign student Christian organizations and transferred them to the care of the United Student Christian Council.[106] For half a century, American Christian organizations and missionaries made unusual efforts at expanding American Christian culture to other societies through the education of the students. The service programs such as the Port-of-Entry, Home Hospitality, and Summer Conferences proved to be valuable for foreign students, especially in helping them make social, psychological, and cultural adjustments in the United States. Many foreign students were touched by the Christian spirit of the services that they received during a time when they constantly encountered racial discriminations in their daily life. The educational endeavor of Christian groups at shaping foreign students into future Christian leaders resulted in the formation of various student Christian associations and the conversion of students to Christian beliefs. These were a clear indication of the success of CFRFS and the YMCA's endeavor in building the Christian character of the students.

Although the education aimed to imbue foreign students with Christian doctrines and to train them to be indigenous leaders of Christianity, it nonetheless contributed to the political liberalization of the students from non-Western societies. The students embraced the political concepts of freedom, equality, and democracy when they were exposed to Western learning in American universities. They did not just acquire the knowledge of modern technology and sciences. The students cherished the political ideals of liberty and equality and expected them to be indiscriminately practiced in American society. Through their own cross-cultural experiences, the students came to grapple with the ideals of Christian teachings and the reality of a Christian society. They criticized racism in America and challenged the practice of racial inequality by missionaries in their home countries. Their criticism forced Christian leaders to rethink matters such as race relations, mutual respect, and the fair treatment of native peoples in missionary work as well as social practice at home in America.

The original plan by American Christian leaders to shape the students into servants for the Christian mission turned out to be a re-educational process for the Christian leaders themselves. They realized that ecumenical fellowship could not be established when equality and mutual respect between different races were not fully implemented. In a sense, the students served as agents for social progress by challenging racial discriminations in American society and among missionaries abroad. Moreover, the programs of CFRFS, the YMCA, and the Cosmopolitan Clubs encouraged an international sensibility among Americans and made racial equality a real issue for many to ponder.

## NOTES

1. John Kuo Wei Tchen, *New York before Chinatown: Orientalism and the Shaping of American Culture, 1776–1882* (Baltimore and London: The Johns Hopkins University Press, 1999). For the discussion of others and otherness, see Elizabeth Hallam and Brian V. Street, eds., *Cultural Encounters: Representing "Otherness"* (London and New York: Routledge, 2000); Gisela Brink-Gabler, ed., *Encountering the Other(s): Studies in Literature, History, and Culture* (Albany, NY: State University of New York Press, 1995).

2. William Reginald Wheeler, Henry Hall King, and Alexander Barkolow Davidson, eds., *The Foreign Student in America* (New York: Association Press, 1925), 270.

3. Two other Chinese, Wong Shing and Wong Foon, also came to the United States with Yung Wing. But Wong Shing, because of poor health, returned to China soon afterward; Wong Foon, upon graduation from Monson, went to the University of Edinburgh to study medicine in 1850. For details, see Yung Wing, *My Life in China and America* (New York: Henry Holt and Company, 1909).

4. Stewart E. Fraser and William W. Brickman, eds., *A History of International and Comparative Education* (Glendale, IL: Scott, Foresman and Company, 1968), 378–380.

5. Jonathan D. Spence, *The Search for Modern China* (New York: W. W. Norton, 1999), 218.

6. Wen-Han Kiang, *The Chinese Student Movement* (New York: King's Crown Press, 1948), 15.

7. Jerome Dean Davis, *A Maker of New Japan, Rev. Joseph Hardy Neesima* (New York: Fleming H. Revell Company, 1894).

8. *Report of the United States Commissioner of Education for the Year 1904* vol. 2 (Washington, D.C.: Government Printing Office, 1906), 1423.

9. Samuel Paul Capen, *Opportunities for Foreign Students at Colleges and Universities in the United States,* United States Bureau of Education, Bulletin No. 27 (Washington, D.C.: Government Printing Office, 1915), 57.

10. For the Soong sisters and their family, see Emily Hahn, *The Soong Sisters* (New York: Doubleday, 1944); Cornelia Spencer, *Three Sisters: The Story of the Soong Family of China* (New York: John Day Co., 1939).

11. *The Unofficial Ambassadors* (Annual Report of the Committee on Friendly Relations Among Foreign Students, 1936), 3. CFRFS box #2, YMCA Archives, University Libraries, University of Minnesota, Minneapolis, MN.

12. Wheeler et al., *The Foreign Student,* 163; Charles Hurrey, "The Migrating Student," n.d., folder titled "Charles Hurrey, 1922–1938," Hurrey Papers, YMCA Archives.

13. Guy S. Metraux, *Exchange of Persons: The Evolution of Cross-Cultural Education* (New York: Social Science Research Council, Report 9, June 1952), 42.

14. Mott's first weeks at Cornell were lonely, and the friendly calls from senior students of the Christian Association made an indelible impression on him and a lasting impact on his career. Mott realized the great strategic value of the Christian Association to relate a student to the organization through acts of kindness. He joined the association and after much

struggle with himself gave up his original ambition of a political career and decided to dedi-
cate himself to the mission of spreading Christian gospel in the world. See Basil Mathews,
*John R. Mott, World Citizen* (New York: Harper and Brothers, 1934); C. Howard Hopkins,
*20th Century Ecumenical Statesman: John R. Mott, 1865–1955, A Biography* (Grand Rapids,
MI: William B. Eerdmans Publishing Company, 1979).

15. Kenneth S. Latourette, *World Service: A History of the Foreign Work and World Service
of the Young Men's Christian Associations of the United States and Canada* (New York:
Association Press, 1957), 38–39; Mathews, *John R. Mott*, 28–37.

16. J. M. Clinton to John Mott, 14 December 1911, folder titled "Correspondence
1908–1918," CFRFS box #10, YMCA Archives.

17. Merle Curti, *Peace or War: The American Struggle, 1636–1936* (Boston: J. S. Canner,
1959), 202–205.

18. Ibid., 209.

19. Charles Chatfield, *For Peace and Justice, Pacifism in America, 1914–1941* (Knoxville,
TN: The University of Tennessee Press, 1971), 16.

20. Wheeler et al., *The Foreign Student*, 268–269.

21. Curti, *Peace or War*, 212.

22. Wheeler et al., *The Foreign Student*, 269–270.

23. For the specific chapters of the Cosmopolitan Clubs at the time, see Wheeler et al.,
*The Foreign Student*, 269.

24. Harry Edmonds to Rockefeller Jr., 11 March 1921, folder 68 (unprocessed), box 10,
RG III 2G, Rockefeller Family Archives, Rockefeller Archive Center (RAC), North
Tarrytown, NY. Edmonds was the director of New York Intercollegiate Cosmopolitan Clubs
(not affiliated with the ACC), and he used the 1913 ACC Convention and those in the following years to illustrate his point.

25. Stewart Fraser, ed., *Governmental Policy and International Education* (New York: John
Wiley and Sons, 1965), 93.

26. Latourette, *World Service*, 74.

27. John Mott to Andrew Carnegie, 9 March 1914, folder titled "Correspondence,
1908–1918," CFRFS box #10, YMCA Archives.

28. Mathews, *John R. Mott*, 414–415; Latourette, *World Service*, 74; Mary Thompson, ed.,
*Unofficial Ambassadors: The Story of International Student Service* (New York: International
Student Service, 1982), 22–23.

29. See Mathews, *John R. Mott*, Chapter XX, for Mott's strategy of fundraising.

30. Mott to Carnegie, 8 May 1912, "Correspondence, 1908–1918"; Mott to James
Bertram, secretary of the Carnegie Corporation of New York, 14 March 1914, folder titled
"Correspondence, 1908–1918," CFRFS box #10, YMCA Archives.

31. "Report of the Committee to Promote Friendly Relations Among Foreign Students for
the Year 1911," 1, folder titled "Correspondence, 1908–1918," CFRFS #10, YMCA
Archives.

32. Ibid.

33. Countries that formed the joint forces included Great Britain, Germany, France, the
United States, Russia, Japan, Italy, and Austria.

34. For a detailed discussion of the Boxer Indemnity and its remissions by some powers,
see Yam Tong Hoh, "The Boxer Indemnity Remissions and Education in China" (Ph.D. diss.,
Teachers College, Columbia University, 1933).

35. A total of about $18 million was authorized to be returned to China by the U.S. gov-
ernment in 1908 and 1924 for educational purposes.

36. Isaac Kandel, *The United States Activities in International Cultural Relations* (Washington, D.C.: American Council on Education, 1945), 80–81; Thomas Bailey, *A Diplomatic History of the American People* (New York: Appleton-Century Crofts, 1964), 529.

37. Benjamin Schmoker, *Oral History*, n.d., YMCA Archives, 4–5, 8.

38. "Report of the Committee to Promote Friendly Relations among Foreign Students for the Year 1911," 1, YMCA Archives. Please note that the number of Chinese students was very possibly inaccurate due to the lack of systematic surveys. The number might have included those in Canada, because the committee drew data from the membership of the Chinese Student Christian Association of North America.

39. John Mott to Andrew Carnegie, 8 May 1912, folder titled "Correspondence, 1908–1918," CFRFS box #10, YMCA Archives.

40. Ibid.

41. Schmoker, *Oral History*, 14.

42. Ibid.

43. CSCA Bulletin No. 2, 15 October 1921, Collection of Chinese Student Christian Association in North America, RG #13, Special Collections, Yale Divinity School Library, 6; Schmoker, *Oral History*, 8–10.

44. Resolution of the Carnegie Corporation of New York, 14 March 1914, folder titled "Correspondence, 1908–1918," CFRFS box #10, YMCA Archives.

45. Mott to Carnegie, 9 March 1914, "Correspondence, 1908–1918"; Mott to Bertram, 14 March 1914, "Correspondence, 1908–1918."

46. Carnegie to Gilbert A. Beaver, 25 February 1915; R. A. Franks, treasurer of the Carnegie Corporation of New York, to Beaver, March 4, 1915, folder titled "Correspondence, 1908–1918," CFRFS box #10, YMCA Archives.

47. This suggestion was taken seriously by non-Western students. CSCA printed a pamphlet in 1922 detailing the appropriate manners for Chinese students to follow in the United States. It covered posture and dress for general appearance, manners of conversation, calling and visiting, at the dinner table, and respect for personality and privacy. ("Friendship," box 2, folder 37, CSCA Collection, RG #13, Special Collections, Yale Divinity School Library.)

48. Williard Lyon to Charles Hurrey, 3 July 1914, folder titled "Correspondence, 1908–1918," CFRFS box #10, YMCA Archives.

49. Thompson, *Unofficial Ambassadors*, 24–25.

50. In 1928–1929, the CFRFS underwent an organizational restructuring. In the late 1920s, CFRFS had financial problems and was forced to cut staff travel that aimed at direct contact with students on campuses and in the communities. Moreover, the CFRFS Board disbanded the Latin American Student Association and Indian Student Association, which much distressed Hurrey—who felt that the isolation of Latin American students from the North American Christian Movement was a grave mistake. Meanwhile, CFRFS' work often "encroached" into the realm of the Student Division of the YMCA, which regarded as its responsibility the contact with foreign students in campus-based programs and at conferences. Misunderstanding and differences between CFRFS and the Student Division were reduced by the appointment of David Porter, national secretary of the YMCA Student Division, to serve on the CFRFS Board, and Elmer Yelton, executive secretary of CFRFS, to serve on the National Student YMCA Board. Because CFRFS and its programs relied heavily on the financial support of the International Committee of the YMCA, there was questioning as to the relationship between the two. A special committee of the YMCA investigated the situation and recommended that CFRFS should not be subordinated in any way to the established departments of the YMCA, nor should it be merged with either the Foreign Division or the Student Division

of the YMCA. After much discussion between the leaders of the CFRFS Board and members of the National Council of YMCAs and its International Committee, it was agreed that the International Committee continued to produce an annual subsidy for CFRFS but give it a free hand in all its operations. At the same time, an administrative board of 12 was formed to supervise the work of CFRFS—especially the raising of a budget and the control of funds. Four of the board members were appointed by the Foreign Committee of the YMCA and four by the Student Division of the YMCA, and the remaining four were chosen by these eight members. Such a structure continued until 1945, when another major change took place. See the "Plan for Administration of the Service of Friendly Relations among Foreign Students," folder titled "Correspondence and Reports, 1920–31," CFRFS box #10A, YMCA Archives; Thompson, *Unofficial Ambassadors,* 53–55.

51. Charles Hurrey to John Mott, 13 February 1917, Hurrey Papers, YMCA Archives.

52. Schmoker, *Oral History,* 39–41.

53. Charles Hurrey's speech at the Cosmopolitan Club Convention, 15 December 1920, folder titled "Correspondence and Reports, 1920–31," CFRFS box #10A, YMCA Archives.

54. Charles Hurrey, "Report of Progress of the Committee on Friendly Relations among Foreign Students," 1 January 1916, folder titled "Articles and Reports, 1916–1920," CFRFS box #10, YMCA Archives.

55. Ibid.

56. Charles Hurrey, "Obligation to Seven Thousand Future Leaders of One Hundred Nations," n. d., folder titled "Articles and Reports, 1916–1920," CFRFS box #10, YMCA Archives.

57. "Statement Regarding a More Effective Service for Foreign Students in the United States," CFRFS, December 1923, folder titled "Correspondence and Reports, 1920–31," CFRFS box #10A, YMCA Archives.

58. "Association Work with Foreign Students," memo from a conference of Hurrey, Yelton, Porter, and Lyon, September 1922, folder titled "Correspondence and Reports, 1920–31," CFRFS box #10A, YMCA Archives.

59. Hurrey, "Obligation to Seven Thousand Future Leaders of One Hundred Nations."

60. Hurrey, "Report of Progress of the Committee on Friendly Relations among Foreign Students."

61. *The Unofficial Ambassadors,* (1933), 5–7.

62. Hurrey, "Report of Progress of the Committee on Friendly Relations among Foreign Students," 1 January 1916; Thompson, *Unofficial Ambassadors,* 4–8.

63. Charles Hurrey, "A Call for United Effort," n.d., folder titled "Articles and Reports, 1916–1920," CFRFS box #16, YMCA Archives.

64. "Minutes of Conference of Foreign Student Secretaries," 23–24 September 1924, folder titled "Minutes and Statements, 1916–1945," CFRFS box #14, YMCA Archives.

65. In a sense, the International House of New York grew out of the intercollegiate Christian student movement. See Chapter 3 for a discussion of the International House Movement.

66. Charles Hurrey to John Mott, 6 October 1919, folder titled "Charles Hurrey, 1911–1921;" Charles Hurrey to John Mott, 30 October 1926, folder titled "Charles Hurrey 1922–1938," Hurrey Papers, YMCA Archives.

67. Charles Hurrey to Harry Edmonds, 11 October 1928, folder titled "Harry Edmonds," Drawer 1, International House New York Archives.

68. See later chapters.

69. Charles Hurrey, "Review of Foreign Student Situation since 1920," n.d., folder titled "Charles Hurrey, 1922–1938," Hurrey Papers, YMCA Archives.

70. Charles Hurrey, "The Committee and its Activities," and "Toward International Cooperation," n.d., folder titled "Articles by C. Hurrey, 1915–1937," Hurrey Papers, YMCA Archives.

71. *The Unofficial Ambassadors* (Annual Report of CFRFS, 1930), 3.

72. Hurrey, "The Committee and its Activities"; *The Unofficial Ambassadors* (1930), 3–4; Wheeler et al., *The Foreign Student,* 137.

73. George Day to Charles Hurrey, 13 February 1923, folder titled "Correspondence and Reports, 1920–1931," CFRFS box #10A, YMCA Archives.

74. The restrictive immigration laws of the 1920s also pushed more foreign students to Europe, which threatened to undermine the international education movement in the United States and thus caused concerns among international educators. See Chapter 2 for a detailed discussion.

75. Wheeler et al., *The Foreign Student,* 136.

76. Ibid.

77. Ibid., 135.

78. Hurrey, "The Committee and its Activities"; *The Unofficial Ambassadors* (1930), 2–3.

79. *The Unofficial Ambassadors* (1930), 2.

80. Ibid.; Wheeler et al., *The Foreign Student,* 229.

81. George Day to John Mott, 11 July 1922, folder titled "Correspondence and Reports, 1920–1931," CFRFS box #10A, YMCA Archives.

82. Ibid.

83. George Day to Elmer Yelton, executive secretary of CFRFS, 7 July 1922; G. Day to John Mott, 11 July 1922, folder titled "Correspondence and Reports, 1920–31."

84. CFRFS contended with the IIE to keep the data gathering as its project but eventually lost it to the IIE when data collecting became more professionally administered.

85. Chapter 2 discusses the development of IIE.

86. "Statement Regarding a More Effective Service for Foreign Students in the United States," by CFRFS, December 1923, folder titled "Correspondence and Reports, 1920–31."

87. Hurrey, "The Committee and its Activities," 5.

88. Hurrey, "Obligation to Seven Thousand Future Leaders of One Hundred Nations."

89. "Factors and Problems of Foreign Students," n.d., folder titled "Correspondence and Reports, 1920–31," CFRFS box #10A, YMCA Archives.

90. They included the University of Illinois, the University of Michigan, American University, George Washington University, Temple University, the University of Florida, the University of Chicago, and Cornell University. For a detailed discussion of foreign student advisors, see Chapters 5 and 6.

91. M. Robert B. Klinger, "The Development of National Association for Foreign Student Affairs from 'Idea to Institution,'" *Governmental Policy and International Education,* edited by Stewart Fraser (New York: John Wiley and Sons, 1965), 99.

92. "Reports and Memoranda, 1926–1930," 90/f-12, folder file 17, Special Collections, University Library, University of Pittsburgh.

93. Hurrey, "Review of Foreign Student Situation Since 1920," 3–4.

94. Day to Hurrey, 13 February 1923, "Correspondence and Reports, 1920–31."

95. "Statement Regarding a More Effective Service for Foreign Students in the United States," by CFRFS, December 1923, folder titled "Correspondence and Reports, 1920–31."

96. Hurrey, "Review of Foreign Student Situation Since 1920," 7–8.

97. Charles Hurrey, "Foreign Students Shocked Our Complacency," folder titled "Charles Hurrey, 1922–1938," n.d., 5–6, Hurrey Papers. The criticism was expressed by foreign students in their letters to the CFRFS or in the articles published in their organizational newsletters.

98. *The Unofficial Ambassadors* (Annual Report of CFRFS, 1932), 3.

99. Ibid.

100. Ibid.

101. Hurrey, "The Committee and its Activities," 5.

102. Hurrey, "Review of Foreign Student Situation Since 1920," 8.

103. Charles Hurrey, "Foreign Students and the Federation," n.d., 3, folder titled "Charles Hurrey Articles," Hurrey Papers, YMCA Archives.

104. Ibid.

105. *The Unofficial Ambassadors* (Annual Report of CFRFS, 1934), 4.

106. The committee retained its relationship with the Chinese Student Christian Association, however, until 1951 when the Cold War and the political change in China brought that to an end. (CSCA news release on June 21, 1948, CSCA folder 1948; Ruth Haines, "Report to J. Benjamin Schmoker, General Secretary, Committee on Friendly Relations," CFRFS box #3, YMCA Archives.

# Chapter 2

## Cultural Internationalism: Educational Exchange and Cultural Understanding for World Peace

While Christian organizations focused their programs on foreign students, educational agencies—with the support of philanthropic foundations—developed a series of educational exchanges during the inter-war years. Studies conducted by the American Council on Education (ACE) showed that by 1925, more than 120 organizations in the United States were engaged in the work of international educational activities.[1] Their programs emphasized international intellectual cooperation and cultural understanding as ways to develop an international outlook and to maintain world peace. The remarkable growth of international educational activities demonstrated the contemporary belief that education shaped people's views and that American democratic values could be spread abroad through educational exchange to contribute to world peace. In this context, educational efforts to understand different cultures appealed to various Americans as an essential means of overcoming the ignorance and irrational nationalism that led to war.

International cultural understanding was a prominent aspect of the Peace Movement in the 1920s.[2] Historian Akira Iriye has used the term "cultural internationalism" to describe the cultural approach to world order.[3] Philanthropic foundations and the East Coast elite played an active role in the educational/cultural efforts to promote world peace after World War I. Cultural internationalists believed that human contact and cultural understanding between different nations were important in developing international goodwill and friendship. They established various kinds of educational exchange programs and fellowships. In addition, Junior Year Abroad and Summer Schools Abroad programs became increasingly popular at American universities and colleges in the inter-war years. The immigration laws of the 1920s, however, posed restrictions on the coming of foreign students and scholars to the United States. The IIE and the ACE eventually worked out with the immigration commissioners a self-monitoring system to keep track of foreign students. This chapter examines the rise of international educational exchange, especially the role of IIE in championing educational exchange and cultural internationalism. It also discusses the key part that the Carnegie and Rockefeller philanthropies played in the development of IIE and the international education activities in the inter-war years.

## WORLD WAR I AND CULTURAL INTERACTIONS VIA EDUCATIONAL ACTIVITIES

The First World War brought the United States into closer contact with other nations than ever before. The war experience motivated an increasing number of organizations to devote their efforts to the mission of intellectual cooperation for friendly relations between nations. In 1915, a group of American educators founded the Society for American Fellowships in French Universities, which established several fellowships for American students in France.[4] In 1918–1919, the Association of American Colleges initiated a similar program by sponsoring groups of French schoolgirls to study in the United States.[5] This new enthusiasm for a French connection illustrated the impact of the war on the development of American intellectual cooperation and student exchanges with allied countries. Strong anti-German sentiment during and after the war propelled the United States to orient its higher education toward French and English universities rather than to continue its ties with German universities.[6] The statement of the Society for American Fellowships in French Universities declared that its purpose was to "assist in establishing, in its proper place of eminence in the mind of the American public, the standing and repute of French scholarship," and "to readjust the true balance, which, for various reasons, has long existed in this country in favor of the German universities."[7]

The American University Union in Europe was another private educational agency established during the war. This organization maintained offices in London, Paris, and Rome to supervise the affairs and progress of American students in England, France, and Italy. The union in Europe was first established at the University Club, New York City on July 6, 1917, by a group of professors and student secretaries from elite universities such as Yale, Columbia, Harvard, Johns Hopkins, and the University of Michigan. In association with The Red Cross, the International Committee of the YMCA, and the War Department, the union in Europe aimed "to meet the needs of American university and college men who are in Europe for military or other service in the cause of Allies."[8] After the war, the union helped

American young men and women with educational processes in France, Italy, and England. Moreover, various European immigrant groups in the United States, which maintained close ties with their home countries, kept an active interest in furthering the relations between their adopted country—the United States—and their homelands. Organizations such as the Netherlands-America Foundation, the Italy-America Society, and the American-Scandinavian Foundation provided funds for exchange studies in the United States and in their home countries.[9]

Cultural and educational exchange activities were not confined to European countries alone. The Pan-American Union assisted Latin American students with information about free courses and college scholarships in the United States. Particular interest was shown to Mexican students. For example, in 1917 the Peace Committee of the Philadelphia Yearly Meeting of Friends appealed to 500 colleges and universities for special grants to Mexican students. In 1920, the Mexican-American Scholarships Foundation was formed with the efforts of Will Peairs, vice president of the Chamberlain Medicine Company, Des Moines, IA, and the American Chamber of Commerce in Mexico.[10]

The American Council on Education, which was founded in 1918 to serve as a channel of communication between educational associations and the federal government for war efforts, acted as a clearinghouse of opinions and as a starting point of action in the American educational world. The ACE organized seven new committees to deal with specific and immediate problems confronting American higher education during the war. One of them was the Committee on International Educational Relations, which cooperated with the American Association of University Professors, the Pan-American Union, the U.S. Bureau of Education, and other agencies on the standards of determining academic credits for exchange students.

In 1919, the Institute of International Education was established for the specific purpose of providing professional services to international educational activities. The IIE initially concentrated on administering fellowships for foundations and governments and providing educational information for both foreigners coming to the United States and Americans going abroad. IIE was originally formed by a group of intellectual statesmen in New York City who were concerned with the country's international role and stature.[11] But Nicholas Murray Butler, Elihu Root, and Stephen P. Duggan played a key role in the inception of the IIE. Butler was president of Columbia University and a founding trustee of the Carnegie Endowment for International Peace (CEIP). Root, who was a lawyer by profession but had served as secretary of war and secretary of state, was also a founding trustee of the Carnegie Corporation and president of the Carnegie Endowment for International Peace. Root and Butler were prominent peace advocates, and both later won the Nobel Peace Prize. Duggan was a professor of government and international relations at the City College of New York and used to meet with a group of intellectuals for regular luncheon discussions of issues of war and peace. The luncheon group included Paul Kellogg, editor of *Survey Magazine*, Norman Hapgood, editor of *Harper's Weekly*, Charles A. Beard, professor of history at Columbia, Joseph Chamberlain, professor of public law at Columbia, and Charles Howland, a New York lawyer. The luncheons, recalled Duggan, were often scenes of argument rather than discussion but served as a channel for expressing and exchanging opinions and of placing convictions before the bar of criticism.[12] The luncheon group, through which Duggan developed personal contact with people who were important in his future career, formed itself as the League of Free Nations Association after the war and then became the Foreign Policy Association in 1921.[13]

Duggan became acquainted with Nicholas Butler when he helped organize a conference on American foreign policy under the auspices of the Carnegie Endowment for International Peace in the spring of 1917. Shortly afterward, Duggan presented Butler a plan of establishing an Institute of International Relations to promote the learning of international affairs in American colleges and universities. Butler was the director of the Carnegie Endowment for International Peace at the time, and the two men had previously discussed the possibility of organizing an institution for the purpose of helping Americans gain a better understanding of foreign nations and assisting foreign peoples with obtaining accurate knowledge of the United States. Duggan was shocked at the general ignorance of international affairs in American society when World War I broke out:

I had watched with growing anxiety the constantly increasing friction between Great Britain and Germany, and the positions that were being taken by the Great Powers on the diplomatic battleground. When World War I finally broke out it was like a bombshell to the American people. They had for nearly a generation devoted themselves almost exclusively to domestic affairs and they were woefully ignorant of the background of the war and the issues involved.[14]

Duggan felt that the media pumped out much misinformation of international affairs for the American general public. "Our people have been deluged with misinformation by newspapers, magasines [sic] and platform these past four years."[15] In the plan that he submitted to Butler, Duggan suggested that an institute be created to serve as a source of accurate information for organizations and individuals interested in international affairs. The institute, he hoped, would raise public interest in international relations by organizing conferences on international affairs and by acting as an advising agency in the educational exchange of teachers and students. The Carnegie Endowment for International Peace did not adopt his plan, however.[16]

Unaware of the suggestion that Duggan had made to Butler, Professor William Schofield of Harvard University, chairman of the Committee on

International Educational Relations of the ACE, sent Butler a proposal for a bureau to coordinate the interchange of teachers and students and asked the Carnegie Endowment for a grant of $25,000. Butler was favorably impressed with the proposal but wanted the committee to further define its goals and procedures. He also suggested that Duggan be added to the committee. In September 1918, the committee formally submitted the proposal to the Carnegie Endowment for International Peace with a supporting letter from Secretary of State Robert Lansing. Butler forwarded the proposal to the Carnegie Corporation, believing that it fell into the corporation's realm of interest. But the proposal was returned with the statement that the corporation had deferred taking the project into consideration.[17] Not discouraged, Duggan revised his plan and sent it to Butler again, urging him for quick action. Duggan worried that international interest and activity would not be maintained after the war, when problems of domestic politics began to take priority. He emphasized that the main question at the moment was where to find the financial support for undertaking the plan.

Even before the war, Butler had made an argument about the importance of international mindedness in keeping the balance of power. He explained, "In striving to gain the international mind, it is necessary first of all to learn to measure other peoples and other civilizations than ours from their own point of view and by their own standards rather than by our own."[18] Duggan agreed with Butler's argument for an "international mind" in the debate of means to maintain world peace. He believed that irrational nationalism was the cause of war. Like some of his contemporaries, Duggan viewed nationalism as a result of national education. Similarly, he thought that education could also be used to cultivate international mindedness. If a new way of education was used to teach people how to appreciate other nations and cultures, then nationalism could be mitigated, if not eliminated. As a progressive educator, Duggan saw education as a vehicle to promote social change and progress. In short, his interest in international affairs, his concern over world peace, and his faith in education as a social panacea led him to believe that international education was a process by which individuals could learn to transcend their own national points of view and understand and appreciate the values, attitudes, and ideas of peoples who were different from themselves. Duggan also regarded the educational travel of teachers and students between different nations as one of the most effective ways to cultivate people with international mindedness. In his opinion, educational travel offered people opportunities to observe other nations firsthand and to make their own country understood through direct contacts with other peoples. If educational travel was systematically organized, it could help abate prejudices and misunderstandings and contribute to the appreciation and understanding of other societies and peoples.

Duggan, Butler, and Root had frequently discussed the implications of peace after the war and the relations of international mindedness to world understanding.[19] At these discussions, Butler began to give further consideration of the two proposals submitted by Duggan and Schofield, respectively. In December 1918, drawing on the best features of the two proposals, Butler drafted a version of his own international institute. His proposal included Plan A and Plan B. Plan A proposed an institute of education in the "technical and narrow sense of the word" to be subsidized by the Carnegie Corporation; Plan B called for an institute for furthering educational exchange in a much broader sense to be supported by the Carnegie Endowment. The educational exchange activities covered by Plan B included not only exchanges of teachers, students, and researchers, but also exchanges in the fields of commerce, industry, finance, and technical skills. On January 7, 1919, Butler received a notice from Henry Pritchett, president of the Carnegie Foundation for Advancement of Teaching, telling him that he had talked with Elihu Root about his proposal and that Root was in favor of going ahead with Plan B. A few days later, Butler formally presented his proposal to the executive committee of the Carnegie Endowment and requested that Stephen Duggan be named director of the new institute.[20]

The institute was established on February 1, 1919, as a department of the Carnegie Endowment for International Peace (CEIP). In order to guide the policy of this new institute, the CEIP asked representatives of the American Council on Education, the American University Union in Europe, and other organizations to form an administrative board for the institute.[21] Butler and Duggan named the new organization the Institute of International Relations, but Elihu Root did not agree because the name did not evoke its educational mission. Subsequently, Duggan accepted Root's suggestion and on March 15, 1919, the Institute of International Education was officially announced. The general goal of the IIE was "to develop international good will by means of educational agencies" but specifically was "to act as a clearinghouse of information and advice" for Americans and foreigners on educational exchange.[22] Duggan solicited the cooperation of American colleges and universities in this endeavor of international educational exchange. Some universities responded enthusiastically, but many remained passive. In order to achieve greater efficiency, the IIE created divisions to deal with specific institutions and world regions, with Duggan responsible for Europe, Paul Monroe for the Far East, Peter H. Goldsmith for Latin America, Virginia Newcomb for women's colleges, and Margaret C. Alexander for the International Relations Club.

## INITIAL PROGRAMS OF PROFESSOR AND STUDENT EXCHANGES

The IIE first concentrated on the exchange of professors and students to promote understanding and goodwill between nations. Before World War I, academic exchanges had been sponsored by a few isolated programs such as the Rhodes Scholarship Program, the Fellowship Program of the American Association of University Women, and the Kahn Foundation for the Foreign Travel of American Teachers. But the war disrupted these exchange programs. Duggan was anxious to revive them in structuring a new educational exchange system. He encouraged universities to participate in professor and student exchanges and to organize exchanges in a more cooperative manner. But the American Council on Education and the American University Union in Europe had already been working in the field of educational exchanges when the IIE was established. In order to avoid duplication and unnecessary competition, leaders of the IIE, the ACE, and the union worked out a cooperative partnership. Subsequently, the union's offices in Europe would represent the IIE abroad while the IIE would represent the union at home in the United States to deal with exchange affairs. In the spring of 1919, the IIE sent a questionnaire to 250 higher educational institutions to find out their interest in and needs for educational exchange. The IIE wanted to know on what conditions they would receive foreign professors and students and on what conditions they would send their own professors and students abroad. Duggan visited educational leaders on campuses across the country to promote educational exchange. After domestic surveys were done, Duggan left for Europe to introduce his new organization to European educational authorities, university officials, and prominent intellectuals.[23] He hoped to stimulate their interest in educational exchange with the United States.

Duggan's visit to European universities soon revealed that it was impossible to develop a systematic professor exchange based on pre-war practice, which typically had the sending countries bear the expenses. European universities were congested with students returning from the war, and teachers were in short supply. Devastated by the war, European universities could not spare teachers or professors for exchange, but they were anxious to have Americans as visiting professors. Duggan talked about his European experience with Paul Monroe of Teachers College, Columbia University, who was an enthusiastic advocate for international education. Monroe sat on both the administrative board of the IIE and the Committee on International Educational Relations of the ACE.[24] He indicated that American professors on sabbatical leave might be interested in teaching abroad if their traveling expenses were covered. Duggan forwarded Monroe's suggestion to the Carnegie Endowment for International Peace and asked for financial support. The CEIP responded with a grant of $12,500 for the traveling expenses. In selecting professors for exchange, the IIE paid special attention to the applicants' personality and scholarship, because they were to represent the United States during their teaching mission abroad and to "do great service to the development of international good will."[25] By 1923, 45 American professors on sabbatical leave benefited from the grant by participating in the program.[26] In contrast, the IIE did not have funds to sponsor visiting professors from foreign countries. Duggan thus encouraged American universities, whenever they could, to support foreign visiting professors on their own. With the recommendation of American scholars, dozens of prominent professors from Europe, Canada, and India came and lectured at several major American universities, mostly on the East Coast.

Meanwhile, Duggan sought opportunities for student exchange. He wanted to set up fellowship programs for American students to go abroad and for foreign students to come to America. But there was no funding for such programs. Duggan, who was deeply troubled by the devastating situation of European universities, thought of creating a Foreign Student Revolving Scholarship Fund with a long-range objective of building cultural bridges connecting the two sides of the Atlantic. According to his plan, the fund would provide financial assistance in the form of loans to European students who planned to study in the United States. Committees would carefully select the students for proper educational institutions. The students were to pass specially designed examinations and pursue post-college education in America for four years, followed by a year of practical training if they wished. Special persons were to be assigned to guide the students in their academic and personal matters and to send regular reports to the fund on students' progress.[27] Duggan thought that a foreign student should also make friends, travel, and become familiar with American life and institutions while he or she was in the United States. He believed that the important experience beyond academic and professional training would make the student's sojourn in the United States more meaningful. However, his plan did not go beyond the stage of conceptualization and was revived only after World War II when the U.S. government called upon the IIE to help administer government exchange programs. Most of the ideas expressed in the Foreign Student Revolving Scholarship Fund were then practiced in the administration of government exchange programs.[28]

In developing student exchange programs, the IIE cooperated with organizations that had educational relations with foreign countries—organizations such as the Pan-American Union, the American-Scandinavian Foundation, the Italy-America Society, the Council on Foreign Relations, the International Federation of University Women, and the Committee on Friendly Relations Among Foreign Students. As a result, various student tours were organized and fellowships were established. For instance, with the help of the Italy-America Society, the Alliance Française, and the American-Scandinavian Foundation, the IIE successfully arranged educational tours for American students to those countries.[29] Moreover, IIE leaders sat on the boards of various organizations, with Duggan as chairman of the Committee on Education of the Italy-America Society, Paul Monroe as chairman of the Educational Committee on the Near East, and Virginia Newcomb as the executive secretary of the Committee on International Relations of the Association of Collegiate Alumnae.[30]

Furthermore, the IIE worked with various foundations and foreign governments to publicize and administer their exchange scholarships. For instance, the IIE helped the American Council on Education and the Office Nationale des Universités et Ecoles Françaises to select students to receive exchange scholarships. It also helped administer fellowships for library work and public health that were established through the cooperation of the French government, the American Library Association, and the Carnegie Endowment for International Peace. In 1922, the Czechoslovakian government called upon the IIE to arrange its scholarship students to study in the United States. The American Chamber of Commerce of Mexico City also authorized the IIE to administer the scholarships that it had established for Mexican students to study at American universities. When a large number of American women tried to study at the women's colleges at Oxford in the early 1920s, the IIE was asked to pre-screen the applicants' credentials and recommend the best for admission.[31]

As an information clearinghouse, the IIE helped foreign students secure American university scholarships and American students opportunities to go abroad. Every day, it received inquiries from foreign and American students about scholarship information. This demand prompted the IIE to further investigate the availability of fellowships for student exchanges. It published two booklets for interested students in the early 1920s: *Fellowships and Scholarships Open to Foreign Students for Study in the United States* and *Fellowships and Scholarships Open to American Students for Study in Foreign Countries*. In addition, the IIE also published other booklets to help students get acquainted with the education of other countries. Those booklets included *Opportunities for Higher Education in France* (1919), *Opportunities for Graduate Study in the British Isles* (1919), *Opportunities for Higher Education in Italy* (1920), *Guide Book for Foreign Students in the United States,* and *Bibliography on the United States for Foreign Students* (1922). The *Guide Book for Foreign Students* was the first of its kind and was highly welcomed by foreign students and educational officials alike. A second edition of *The Guide Book* was printed the next year to satisfy large demands.

In conducting foreign student exchanges, the IIE was most concerned with three major issues: 1) proper orientation, 2) proper classification, and 3) fellowships.[32] As an increasing number of foreign students came to America after World War I, the country was replacing Germany as the rendezvous for foreign students. But few universities in the United States had undertaken any measures like those used in pre-war Germany to secure the effective orientation of foreign students. Investigations by the IIE indicated that practically nothing had been done for the orientation of foreign students at many American colleges and universities. But the Cosmopolitan Clubs at various universities were making a special effort to enroll foreign students in the clubs and to help them get acquainted with one another and with American students through dinners, dances, lectures, and concerts. One of the most helpful activities of the clubs was to invite foreign students to come to American homes for weekends. Similarly, the IIE recognized the extraordinary work that the Committee on Friendly Relations Among Foreign Students had been doing on behalf of foreign students. The IIE and the ACE urged universities with large numbers of foreign students to make adequate provisions for the supervision of the social as well as intellectual lives of foreign students. Consequently, some institutions of higher learning appointed faculty advisors to foreign students or formed committees on foreign student affairs.

Proper classification of foreign students was a challenging task for the IIE. There was confusion over the academic credentials of foreign students at American universities and colleges. For instance, graduates of one Chinese institution had been accepted for entrance at American colleges all the way from freshman to senior classes, which led to friction as well as resentment between institutions and students. In order to reduce confusion and better serve educational exchanges, the IIE attempted to establish an adequate system of academic evaluation of foreign credentials. It sent a questionnaire to colleges and universities with large numbers of foreign students, making inquiries about the institutions from which their foreign students came, the credentials that their foreign students sent in, and the evaluation of those credentials. The survey laid the groundwork upon which the IIE, the ACE, and the union in Europe eventually established the standards of credential evaluation that won the approval of both foreign and American educational authorities.[33]

Fellowships were essential for foreign students to come to the United States because American tuition was—comparatively speaking—exceptionally high. In addition to providing general information about scholarships, the IIE made special efforts to help students in an emergency. In 1921, the wretched condition of the expatriated Russians attracted the general attention of American society. Duggan appealed to American universities and philanthropic organizations for tuition fellowships and other assistance for Russian students. Fifty Russian students benefited from the new fellowships set up to enable them to continue their studies. In addition, the Rockefeller Foundation contributed a fund of $15,000 to aid those Russians who could not find a job or a fellowship.[34]

Besides the exchange programs of professors and students, the IIE also supervised the International Relations Clubs (IRC), which were officially known as the International Polity Clubs under the American Association for International Conciliation. The IRC existed at about 40 colleges and universities across the country to convey knowledge of international affairs at a time when many small colleges did not have courses on international relations and the "group system" in large universities prevented students from electing courses in the subject. Duggan took promoting the work of the IRC as his personal responsibility. He toured the country to give lectures on international relations at many colleges. Books, magazines, and other literature on world history and international relations were sent to IRC-affiliated institutions. In addition, the IIE prepared and published numerous syllabi for the IRC.[35] In 1924, the Carnegie Endowment of International Peace took over the IRC when financial support for the IIE was transferred to the Carnegie Corporation.[36]

## IMMIGRATION LAWS AND FOREIGN STUDENTS

In the early 1920s, the U.S. government adopted the most restrictive immigration policy in its history for fear of an influx of undesirable immigrants from Asia and war-ravaged Europe amidst a growing hysteria about communists and foreigners "perpetrating" domestic radicalism. Nativist sentiments surged in post-war American society, and Congress passed the Dillingham bill in 1921, which assigned immigration quotas to particular nationalities based on the 1910 census. In 1922, Congress extended the Dillingham bill for two more years. When the Dillingham bill was about to expire, the nativist forces led by Albert Johnson, a Republican from Washington State, successfully turned the bill into law in 1924. The new immigration law of 1924 restricted "the undesired immigrants" by moving the baseline census back to 1890 and reduced the quotas from 3 percent to 2 percent.[37] The law, as the nativists desired, excluded Asians who were defined as ineligible for citizenship and restricted immigrants mostly from Southern and Eastern Europe. As the law contained no specific provisions in regard to foreign students and scholars, they were thereby included in the quota of immigrants allotted to their countries. The immigration laws thus greatly affected the entry of foreign students into the United States. A considerable number of foreign students, thereafter, were detained at Ellis Island for deportation because the quota from their countries had been exceeded. The IIE reported in 1922: "Because of the new immigration law of 1921, foreign students experienced considerable hardship during the past year."[38]

In face of this new obstacle to international educational exchange and contact, the IIE and CFRFS criticized the new immigration laws and the harassment of foreign students at immigration stations. Duggan corresponded with the commissioner general of immigration at Washington, D.C. and held sessions with the commissioner of immigration at Ellis Island to seek improved treatment of foreign students. His effort resulted in an agreement with immigration authorities whereby a foreign student who complied in all respects with the immigration law was to be admitted although the quota of the country from which the student came had been exceeded. However, such a student was required to give a bond in the penalty of $500 that he would leave the country within a year.[39] Immigration officials soon discovered that the agreement with a bond in reference to foreign students was exploited by some impostors. The IIE therefore cooperated with immigration officials in the following matters. First, for convenient checking at Ellis Island, the IIE furnished the commissioner of immigration at Ellis Island with a list of *bona fide* students who had been admitted into American colleges and universities. In conformity with this action, a letter was sent to the colleges and universities requesting them to keep the IIE informed of any students admitted from foreign countries. Second, the IIE helped immigration officials evaluate official academic certificates and statements that students brought with them. Third, when the *bona fide* students came in the excess of quota, they would be paroled in the care of the IIE rather than being detained at Ellis Island, and the IIE would keep track of such students for immigration offices.[40]

The immigration laws of the 1920s gave rise to disturbing experiences of foreign students at the port of entry. Despite the efforts of the IIE and CFRFS to seek cooperation with immigration officials, misunderstandings and unpleasant incidents still occurred. IIE officials felt that special efforts should be made especially in regard to foreign women students, because parents of those students relied on the IIE to safeguard their children's orientation in the new American environment. Hence, IIE representatives met female exchange students on board ships and arranged their passage through customs. Provision was also made for their temporary stay at the International House of New York while they were in the city. The IIE assisted them with railway tickets, and when they arrived at their destination, they were usually received by a representative of the faculty from the school they were attending.[41] However, IIE extended assistance only to its fellowship students, who constituted a small percentage of the entire foreign student population in the United States. The majority of the students sought the assistance of the port-of-entry service that CFRFS offered.

The restrictive immigration laws discouraged foreign students from coming to the United States and adversely affected the progress of educational exchange in general. For this reason, Duggan wrote Congressional committees on immigration, suggesting the incorporation of certain provisions in the new immigration law to protect foreign students. He pointed out the negative effect of the restrictive immigration law on foreign students and reiterated the IIE's policy of encouraging student migration for the improvement of international understanding and peace. Specifically, Duggan made the following suggestions to amend the new immigration laws. First, an alien wishing to study in the United States should present a diploma from an accredited secondary school (with an English version), showing the eligibility for admittance to an American college or university. Second, any alien provided with such documents should be permitted to land without hindrance and to remain in this country as long as he or she continued to be a *bona fide* student. Third, at the end of each academic year, the alien student should present to the immigration authorities a statement from his or her American college or university in which he or she was studying, certifying that he or she had completed the year's work and intended to continue his or her studies there next year. Fourth, the wife and minor children of an alien student should be admitted to this country and allowed to remain as long as such student was continuing his studies in the United States.[42] Duggan's suggestions were largely accepted by the government in reshaping the policy regulating foreign students and scholars.

## THE CARNEGIE CORPORATION, THE LAURA SPELMAN ROCKEFELLER MEMORIAL, AND THE RESTRUCTURING OF THE IIE

In the spring of 1923, just as the IIE was making strides at promoting educational exchanges on American campuses, the executive committee of the Carnegie Endowment for International Peace decided to stop funding the IIE effective the next fiscal year. To Duggan, this news was a terrible blow. The reason for CEIP's decision was its financial incapability to support the IIE anymore. Indeed, the entire budget of CEIP was reduced by $128,000 that year.[43] But there were speculations that the CEIP might have ceased the support not merely because of budgetary difficulty. Documents of the Laura Spelman Rockefeller Memorial indicate that as early as January 8, 1923, Pritchett, Keppel, Woods, and Ruml—leaders from the Carnegie and the Rockefeller philanthropies—had already had a conference in regard to CEIP's stand on the IIE and the possible future support to the IIE from the Laura Spelman Rockefeller Memorial.[44] At this conference, Pritchett mentioned "that he was in California when the Peace Endowment reached its decision with reference to the Institute, and felt that had he been present things would have been different. He felt that Carnegie Corporation might support the Institute for a year giving it opportunity to turn around."[45] Meanwhile, Elihu Root, chairman of the executive committee of the CEIP, wrote Arthur Woods of the Laura Spelman Rockefeller Memorial, recommending the IIE. He mentioned that IIE was "urgently needed" for those who were interested in international affairs.[46]

Leaders of the Laura Spelman Rockefeller Memorial actually had an interest in the educational needs of foreign students in American colleges and universities. They considered the assistance to foreign student education an important contribution to promoting international goodwill and understanding. The trustees of the memorial felt that the IIE was an important instrument through which the memorial's work on the welfare of foreign students in this country, especially "that portion related to the more strictly educational needs, could be carried out."[47] At the same time, presidents of colleges and universities also indicated to leaders of the memorial that the IIE had provided an extremely valuable service as a central clearinghouse on educational exchange information and had helped formulate policies regarding foreign students.

In 1924, the Carnegie Corporation and the Laura Spelman Rockefeller Memorial attempted to create a comprehensive system of international educational exchange and foreign student education in the United States.[48] They asked leaders of the ACE, IIE, and CFRFS to define the field in which each of them was working. CFRFS cooperated with the hope of getting grants from the philanthropies to support its work.[49] When the Carnegie Corporation and the memorial failed to bring the three organizations together to work in an integrated system, they decided to restructure the IIE and turn it into a single most important agency representing the United States in international educational affairs. The Carnegie Corporation and the memorial suggested that the IIE form a new board of directors and get incorporated into an independent enterprise. This reorganization of the IIE was regarded "as a going concern [which] represents a natural point of departure for work with foreign students" and international educational exchange.[50]

The IIE could not carry on its functions without funding during the transition, however. Back in May 1923, Pritchett had mentioned that the Carnegie Corporation would give the IIE one year of support. IIE leaders lost no time in campaigning for stronger financial support from the Carnegie Corporation and the Laura Spelman Rockefeller Memorial while they complied with the reorganization plan. In December 1923, representatives of the ACE, the union in Europe, and the IIE agreed to absorb the union into the ACE's administrative system. The Laura Spelman Rockefeller Memorial and the Carnegie Corporation assisted with the rearrangement of the international work of the three organizations and shared the financial support of international education activities. The Carnegie Corporation provided an annual grant of $35,000 to the IIE for five years while the Laura Spelman Rockefeller Memorial made a matching grant to ACE for its international work and for the maintenance of the union offices in Europe.[51] Previously, the union and the ACE had been supported primarily by the annual contributions of American universities and colleges. The financial resources of the Carnegie Corporation and the memorial helped complete the reorganization of the IIE in 1927 and eventually shaped the administrative structure of American educational exchange programs.

The need for the change was multifaceted. First, the duplication of work was apparent as many agencies engaged in international education affairs. It became imperative that a national organization be established to administer the work of international education. Second, the reorganization of the IIE was expected to stimulate more interest in international education among American colleges and universities. Beardsley Ruml of the memorial reported, "American educational institutions as a group had become apathetic with reference to the foreign student and the international problems of education, and that this work would be more efficiently and more enthusiastically administered by an institution in which these international problems were of primary consequences."[52] Subsequently, representatives of the

ACE, the union, the IIE, the Carnegie Corporation, and the Laura Spelman Rockefeller Memorial held several conferences during 1925–1927 in an attempt to integrate international education activities in a single organization so as to avoid duplication and confusion. They finally agreed that the administration of international educational affairs should be concentrated in the IIE. As far as the three educational agencies were concerned, the union was to become a subsidiary of the IIE, and the ACE was to devote its attention to domestic educational affairs and to turn over to the IIE all matters relating to international education, which included exchanges of professors and students, advice and correspondence, and the studies of policies and practices. In order to enable the IIE to carry out its increased responsibilities at home and abroad, the Carnegie Corporation increased its annual grant to the IIE to $60,000 in 1927; the memorial, correspondingly, increased its annual grant to the ACE to $50,000 for the transitional development of the IIE.[53]

After the restructuring, the IIE increased the representation of professional associations on its board of directors, which included the American Council on Education, the Association of American Universities, the Association of State Universities, the Association of American Colleges, the American Association of University Professors, the National Education Association, the American Association of University Women, the American Association for the Advancement of Science, the National Research Council, the Social Science Research Council, the American Council of Learned Societies, the American Committee on Intellectual Cooperation, and the American Library Association.[54] Foreign educational organizations and educators were requested to contact the IIE on international educational affairs.[55] Major activities of the IIE included the maintenance of a central clearinghouse for international education information, planning student tours, negotiating the evaluation of equivalent credits and degrees between American and foreign educational institutions, collecting statistics, administering fellowships and scholarships for exchange, and handling immigration problems affecting foreign students.

In considering further funding for the IIE, the Carnegie Corporation performed an evaluation of the IIE in international education. IIE leaders, after the experience with the CEIP, were anxious to make sure that funding from the Carnegie Corporation would come through. They used prominent educators and civic leaders such as Paul Monroe, Mongenthan, and Anson P. Stokes as a lobbists to work on Frederick Keppel, president of the Carnegie Corporation, to secure from him the assurance of adequate support for the IIE. Anson Stokes, who was general secretary of the American Union and an active civic leader, carried an unusual weight on policy decision due to his active leadership in the educational realm.[56] In the end, their effort bore fruit. The Carnegie Corporation decided on November 17, 1927, that it would continue to support the IIE for another 10 years starting January 1,

1929 with an annual grant of $60,000. This grant, however, depended upon the IIE's securing of a similar sum from other sources. IIE leaders, therefore, requested the board of trustees of the Laura Spelman Rockefeller Memorial to continue cooperation with the Carnegie Corporation "in this important educational enterprise by renewing for another term of years from January 1, 1929, its grant of at least $50,000 a year towards 'the development of the Institute of International Education.'"[57] The trustees of the memorial, however, declined to permanently support the IIE. Director Ruml of the memorial pointed out that "since the work of the Institute, though important, is not closely connected with the Memorial's special interests, it would seem desirable to indicate to the Institute the Memorial's inability to assume a permanent commitment to the Institute."[58] Ruml even questioned whether the memorial's appropriation to the IIE should exceed $40,000 a year for the operation of the union offices in Europe, should the memorial continue to support the IIE. Finally, the memorial made a 10-year terminal grant of $240,000 to support the IIE's general operations, with the goal of giving the IIE the flexibility to plan its programs and obtain support from other sources. Ruml notified Duggan, "The Memorial would appreciate it if no public announcement were made of this gift, other than that which is made as a routine matter in your regular annual report."[59] The grant set the condition that no more than $40,000 should be withdrawn annually and that $1 should be obtained from other sources for each dollar paid by the memorial.

After the Rockefeller Foundation took over the memorial in the 1929 reorganization of the Rockefeller Boards, the Rockefeller Foundation assumed no responsibility to continue the support to the IIE. But in 1936, when the memorial grant was exhausted, the IIE asked the Rockefeller Foundation for further support. President Keppel of the Carnegie Corporation also urged the Rockefeller Foundation to continue the sponsorship. He even made "threats" and reminded Raymond Fosdick that "the Foundation and our Corporation came to an understanding at the behest of Anson Stokes, whereby you would look after the Union, and we would put in approximately the same amount for the Institute of International Education (Duggan's show)." He further explained, "It would have been difficult for us under the terms of our charter to support enterprises in Europe. We have been fully satisfied with our side of the bargain, and are looking forward to supporting the Institute as long as Duggan is in the saddle."[60] With the urge of the Carnegie Corporation, the executive committee of the Rockefeller Foundation made a provision of $20,000 to the IIE on February 19, 1937 as a supplement to the final appropriation of the memorial.[61]

## EXPANSION OF NEW PROGRAMS

With the financial support from the Carnegie Corporation and the memorial, the IIE was able to implement various new programs of educational exchange and intellectual cooperation in the 1920s and 1930s. These programs included Summer Schools Abroad, Junior Year Abroad, Exchange of Industrial Management Studies, Exchange with Latin America, and Exchange Fellowship Programs.

## Summer Schools Abroad

The 1920s witnessed a growing interest among American youth in going to Europe. The IIE and other educational organizations helped arrange summer tours for American college students. Steamship companies, whose trans-Atlantic business was unfavorably affected by the drop of immigrant passengers, seized the new interest of college students in traveling to Europe. They tore out the accommodations in the steerage of some ships and created what was known as Student Third Class, which included staterooms, dining rooms, and recreation facilities. Those rooms and facilities, while not equal to that of Second Class, were much better than the old steerage. Companies advertised these new accommodations at reduced prices for students exclusively. Hundreds of thousands of American students spent their summer vacations in Europe, and many foreign students traveled to the United States. But the easy access to trans-Atlantic travel also gave rise to incidents of "excessive drinking and freedom of conduct" of some American students, which not only caused concerns for the students' parents but also invited criticism of American education in European countries.[62] The IIE was challenged to take actions to help young Americans better adjust to European societies and to make the tours more educationally profitable.

The IIE cooperated with European universities to create summer courses for American students, primarily in language studies. These summer sessions were first offered at various French universities and then extended to Berlin, Heidelberg, Hamburg, Vienna, Rome, Geneva, Madrid, and later to Puerto Rico and Mexico City when American students traveled to Latin America.[63] The growth of summer schools in European countries was particularly remarkable (see Table 2.1). In 1929, there were 104 summer schools in 12 European countries; by 1933, more than 150 summer schools were operating in 16 European countries. Americans played a significant part in the summer schools of these countries. Statistics of 1931 and 1932 show that even in the early years of the Depression, nearly 3,000 Americans attended European summer schools annually.[64] Many Americans attended these schools for language and cultural studies. The IIE regarded courses in language, literature, and history of a foreign country particularly advantageous for American students to take in the summer session of a university abroad. It urged American higher educational institutions to grant credits for these summer courses as long as they were of equal standards.

**Table 2.1**

## Number of Summer Schools in European Countries, 1929–1933

| Country/Year | 1929 | 1930 | 1931 | 1932 | 1933 |
|---|---|---|---|---|---|
| Austria | 3 | 6 | 5 | 4 | 5 |
| Belgium | 3 | 2 | 3 | 3 | 3 |
| Czechoslovakia | | | 1 | 1 | 2 |
| Denmark | 2 | 3 | 2 | 2 | 2 |
| France | 22 | 23 | 24 | 25 | 27 |
| Germany | 21 | 25 | 19 | 32 | 30 |
| Great Britain | 21 | 20 | 22 | 20 | 32 |
| Hungary | 1 | 1 | 1 | 1 | 1 |
| Italy | 9 | 11 | 9 | 12 | 15 |
| Yugoslavia | | 2 | 2 | 3 | 3 |
| Netherlands | 2 | 3 | 3 | 4 | 3 |
| Poland | | | 1 | 2 | 1 |
| Portugal | 1 | 1 | 1 | 1 | 0 |
| Romania | | | 3 | 1 | 1 |
| Spain | 9 | 10 | 10 | 12 | 13 |
| Sweden | | | | 1 | 2 |
| Switzerland | 10 | 10 | 13 | 11 | 15 |
| Ireland | | 1 | | | |
| Total | 104 | 118 | 119 | 135 | 155 |

Sources: *Fourteenth Annual Report of the Director* (New York: IIE, 1933), 29.

## Junior Year Abroad Program

Summer Study Abroad inspired another program at universities and colleges: the Junior Year Abroad Program. The program was first started at the University of Delaware. In the fall of 1922, the University of Delaware sent

Professor Raymond W. Kirkbride to France to investigate the possibility of organizing a program of French studies that the University would accept in lieu of the regular work of the junior year. As a result of his visit, nine students in the sophomore class were selected in the spring of 1923 to be part of an experiment that would "test the wisdom of interrupting an American student's college career by sending him abroad for his junior year" and crediting the year's study abroad toward his college degree. The selected students were men of excellent scholastic standing, proficient in French, and of a temperament that gave promise of quick adaptability to a strange environment. They left the United States in July 1923, stayed for three months at the University of Nancy, and participated in an intense course in French. Then, they moved to Paris where they were matriculated at the Sorbonne. During the entire year, students pursued a carefully organized program known as Cours de Civilisation Française, which was designed to give the student an adequate knowledge of French civilization and culture. The studies included language, literature, history, geography, science, industries, and institutions of France as well as courses in art, music, economics, and philosophy. In Nancy and Paris, each student lived in a carefully selected French family as the only foreign member of the family. The students pursued their studies under the daily supervision of Professor Kirkbride. They also attended the best plays and operas, visited museums, libraries, and churches, and made weekend trips to places of interest outside of Paris. The success of the first group of Junior Year Abroad Program had a far-reaching impact on American college students and encouraged the University of Delaware to accept students from other institutions to participate in the program. Enrollment of the Junior Year Abroad Program increased to 80 in subsequent years.[65]

The University of Delaware Program was open to male students only, however. In 1924, Smith College received numerous requests from students and their parents asking for junior-year abroad studies—especially in France. In response to the requests, President Neilson of Smith College asked Professor Cattanes to investigate the possibility of starting a junior-year abroad program. As a result of her efforts, a one-year program of studies abroad was organized in the way that would justify Smith College faculty in accepting it in lieu of the junior year study at the college. In September 1925, a group of 40 juniors of excellent scholastic standing and ability to use French went to join Professor Cattanes in France for a year of study at the Sorbonne. The students went through an intensive course in French at Grenoble before beginning courses in Paris in November. The Smith College group also participated in extracurricular activities similar to those of the University of Delaware Program.[66] The Junior Year Abroad Program of Smith College offered an alternative for female students at various colleges to spend a year abroad during their college education.

Certain conditions helped promote the success of the Junior Year Abroad Program. First, the program had the hearty support of French educational authorities and the approval of interested American faculty. Second, students were carefully selected with the criteria that each student, in addition to scholastic excellence, must possess an ability to concentrate and engage in hard and continuous work. Third, the supervision of a faculty member was indispensable for the success of the program. And finally, the preliminary three months' intensive course in French was essential for the success of the rest of the program. In a technical college or in one with a highly science-oriented curriculum, however, it was difficult to organize such a program because of the very emphasis on humanities in the Junior Year Abroad Program. The acceptance of such a program also depended largely upon whether the subjects covered in the Cours de Civilisation Française would compare favorably with those in the junior year of home colleges.

To participate in the Junior Year Abroad Program, a student had to bear the necessary expenses. Both Smith and Delaware charged the student the same tuition for the year abroad as at home. In addition, the student must meet his or her traveling and incidental expenses. This situation posed difficulties for students who could greatly profit from the experience but were not able to pay. Although the IIE did not encourage individual undergraduates to study abroad for fear that they would become denationalized in a foreign country, it saw the advantage of the Junior Year Abroad Program with careful supervision of a faculty member over the undergraduate students. The IIE cooperated with Smith College and the University of Delaware to solve the problem of financial constraint for certain students by forming a committee to administer the program. The Committee on Foreign Travel and Study donated to the IIE five special fellowships for the Junior Year Abroad Program. The IIE hoped that the Junior Year Abroad Program, which had passed the experimental stage and had become a permanent feature of international education at American colleges, would expand into other countries besides France. Director Duggan of the IIE believed, "Such an agency in the development of international good will should be used in connection with all the countries of Europe with which we have close intellectual cooperation."[67] With the assistance of the IIE and other concerned institutions, the Junior Year Abroad Program was extended to Germany. In the fall of 1930, a center was established at the University of Munich to organize American Junior Year Abroad Program courses similar to those at the Sorbonne. About 90 colleges and universities in the United States granted credit for work done abroad under the Delaware and Smith programs in 1930. The Junior Year Abroad Fellowships, which the University of Delaware offered through the IIE's administration, also became an important part of the Program.[68] In 1937, a small group of students in the Junior Year Abroad Program was sent to study in Geneva and thus extended the program to Switzerland.[69]

## Exchange of Industrial Management

Educational exchange with European countries also expanded from cultural and scientific studies to industrial management. In the late 1920s, several European countries delegated their embassies in Washington, D.C. to negotiate internships for their students to study industrial management in America. As a result, the Bureau of Immigration and the Labor Department reached an agreement that permitted university graduates from certain European countries to enter the United States on nonquota visas to secure employment in American industrial plants. This work-study program also gained the support of the American Federation of Labor on the condition that the students were restricted in numbers and were carefully supervised. Application for the program was made through the legation of a European country in Washington, D.C., and the IIE helped administer the program. The students, known as work students, were carefully selected and expected to occupy executive and managerial positions in their home industrial plants after the training in the United States. American leaders were confident about the country's scientific business management methods and wanted others to emulate them. The work students were to study "American efficiency methods in industrial management and the relations between workers and managers, which are on a happier footing in this country than in European countries."[70] The length of the study of American industrial management varied from one to two years. In 1929, about 150 work students came from Germany. Then, the program was extended to Poland, Czechoslovakia, Austria, the Scandinavian countries, Great Britain, Switzerland, and Hungary.[71] Some of the students were also placed in banking and commercial enterprises to learn modern management methods. They were paid regular wages attached to their positions and were usually allowed to stay only for one year. But in 1931, when the job market deteriorated during the Depression, the commissioner of immigration requested the discontinuation of the program and the Department of Labor withdrew the privilege to the students.[72]

## Exchange with Latin America

In the early 1930s, the United States began to pay more attention to cultural relations with Latin American countries. After President Hoover's tour to South America in 1929, the Carnegie Endowment for International Peace made a grant to the Pan American Union for the purpose of inviting Argentine and Brazilian scholars to visit the United States. In 1931, Duggan spent half a year in South American countries, meeting with government and educational officials to further stimulate educational visits of Latin American scholars to the United States. The Carnegie Endowment for International

Peace followed up Duggan's visit with a grant of $4,000 to sponsor a group of Chilean scholars to the United States. At the same time, the IIE proposed that a group of distinguished American scholars make a trip to South America for educational exchange. The proposal received support from the Pan American Union and approval from the State Department. In addition, the IIE established a summer school at Rio de Janeiro, Brazil in 1929 and another one at Lima, Peru in 1932. But political chaos and natural disasters disrupted the IIE's attempts to consolidate summer programs in Brazil and Peru.[73] Nonetheless, student exchange with Latin America continued, although it was organized differently from that with European countries. Latin American students tended to focus on the study of medicine, engineering, technical research, agriculture, journalism, and education in the United States. But they went to Europe to study philosophy, art, and music. In contrast, only a small number of Americans went to Latin American countries to study sociology, archaeology, anthropology, and ethnology in the 1930s.[74] American educational exchange with Latin America began to take a dramatic turn, however, with President Franklin Roosevelt's "Good Neighbor Policy" and the outbreak of World War II. We will discuss these new developments in Chapter 5.

## Fellowship Programs

Fellowship programs constituted the main work of the IIE. Private organizations and different governments around the world entrusted fellowships to the IIE for their administration. In 1926, the number of fellowships entrusted to the IIE was 148 (see Table 2.2), but by 1938 the number had increased to 375 (see Table 2.3). Those fellowships covered tuition and room and board. Because of the high cost of travel, some candidates could not afford to come to the United States even though they were offered fellowships. Therefore, travel grants were established to facilitate certain exchanges. In addition, there were fellowships that were not operated by the IIE. They included the Rockefeller Foundation fellowships for 150 graduate appointees annually from 40 different countries, the Commonwealth Fund of 40 fellows every year from Great Britain to study in the United States, the Barbour Fellowships at the University of Michigan for young women from Asia, and the American Scandinavian Foundation scholarships for student exchange.[75] Those fellowships reflected the strong cultural internationalist sentiment in the 1920s.

Although the increase of IIE fellowships was remarkable during the 1920s and 1930s, exchanges conducted via these fellowships were of a relatively small number. For instance, the 191 fellowship recipients from abroad in 1938 constituted a mere 3 percent of the entire foreign student population in the United States. But the significance of these fellowships should not be

**Table 2.2**

## Student Exchange Fellowships to and from the United States, 1926

| Names of Fellowships | From | To | Total |
|---|---|---|---|
| American Field Service Fellowships for French Universities | 11 | | 11 |
| Franco-American Fellowships | 21 | 25 | 46 |
| American German Student Exchange Fellowships | 20 | 35 | 55 |
| American Czechoslovak Exchange Fellowships | 5 | 5 | 10 |
| American Hungarian Exchange Fellowships | 5 | 5 | 10 |
| Willard Straight Fellowship for China | 1 | | 1 |
| Fellowships for the Junior Year Abroad | 5 | | 5 |
| Postes d'Assitant for French Universities | 10 | | 10 |
| Total | 78 | 70 | 148 |

Sources: *Seventh Annual Report of the Director* (New York: IIE, 1926), 13–15.


**Table 2.3**

## Student Exchange Fellowships to and from the United States, 1938–1939

| Names of Fellowships | From | To | Total |
|---|---|---|---|
| American Czechoslovak Student Exchange | 5 | 13 | 18 |
| Franco-American Student Exchange | 55 | 44 | 99 |
| American German Student Exchange | 39 | 54 | 93 |
| American Hungarian Student Exchange | 3 | 5 | 8 |
| American Italian Student Exchange | 17 | 15 | 32 |
| American Japanese Student Exchange | 1 | 1 | 2 |
| Latin American Student Exchange | 3 | 35 | 38 |
| American Spanish Student Exchange | | 2 | 2 |
| Swiss American Student Exchange | 11 | 10 | 21 |
| American Field Service Fellows | 1 | 4 | 5 |
| Carnegie Art Scholars (Summer) | 20 | | 20 |

| Names of Fellowships | From | To | Total |
|---|---|---|---|
| Advanced Science Fellow for France | 1 | | 1 |
| Fellows of Société des Amis de L'Université de Paris | 2 | | 2 |
| Junior Year Students in Paris | 14 | | 14 |
| Fellow of Germanistic Society of America | 1 | | 1 |
| Munich Junior Year Students (varying grants) | 7 | | 7 |
| Salzburg Summer Scholar | 1 | | 1 |
| Pan American Airways System Travel Fellows | | 4 | 4 |
| Special Appointee from Bulgaria | | 1 | 1 |
| Special Appointee from Finland | | 1 | 1 |
| Special Appointee from Great Britain | | 1 | 1 |
| Special Appointee from Holland | | 1 | 1 |
| Special Appointee from Ireland | | 1 | 1 |
| Special Appointee from Norway | | 1 | 1 |
| Special Appointee trom Sweden | | 1 | 1 |
| Total | 181 | 194 | 375 |

Sources: *Nineteenth Annual Report of the Director* (New York: IIE, 1938), 56–57.

ignored. The fellowships were established for the purpose of enabling "bright, capable, and typical students to study abroad who because of economic restriction would otherwise be unable to do so." Fellowship students, upon returning to their homelands, were expected to become leaders in their communities and to influence public opinion in favor of international understanding. Candidates were instructed that fellowships were created as a valuable instrument for international understanding and only incidentally for the personal advantage of the fellows. They were expected to serve as sources of information concerning the life and institutions of the countries in which they studied. Each American student sent abroad was required to write two reports during the academic year on his impressions of the people of the country he studied, particularly on the university organization and administration and on students' attitudes toward life. The confidential reports written by American students helped the IIE to form new exchange policies.[76]

Drawing upon its experiences, the IIE developed principles in regard to the administration of fellowships. First, the IIE offered fellowships only to graduate students. IIE leaders believed that every young person should have his or her national education before studying abroad. They thought that by the time they graduated from college, the students were usually sufficiently mature to compare justly their own country with a foreign civilization. Early experience in educational exchanges helped shape such a view among IIE leaders than when undergraduates went abroad to study, they did not fit into the administrative scheme in foreign institutions and frequently floundered a considerable time before getting settled. If they stayed many years abroad, they tended to become denationalized. IIE leaders found this situation particularly true with students from Asia and Latin America. For instance, in the 1920s China sent more students to the United States than to all of Europe, and American influence on Chinese education was profound. However, there was serious denationalization of the undergraduate Chinese students that resulted from too prolonged a stay in the United States. These young Chinese had problems readjusting to their own society when they returned to China. In 1924, a group of eminent American educators and a few Chinese scholars who were educated in the United States held a conference on the problems of returned Chinese students. They devoted their meeting mainly to the problem of denationalization and urged Chinese students to secure their general education in China and come to the United States only for graduate work of a specialized kind. They suggested that the Boxer Indemnity Fellowships should be granted to graduate students only. Moreover, the Boxer fellowships should no longer be confined to students from Qinghua College, the preparation school for Boxer Indemnity Fellows, but should also be open to students from all Chinese colleges for the selection of best students. In 1929, the Boxer Indemnity fellowships began to be granted exclusively to graduate students in China. The American leaders of women's education in China also formed an organization, the Committee on Foreign Study for Chinese Women, to select women students who wished to go to the United States. The committee's influence was so powerful that the best women's colleges in the United States refused to receive students whose credentials were not passed upon by the committee.[77]

Second, the IIE's primary consideration in granting a fellowship was based on scholarly merit. Study abroad fellowships were open via competition to all American graduate students. The IIE did not set up its own examination, however; instead, it selected students according to their college performance. The candidates had to show that they had a working knowledge of the language of the country they wanted to study in so that they could participate sufficiently in seminar discussions. The IIE's Committee on Candidate Selection was made up of language professors who were familiar with the conditions in those particular foreign countries. Students must possess the ability to adapt to a new environment and culture for successfully carrying out their studies. Each of the selected American students would read the reports of former fellows who went to the same university. In the case of foreign students, the IIE provided each of the fellowship holders a copy of the

*Guide Book for Foreign Students in the United States* for their adjustment to American education and living. Moreover, in the early 1930s the IIE started an orientation meeting for foreign students upon their arrival in mid September. The orientation meeting was held in International House New York for about three to five days to help foreign fellows to get to know each other and to establish personal connection with IIE representatives. Third, the IIE requested that candidates must clarify a particular subject of study rather than going abroad "for vague and indefinite purposes, such as good will and internationalism." IIE indicated that goodwill was best developed incidentally as a result of contact of a foreigner with his fellow students in the same field of work "where all are measured against one another in the qualities which go to make up a real manhood."[78]

The majority of fellowships for foreign students came from American colleges and universities. In the early fall of each year, the IIE would request information from these institutions as to whether they intended to offer any fellowships for foreign students in the following year or for students from a particular foreign country or countries. The IIE would then work with foreign educational authorities to find the candidates for these fellowships at American colleges and universities. The fellowships for American students to study in foreign countries mainly came from foreign governments. The IIE organized those fellowships under various exchange categories to fulfill a two-way educational exchange.[79] Moreover, individuals and private organizations with a special interest in cultural cooperation with a particular country were also drawn to the IIE to create new exchange programs. For instance, Mr. Coffin, president of General Electric Company, donated a quarter of a million dollars to found "The American Field Service Fellowships for French Universities" in commemoration of the young American ambulance drivers who died in the French service before the United States officially joined the war. The Carl Schurz Memorial Foundation offered an annual fund of $10,000 for the American-German Student Exchange. The Council on Inter-American Relations, cooperating with the National Foreign Trade Council, contributed substantial sums for the support of the IIE's exchange with Latin American countries.[80] From the initiation of exchange fellowships in 1922 to 1938, a total of 1,638 foreign students received IIE fellowships at the value of $1,234,812, and a total of 2,079 American students went abroad on IIE fellowships at the value of $808,621.[81] Table 2.4 summarizes the IIE's educational exchanges from 1922 to 1938.

## CHALLENGES TO EDUCATIONAL EXCHANGE

The entire development of educational exchange was undertaken in face of various challenges. First, the American immigration laws of the early 1920s made it more difficult for foreign students to be admitted into the United

**Table 2.4**

**IIE Educational Exchanges to and from the United States, 1922–1938**

| Regions | To | From | Period covered |
|---------|-----|------|----------------|
| Austria | 49 | 67 | 1928–1938 |
| China | 3 | 3 | 1935–1938 |
| Czechoslovakia | 87 | 127 | 1922–1938 |
| France | 506 | 309 | 1925–1938 |
| Germany | 566 | 642 | 1925–1938 |
| Hungary | 36 | 87 | 1925–1938 |
| Italy | 121 | 103 | 1928–1938 |
| Latin America | 4 | 135 | 1931–1938 |
| Spain | 11 | 19 | 1929–1938 |
| Switzerland | 69 | 92 | 1928–1938 |

Sources: *Nineteenth Annual Report of the Director* (New York: IIE, 1938), 55.

States than into other countries. University officials found the immigration regulations irritating because they spent tremendous time and energy straightening out problems with immigration offices for a relatively small number of students. In 1927, the University of Pittsburgh started a detailed study of the problems of individual foreign students and their status to find out the best solution to the triangular tangle of immigration laws, university procedures, and student mobility. The study continued for three years, and the findings indicated that university admission needed to develop a system that was constructive and helpful to foreign student supervision by taking into account the regulations of immigration laws and government policies regarding student supervision. Ruth C. Mitchell, foreign student advisor at the University of Pittsburgh, shared her work with other university officials in charge of foreign students in her monograph *Foreign Students and the Immigration Laws of the United States.* The booklet, published by the IIE in 1930, informed university officials about the actual operations of the student provisions of the immigration laws and helped universities take a position to protect students' interests.

Second, foreign students in the United States faced new problems when they were restricted from seeking jobs when the Depression began. As unemployment continued to rise in the United States, the Department of Labor issued strict regulations limiting foreign students from work. Congress supported the Labor Department by enacting a statute that gave the secretary of labor absolute control over the status of a foreign student. Regulations issued by the secretary of labor on September 1, 1932, "provide that the foreign student may not engage in 'any gainful occupation' whatsoever," otherwise, they would be deported.[82] Leaders of the IIE worried that some students might face extreme difficulty in supporting themselves under the new regulations. To help the needy students maintain their status as *bona fide* students, the Committee on Emergency Aid to Chinese Students,[83] which was set up in 1927 to assist Chinese students when their funds were cut short by political crisis in China, extended aid to all foreign students in 1932. By October 1932, 46 students from Asia and Eastern Europe were helped with funds from the committee. All of them would have been deported from the United States if not for the action of the committee.[84]

The regulations of the Labor Department caused an outcry among individuals and organizations concerned with foreign students and international understanding. They pointed out that foreign students often picked up work unfilled by American students, such as foreign language tutoring and translation. In his letter to the editor of *The New York Times*, Chauncey Belknap, a member on the Board of Governors of International House New York, defended the legal right of foreign students to work in the United States, citing the 1926 case *United States ex rel. Antonini vs. Curran, Commissioner*. He commented, "It would be a tragedy to send them [foreign students] home embittered with the thought of America as a country where, for foreign students, education has become a privilege of the rich, and the poor are denied even the right to work their way through college."[85] Duggan questioned, "Ought the international educational and cultural relations of the United States be placed under the control of the Department of Labor which, almost of necessity, will look upon the whole matter as a problem of employment?"[86] Duggan suggested, "Were the determination of student status and professor status to be placed in the Office of Education of the Department of Interior some causes of international misunderstanding would be moved. Even without such a transfer of supervision the situation would be improved, were the officials of the Department of Labor to consult the Office of Education before issuing regulations concerning foreign students and professors."[87] Duggan argued publicly for the establishment of a Department of Education in the U.S. government to take responsibility for American cultural relations with other countries.[88] The IIE also cited existing treaties and legislation in its publication "The Foreign Teacher: His Legal Status as Shown in Treaties and Legislation" to help foreign teachers deal with the new government policy.

After many endeavors by organizations like the IIE, CFRFS, the International Student Committee, and International Houses, some improvements were made in 1934 with regard to the work permit for foreign students. Characterizing the issue in contemporary political discourse, international educators called the improvements "The New Deal and the Immigrant." Under this new deal, foreign students were again allowed to work a limited number of hours to support themselves. With this change of policy, officials at the port of entry also made the entrance of foreign students easier.[89]

During the Depression, colleges and universities were obliged to assign as many fellowships as possible to American students, and money for foreign students became scarce. Although colleges and universities still offered limited fellowships for students and professors from abroad, their enthusiasm and optimism in international peace via education were greatly weakened in the face of deteriorating international relations of economics and politics. Moreover, in the late 1930s educational exchange faced serious international challenges. The growing tensions between nations projected a dark future and cast malicious clouds over the educational exchange for world peace. When Germany annexed Austria and Czechoslovakia by force in 1938–1939, objection to the American-German exchange was filed with the IIE on the assumption "that German students were disguised Nazi propagandists." There were accusations that IIE-sponsored German students engaged in propaganda in American colleges. The IIE requested the 60 institutions that had offered German students fellowships to provide definite information on the matter. Among the 55 institutions that responded, 47 stated "that German students behaved as did the foreign students generally," working hard to learn as much as possible in the fields of their study; and "the other eight made only qualified objection."[90] But under great pressure, IIE nonetheless withdrew from the American-German Student Exchange in 1938.

During World War II, the IIE continued its educational exchange with Europe—especially the expansion of American Scandinavian exchange and fellowships for British students. The fastest growth of exchange, however, was with Latin America in those years. The program with Latin America was greatly encouraged by the Division of Cultural Relations of the State Department, which actively sought the expertise of the IIE in cultural exchanges to help develop government-sponsored exchange programs. The cooperation of the IIE and the State Department, which we will discuss in later chapters, set the stage for the government to tap private resources for cultural diplomacy during the Cold War. IIE was created to respond to the new challenge of international relations after World War I, with the aim of developing international goodwill and understanding through international intellectual cooperation and educational exchange. With the financial support from the Carnegie Corporation and the Laura Spelman Rockefeller Memorial, the IIE grew into an important agency representing the United States in international educational affairs. In cooperation with educational institutions and organizations, it made remarkable accomplishments in the inter-war years—although educational exchange programs were still carried out on a relatively small scale. In addition to creating opportunities for foreign students and scholars to come to the United States, Duggan labored assiduously to "internationalize" American education with the Fellowship Programs, Junior Year Abroad Program, and Summer Schools Abroad Program. But the IIE conducted exchanges mainly with Europe, although increased attention was given to Latin America from the late 1930s. IIE programs contrasted with the work of CFRFS, whose emphasis was on students from Asia, the Middle East, Latin America, and Africa. IIE leaders were aware, however, of the importance of educational cooperation with countries in Asia and Latin America. Duggan mentioned that when he traveled to the Philippines, China, and Russia in 1925 and Latin America in 1931, he was impressed with the enthusiasm of these nations to learn from the West to strengthen their national development.[91] Cultural internationalists emphasized educational exchange and intellectual cooperation with a firm belief that educational contact could be instrumental in facilitating the flow of ideas between drastically different societies and in promoting American democratic values for the maintenance of world peace.

## NOTES

1. David Robertson, "International Relations of the United States," *Educational Record* 6 (1925): 91–150.

2. Liping Bu, "Cultural Understanding and World Peace: The Roles of Private Institutions in the Inter-War Years," *Peace & Change* 24, no. 2 (April 1999): 148–171.

3. Akira Iriye, *The Cambridge History of American Foreign Relations* 3, ch. 7 (Cambridge: Cambridge University Press, 1993); *Cultural Internationalism and World Order* (Baltimore: The Johns Hopkins University Press, 1997).

4. Guy S. Metraux, *Exchange of Persons: The Evolution of Cross-Cultural Education* (New York: Social Science Research Council, 1952), 14. Metraux noted in his footnote 31 (page 14) that almost every American institution of higher learning was represented in the list of sponsors for a survey of the opportunities for American students in French universities.

5. Theodosia Hewlett, *A Decade of International Fellowships* (New York: IIE, 1930), 7.

6. For anti-German sentiments in universities, see Carol Gruber, *Mars and Minerva: World War I and the Uses of the Higher Learning in America* (Baton Rouge, LA: Louisiana State University Press, 1975).

7. Metraux, *Exchange of Persons,* 14.

8. Anson P. Stokes Papers, Manuscript Group No. 299, series III, box 176, folder 21, Manuscripts and Archives, Sterling Memorial Library, Yale University; W. R. Wheeler et al., *The Foreign Student in America* (New York: Association Press, 1925), 223–224.

9. Metraux, *Exchange of Persons,* 15–16.

10. Wheeler et al., *The Foreign Student,* 221.

11. For the institutional history of IIE, see Stephen Mark Halpern, "The Institute of International Education: A History" (Ph.D. diss., Columbia University, 1969).

12. Stephen Duggan, *A Professor at Large* (New York: Macmillan, 1943), 14.

13. *Twenty Years of the Foreign Policy Association* (New York: The Foreign Policy Association, 1939).

14. Ibid., 13.

15. Halpern, "The Institute of International Education," 42, 16*f.*

16. *First Annual Report of the Director* (New York: IIE, 1920), 1.

17. Halpern, "The Institute of International Education," 37–41.

18. Nicholas M. Butler, *The International Mind: An Argument for the Judicial Settlement of International Disputes* (New York: Charles Scribner's Sons, 1912), 103–104.

19. *Blueprint for Understanding: A Thirty Year Review* (New York: IIE, 1949), 8.

20. Halpern, "The Institute of International Education," 44–46.

21. "Institute of International Education," n. d., folder 1066, box 106, series 3, Laura Spelman Rockefeller Memorial Archives (LSRM), RAC.

22. *First Annual Report of the Director* (IIE, 1920), 2.

23. Ibid., 3.

24. Paul Monroe was the director of the School of Education at Teachers College, Columbia University. In 1923, he organized an International Institute at Teachers College with a generous gift from John D. Rockefeller, Jr. See Chapter 4.

25. *First Annual Report of the Director* (IIE, 1920), 4–6.

26. The total figure was compiled from IIE annual reports, 1921–1923.

27. Halpern, "The Institute of International Education," 55–56.

28. Current policies concerning foreign student education in the United States resemble much of Duggan's plan in 1921.

29. *Fourth Annual Report of the Director* (New York: IIE, 1923), 6.

30. *Second Annual Report of the Director* (New York: IIE, 1921), 4.

31. Annual reports of the IIE, 1921–1923.

32. *Third Annual Report of the Director* (New York: IIE, 1922), 1–3.

33. *Fourteenth Annual Report of the Director* (New York: IIE, 1933), 9.

34. *Third Annual Report of the Director,* 3.

35. Annual reports of the IIE, 1920–1923.

36. *Nineteenth Annual Report of the Director* (New York: IIE, 1938), 16.

37. Roger Daniels, *Coming to America,* (New York: HarperCollins, 1990), ch. 10.

38. *Third Annual Report of the Director,* 6.

39. Ibid., 6–7.

40. *Fourth Annual Report of the Director,* 1–3. Please note that Ellis Island received immigrants mainly from European countries. Asians, who were the major target of the 1921 and 1924 immigration laws, usually arrived at San Francisco where the IIE had no staff to provide assistance. The IIE was mainly concerned with exchanges with Europe before WWII, and its small staff could pay attention to IIE fellowship recipients only. Asian students were helped to a certain extent by CFRFS and its port-of-entry service if they came in connection with the YMCA.

41. *Seventh Annual Report of the Director* (New York: IIE, 1926), 18.

42. *Third Annual Report of the Director,* 7–8.

43. The *Carnegie Endowment for International Peace Yearbook,* 1923 and 1924 showed the budgetary difference.

44. Henry S. Pritchett was president of the Carnegie Foundation for Advancement of Teaching and trustee of the Carnegie Corporation; Frederick Keppel was president of the Carnegie Corporation; Arthur Woods was chairman of the trustees of the Laura Spelman Rockefeller Memorial; and Beardsley Ruml was director of the Laura Spelman Rockefeller Memorial.

45. Memorandum of the Conference on Foreign Student Problem attended by Pritchett, Keppel, Woods, and Ruml, 8 January 1923, folder 1066, box 106, series 3, Laura Spelman Rockefeller Memorial Archives, RAC.

46. Root to Woods, 27 March 1923, Anson P. Stokes Papers, Manuscript Group No. 299, I ser., box 18, folder 291, Manuscripts and Archives, Sterling Memorial Library, Yale University.

47. Memorandum of the Conference on Foreign Student Problem attended by Pritchett, Keppel, Woods, and Ruml, 8 January 1923, LSRM, RAC.

48. Edward Jenkins to John Mott, 19 March 1924, folder titled "Correspondence and Reports, 1920–1931," CFRFS box #10A, YMCA Archives.

49. "Minutes of Conference of Foreign Student Secretaries," 23–24 September 1924, 3, folder titled "Minutes and Statements, 1916–1945," CFRFS box #14, YMCA Archives.

50. "Institute of International Education," n.d., LSRM, RAC.

51. Beardsley Ruml's draft on resolution to the IIE's grant request in 1928, n. d., folder 1066, box 106, series 3, Laura Spelman Rockefeller Memorial Archives, RAC.

52. Beardsley Ruml's report on the IIE, 1928, folder 1066, box 106, series 3, Laura Spelman Rockefeller Memorial Archives, RAC.

53. IIE letter to Beardsley Ruml, 15 December 1927, folder 1066, box 106, series 3, Laura Spelman Rockefeller Memorial Archives, RAC; *Institute of International Education: Its Origin, Organization, and Activities,* IIE Bulletin No. 1 (New York: March 1, 1928), 4.

54. *Institute of International Education: Its Origin, Organization, and Activities*, 4–5.

55. *Eighth Annual Report of the Director* (New York: IIE, 1927), 9.

56. Stephen Duggan to Anson P. Stokes, 25 October 1927, Anson P. Stokes Papers, Manuscript Group No. 299, series I, box 19, folder 297. Manuscripts and Archives, Sterling Memorial Library, Yale University.

57. IIE letter to Beardsley Ruml, 15 December 1927, LSRM, RAC.

58. Beardsley Ruml's report on the IIE, 1928, folder 1066, box 106, series 3, Laura Spelman Rockefeller Memorial Archives, RAC (1928).

59. Beardsley Ruml to Stephen Duggan, 2 March 1928, folder 1066, box 106, series 3, Laura Spelman Rockefeller Memorial, RAC.

60. Frederick Keppel to Raymond Fosdick, 9 October 1936, folder 1066, box 106, series 3, Laura Spelman Rockefeller Memorial Archives, RAC.

61. Secretary of the Rockefeller Foundation to Stephen Duggan, 23 February 1937, folder 1066, box 106, series 3, Laura Spelman Rockefeller Memorial Archives, RAC.

62. *Seventh Annual Report of the Director,* 8–12.

63. Ibid., 16–17.

64. *Fourteenth Annual Report of the Director,* 28.

65. *Seventh Annual Report of the Director,* 4–5.

66. Ibid., 4–6.

67. Ibid., page 8.

68. *Fourteenth Annual Report of the Director,* 24.

69. *Nineteenth Annual Report of the Director,* 21.

70. *Tenth Annual Report of the Director* (New York: IIE, 1929), 4.

71. Ibid., 3–5.

72. *Nineteenth Annual Report of the Director,* 25.

73. *Tenth Annual Report of the Director,* 5–7; *Fourteenth Annual Report of the Director,* 27; *Twelfth Annual Report of the Director* (New York: IIE, 1931), 7.

74. *Nineteenth Annual Report of the Director,* 41–42.

75. Charles Hurrey, "Foreign Students in the United States," *International Law and Relations*, vol. VI, no. 9, 1937, 6, folder titled "Articles and Reports, 1916–1920," CFRFS box #10, YMCA Archives.

76. *Fourteenth Annual Report of the Director*, 24–25.

77. *Sixth Report of the Director* (New York: IIE, 1925), 10–11; *Fourteenth Annual Report of the Director*, 9–10.

78. *Fourteenth Annual Report of the Director*, 20–21.

79. Ibid., 22; *Nineteenth Annual Report of the Director*, 25; *Twentieth Annual Report of the Director* (New York: IIE, 1939), 3.

80. *Fourteenth Annual Report of the Director*, 22–23.

81. *Nineteenth Annual Report of the Director*, 26.

82. *Thirteenth Annual Report of the Director* (New York: IIE, 1932), 6. In those days, the Department of Labor made the regulations to determine who was entitled to an immigrant's visa, a student's visa, a professor's visa, and so on.

83. The committee members included Del Manzo and Paul Monroe from the International Institute of Teachers College, Columbia University, Stephen Duggan from the IIE, Sidney Gamble and Harry Edmonds from International House New York, Charles Hurrey from the Committee on Friendly Relations Among Foreign Students, and Chih Meng from the China Institute.

84. Folder titled "Foreign Students (1)," box 25, Special Collections, Milbank Library, Teachers College, Columbia University (T. C. Special Collections).

85. Stephen Duggan, "Letters to the Editor," *The New York Times*, September 27, 1932.

86. *Thirteenth Annual Report of the Director*, 7.

87. Ibid.

88. Duggan, "Letters to the Editor."

89. *Fifteenth Annual Report of the Director* (New York: IIE, 1934), 19.

90. *Nineteenth Annual Report of the Director*, 28; *Twentieth Annual Report of the Director*, 4.

91. Duggan, *A Professor at Large*, 45, 51–52, 333.

# Chapter 3

## Liberal Visions in a Conservative Age: The International House Movement

The International House Movement was another major component of cultural internationalism in the 1920s–1930s. It aimed at cultivating "brotherhood" among the young representatives of different nations who were studying in the United States, with the goal of promoting American democracy and international goodwill worldwide. John D. Rockefeller, Jr. sponsored the movement with millions of dollars to build four major International Houses in New York, Berkeley, Chicago, and Paris, respectively. Each of the houses in America was also purported to function as a center to extend internationalism in different regions, especially in the Midwest and in the West, where isolationist sentiment was strong. After World War I, Rockefeller and his associates developed liberal visions of international relations and American leadership of the world.[1] They believed that peaceful international relations depended, to a large extent, on the personal relations of international leaders. Nations could not enjoy harmonious relations if their leaders were not friends who could understand each other. They also believed that "brotherhood" could be forged among peoples of all races if they were educated to understand and appreciate other nations and cultures.

The increasing number of foreign students (most of them graduate students) coming to study in the United States after World War I presented a unique opportunity for American cultural internationalists to advocate American democratic ideals, international goodwill, and cultural and commercial relations directly to the "representatives" of other nations. Most foreign students came from the elite class of their countries and would rise quickly to leadership positions after their return. Rockefeller, Jr. and his associates saw in those young men and women with American education unlimited potential in making progress in their home countries and in building good relations with the United States. In their opinion, the education of these future world leaders would do far better a service than guns and battleships in keeping a peaceful world and developing friendly relations toward the United States. But racial prejudices and social alienation in the United States often kept the students from forming true friendships with Americans. In an effort to improve the social and educational environment for the foreign students and to help cultivate "brotherhood" among them and Americans, Rockefeller, Jr. and his associates launched the International House Movement to put their liberal visions of international relations into practice.

The Rockefeller philanthropy had made numerous efforts at disseminating American democratic ideals and promoting international understanding after World War I. Although the International House Movement appeared as just another program to spread American values and cultural influence, the movement was unique in that it aimed at achieving the ambitious goal of shaping the world with a particular American vision during a time when the U.S. government had abandoned its international leadership by refusing to join the League of Nations. Officers of the Rockefeller philanthropy believed "that the trend of government was in the direction of democratic systems" and that "the success of democratic systems lay in popular education."[2] In their opinion, non-governmental institutions should play a unique role in a democratic society to serve an important purpose to stimulate and guide governmental effort through their initiatives and experiments.

The International Houses embodied a liberal view of international relations with American leadership thereof. The philanthropic cultural internationalists envisioned a peaceful international order based on the "brotherhood" and harmony of all races and nations. However, International Houses, as a miniature of the world, constantly encountered racial tensions, religious contentions, and the strife of different "cliques." In building the houses, Rockefeller and his associates even had to overcome the objection of co-educational residence from certain American universities. In the late 1930s, when military aggression and international crises escalated, the optimistic liberal view of international relations based on "brotherhood" and personal friendship was seriously challenged. Some houses became military training camps during World War II, but the movement only revived with new momentum after the war.

## JOHN D. ROCKEFELLER, JR. AND THE FOREIGN STUDENTS OF THE COSMOPOLITAN CLUB OF NEW YORK CITY

John D. Rockefeller, Jr. first met foreign students at a Sunday supper of the Intercollegiate Cosmopolitan Club of the City of New York just before

Christmas 1920. He was invited to speak about the meaning of Christmas at the auditorium of Earl Hall of Columbia University, where hundreds of students from all over the world gathered. He was so overwhelmed by "the international fellowship so permeating the assembly" that years later he told his advisor, Raymond Fosdick, "It quite bowled me over."[3]

The Cosmopolitan Club of New York was organized in 1909 by Harry Edmonds, an intercollegiate "Y" secretary, after an accidental encounter with a Chinese student on the steps of the Columbia University Library. His casual greeting of "Good morning!" stopped the student, who respectfully replied, "Thank you for speaking to me; I have been in New York three weeks, and you are the first person who has spoken to me!" Edmonds apologized, "New York is a big place and people do not ordinarily speak unless they know you." This incident left Edmonds wondering how many students like that young Chinese man felt New York City a cold, lonesome place? And what effect did this situation have on them? A few days later, Edmonds and his wife, Florence, invited a small group of foreign students to a Sunday supper at their home. A dozen from different national and religious backgrounds came, but they seemed to "have lost their national identity" amidst the warmth of this international gathering, recalled Edmonds. As the Sunday supper continued, the number of students increased. The next year, Harry Edmonds secured the use of Earl Hall for the Sunday supper of all foreign students in the city, and an Intercollegiate Cosmopolitan Club of the City of New York was thus formed with Edmonds as the director.[4] The founding of the club was part of a national movement of Cosmopolitan Clubs on American campuses.[5] The New York Club, however, was not affiliated with the National Association of the Cosmopolitan Clubs (a secular organization) but instead with the Intercollegiate Branch of the YMCA of New York City. It rented the whole fourth floor at 2229 Broadway for an office and set up a foyer for group gatherings.[6] The club aimed at advancing international goodwill and the spread of Christianity (liberally interpreted) through creating friendships between American and foreign students. The Christian mission of the club was deeply embedded in its programs, which included national night, panel discussions of world problems, excursions to places of interest, port authority service to newcomers, and holiday hospitality in American homes for foreign students to get to know American people and their families.

The American families, which held hospitality and dinner parties for foreign students, were of the eminent elite in the business and social circles in New York City. For example, Mr. and Mrs. Andrew Carnegie gave holiday receptions to foreign students for years, and so did Mr. and Mrs. Cleveland Dodge. Carnegie told foreign students at one of his holiday parties, "You will be told that the ideal of America is money, that materialism rules here. This is false. Service is the characteristic of the real American…This is the America I want you to carry home to your countries."[7] Other New York elite such as George Perkins, Benjamin Price, and James Cushman also invited foreign students to their homes. Many a time, a specific group of students was invited to an American home with the invitation cards marked "confidential." For instance, Mr. and Mrs. James Cushman once invited only the European students of the club for a holiday party, and Mr. and Mrs. Rockefeller, Jr. gave a party exclusively for Asian students.[8] This arrangement of "geographic groups" was supposed to facilitate party conversations around one specific continent or region.

In addition to home hospitality, the club also organized students to visit social, economic, political, and religious institutions that "reflected the highest American ideals." Students were enthusiastic about those activities. Moreover, the club helped students in financial difficulties get in touch with prospective employers and jobs and assisted them with scholarships and charities.[9] Despite the relatively high membership fees of $4, more than half of the foreign students in New York City joined the club. In 1921–1922, the club had 723 paid members representing 68 countries and 55 colleges and universities in New York.[10] Edmonds commented that a fine "spirit of neighborliness and comradeship" had pervaded "this large group of young people who are so heterogeneous in respect of national heritage, religious tradition and belief, economic status, and social rank."[11] Through various social services, the club played an important role in promoting contact between foreign students and Americans. Universities, which did not have special offices to look after foreign student affairs, often referred their students to the club for help.

At this moment, John D. Rockefeller, Jr. stepped into the life of the club. After Rockefeller's speech about Christmas, Edmonds asked him if he and his wife would like to have a Christmas party at their house for Latin American students who had not been arranged for such a party yet. The Rockefellers gladly accepted the suggestion. In a letter to his father on December 31, 1920, Rockefeller, Jr. wrote:

We had a most delightful party at our house yesterday afternoon. The guests were some forty young men and women from Mexico, the West India Islands, Central America and South America, who are in New York as students. An extraordinary bright, intelligent, attractive group of young people they are, most of them working to support themselves days and studying nights…We all sat down for supper at little tables in the dining room, after which and before leaving the tables we asked any of the guests who felt so disposed to tell us where they came from, how long they had been here, what they were doing and what their plans were. This resulted in the most interesting experience…John and Winthrop helped Abby and me receive the guests and were perfectly thrilled by the whole experience.[12]

The Edmonds, who participated in the entire evening event of the Christmas party, were also pleased with "their" students. "I have always felt," recalled Edmonds, "that those Latin students were 'raised up' for this occasion…Their responses contributed very significantly to Mr. and Mrs. Rockefeller's interest [in foreign student affairs]."[13]

The numbers of foreign students in the United States increased rapidly after World War I, from 4,222 in 1913 to 6,636 in 1919. Many of the students studied at universities on the East Coast (see Table 3.1).[14] New York State led the country in hosting one-fifth of the foreign student population, a majority of whom enrolled at colleges, universities, and professional schools in New York City. Those students often felt lost in the big metropolitan center and regarded the Cosmopolitan Club as their "home" where they met American students and other foreign students in a friendly atmosphere. Edmonds reported with much exuberance that fellowship flourished and national differences faded through these meetings.

The facilities of the club became limited in the face of increasing needs of the students. Housing was particularly difficult for foreign students in New York City. Harry Edmonds had conducted a survey of the living conditions of foreign students in the city and found that the majority of them lived in isolation from each other and from the American community. He thought that if the club built a home center, with a large portion for residential purposes, the students would have the opportunity to meet and make friends.

**Table 3.1**

**Distribution of Foreign Students in Top Seven States in 1913\* and 1919**

| *Ranking* | *States* <br> *1913/1919* | *Students* <br> *1913/1919* | *Schools* <br> *1913/1919* |
| --- | --- | --- | --- |
| 1 | New York/New York | 697/1210 | 19/36 |
| 2 | Pennsylvania/Illinois | 506/725 | 22/41 |
| 3 | Massachusetts/Pennsylvania | 442/709 | 15/46 |
| 4 | Illinois/Massachusetts | 412/584 | 12/25 |
| 5 | Indiana/California | 303/533 | 12/20 |
| 6 | Michigan/Ohio | 239/415 | 5/35 |
| 7 | California/Michigan | 191/199 | 7/8 |

Sources: Samuel P. Capen, "Opportunities for Foreign Students at Colleges and Universities in the United States," *United States Bureau of Education Bulletin,* No. 27, Whole No. 654 (1915), 57; *Directory of Foreign Students in the United States of America, December, 1919.* Committee on Friendly Relations Among Foreign Students, 1919, 211–212, YMCA Archives.

\*According to Samuel Capen, foreign students tended to go to the states of New York, Pennsylvania, and Massachusetts. These three states entertained 39 percent of all foreign students in the United States in 1913. In that year no foreign students were recorded in the states of Delaware, Oklahoma, Wyoming, and Idaho.

Then, the club would be capable of doing a greater service to international understanding and friendship. With these ideas in mind, Edmonds began a fund drive for the housing project. But he had a hard time raising money after the war, because many of the donations went to war refugee relief. Although many of the New York wealthy showed sympathy and admiration for his cause, few gave him money. Finally, in the summer of 1920 the Dodge family secured $60,000 for the club to buy six lots on the Claremont Avenue side.[15]

Early in 1921, Frederick Osborn, who was the board chair of the club, mentioned to John D. Rockefeller, Jr. the club's plan to build a home center for foreign students. Rockefeller showed much interest and invited Harry Edmonds to discuss the details. He wanted to know whether, if more ample facilities were available, the club could be enlarged and its friendly service extended to a broader circle of young people of the same type, including American students. What Rockefeller had in mind was a vision of promoting international goodwill through students of different nations. In his talk with Rockefeller, Jr., Edmonds emphasized that the new building, as a center for international understanding and goodwill, would help spread the highest ideals of thought, action, and service through its leadership in foreign student affairs. In his opinion, students were future leaders through whom the principles of international justice and brotherhood could be strengthened. If they could live in friendship under the same roof, fellowship and understanding would multiply to make them an effective force in promoting international peace. Rockefeller was enthusiastic about the plan, but Edmonds pointed out that the purchased site was only large enough for half of the building—and the Riverside lots would be needed to complete the project. Rockefeller responded that he would go and take a look. Two weeks later, Rockefeller told Edmonds, "Go to your broker, don't tell him who you represent, but tell him you are prepared to make a *cash* offer of $175,000." With this generous support, Edmonds immediately obtained the land on Riverside Drive that was advertised for $250,000.[16]

Rockefeller, Jr. made a pledge of $1 million to the housing project of the club, and he hoped that his support would enable foreign students to meet Americans on a regular basis and to get to know America in ways not available at the time in the large society. As he attended more of the club's activities, Rockefeller became more convinced that foreign students were "a great force for the promotion of international understanding and good will" and "for building up right relationships in commerce, industry, and trade."[17] He was "thrilled with the far possibilities of the Club" and was glad to "be identified with an undertaking whose possibilities for good seem almost limitless."[18]

## FROM THE COSMOPOLITAN CLUB TO INTERNATIONAL HOUSE NEW YORK

As the club was affiliated with the YMCA, Rockefeller wanted to deed the property to YMCA or to the joint ownership of YMCA and YWCA and then let the "Y" give the club a 99-year lease at a nominal rental. Rockefeller's advisors, although not opposed to any link between the club and the "Y," believed that the independence of the club was essential for its new mission.[19] But Edmonds and Osborn were anxious for the new center to be an organic part of the YMCA and for the property to be vested to the City Branch of the YMCA.[20] The YWCA, due to dissatisfaction with the club's work with women students, argued that the club, as a branch of the YMCA, was interested primarily in male foreign students and that female foreign students were used largely as a form of entertainment for men. "The women's part is just a tail of the kite," protested Miss Marbel Cratty, general secretary of the National Board of the YWCA. Workers in the YWCA at Columbia University openly objected the new center, even though the center meant additional facilities for female foreign students.[21]

Raymond Fosdick represented Rockefeller, Jr. in handling the matter of property ownership. He offered the concerned parties three alternatives: 1) a title vested in an independent board of trustees; 2) a title vested in the YMCA; and 3) a title vested in the YMCA and YWCA jointly. In favor of the first alternative, Miss Cratty pointed out that the increasing accumulation of property by the YMCA and the YWCA "tended to institutionalize the organizations and made them inelastic for new needs." She asked, "Why should we hesitate if it appears that the work we started can be better carried forward in certain instances under new auspices?"[22] Neither the YWCA at Columbia University nor the club had the desire to work with each other.

The antagonism between the club and the Columbia branch of the YWCA resulted from their competition for and different emphasis on the work of foreign students. Edmonds apparently felt that the YWCA was encroaching upon his "sphere" when it moved into Columbia in 1918 and set up a foyer for women foreign students, known as the International Club of Women Students, at a Teachers College dormitory. The YWCA officers felt that no organization associated with the YMCA could possibly handle the work of female foreign students the way they wanted. The YWCA wanted to have female foreign students separated from the club. But Edmonds was so eager to keep the student movement together that he would prefer to divorce the whole student movement in New York from the YMCA rather than "cut it up into pieces."[23]

In the Progressive Era, feminists had used separatism as one of the strategies to achieve equality for women on American campuses.[24] They promoted the separation of women from men in campus life to create a better climate of opportunity for female students who often faced exclusion from men's campus activities and suffered from the triviality and marginality imposed upon them. Separation therefore became a means for the Progressive feminists and the YWCA to establish and maintain an equal position for women on campus. The Columbia YWCA had specific concerns when it complained about the club's neglect of women's interests and worried about their chaperonage.

Because cooperation between the YWCA and the YMCA was impossible, Raymond Fosdick reminded Rockefeller, Jr. of the various advantages of an independent club. He explained that independence would make it easier for the club to "assume responsibility for the entire foreign student problem in New York, regardless of sex," and would also "obviate the awkward machinery of a long-term lease from the two associations to the Cosmopolitan Club."[25] Wickliffe Rose and George Vincent, chief officials of the Rockefeller philanthropy and advisors to Rockefeller, Jr., held similar views.[26] Vincent remained firm "that the best results can be obtained only as complete independence for the new club is achieved."[27] In addition, there were legal problems to deed the property to the "Y." Charters of the YMCA and the YWCA stated that property owned by each organization must be used solely for men and women, respectively. The charters also limited the freedom of the management of any property deeded to the "Y."[28] Under these circumstances, Rockefeller instructed Fosdick to make an appointment with John R. Mott, chairman of the YMCA International Committee, in regard to the club's proposition and to state frankly all sides of the issue. He told Fosdick, "While I should not want to be bound by Mr. Mott's recommendation in the matter, it would be most valuable in reaching a final conclusion."[29]

In the meantime, Rockefeller asked Frederick Osborn to find out the real needs of female foreign students in the city. He also suggested that the club make a permanent arrangement with the YMCA and the YWCA to prevent any overlap of work in foreign student affairs. Osborn's investigation showed that dormitory facilities for female foreign students were, indeed, in urgent need. Osborn reported, "Careful investigation in different directions makes it appear certain that a women's dormitory would be immediately successful and enormously serviceable."[30] He emphasized that proper protection should be afforded to female students. The YMCA and the YWCA, meanwhile, reached an agreement that they would "co-operate in every way possible" with the club in its work and "discontinue all work for foreign students in New York City" so long as the club continued in existence.[31] The Metropolitan Boards of both "Y" associations signed a resolution in April 1921:

Whereas it being deemed wise, to avoid certain difficulties, to reorganize this work [the Club] on a basis which shall be independent of the Young Men's and the Young Women's Christian Associations, although it is clearly intended that the work shall be continued on the highest Christian basis...Be it Resolved that the Young Men's Christian Association and the Young Women's Christian Association...agree that when it [the new Club] becomes a reality and fulfills the needs for work among foreign students in the City of New York, they will not engage in work which would be in any sense competitive or overlapping.[32]

With this resolution, the club began a new phase of life. It ceased to be part of the YMCA and enjoyed independence with Cleveland E. Dodge as the treasurer. It raised $12,000 that year, including a gift of $5,000 from Rockefeller, Jr.[33] Edmonds, who had been director of the Intercollegiate Branch of the YMCA for 16 years, was to continue to work with foreign students as the director of the independent club—soon to be changed to International House New York—and John R. McCurdy succeeded Edmonds as the intercollegiate director, concentrating on the work with American students.[34]

The separation of the club from the "Y" caused concerns among YMCA and church workers. Edmonds assured his colleagues "The new arrangement is to be largely a division of labor. The objectives, the methods, the spirit of both organizations are one." Edmonds further emphasized that the new center of the club "ought to be a Christian home center and lighthouse extending its influence around the world. It is my ambition to have it represent the united interest of the Universities, the Christian Associations, Churches, Missionary Boards, and in fact any agency or anybody that has an interest in the presence and welfare of the large number of foreign students who are in this city."[35] Edmonds was afraid that emphasis of the club's separation from the "Y" would lead to its isolation. He wanted the new center to serve as a clearinghouse for all those who are interested in foreign students.[36]

The property was eventually deeded to a board of five in June 1921, which included the chairman of the International Committee of the YMCA, the president of the National Board of the YWCA, the president of the YMCA of the City of New York, the president of the Metropolitan Board of the YWCA of the City of New York, and the president of the General Education Board. Succession to the membership of the board was to follow these titles, such as the next chairman of the International Committee of the YMCA would be the successor to the board and so on. The board of five, which showcased the compromise, was shortly afterward incorporated into an independent charitable organization under the laws of the state of New York, known as The International Students' Association of the City of New York. Once the new center of the club was completed, a self-perpetuating governing board would be organized for the administration of the property and the management of the enterprise in accordance with the general purposes of the club. The Governing Board was to exercise this function under a 99-year lease from the International Students' Association.[37] The name of the club was to change to International House New York.

## INTERNATIONAL HOUSE NEW YORK: LIFE AND MISSION

Key persons such as Frederick Osborn, Cleveland E. Dodge, Harry Edmonds, and Raymond Fosdick formed a Building Committee for International House New York. But Rockefeller, Jr. and his wife, Abby Aldrich Rockefeller, participated in the entire planning, including the decision on the architect and the specific designs of the facilities and interior decoration. Moreover, the management committee of the club was also restructured to incorporate local and international interests. It selected as members those who possessed influential contacts in the United States and abroad through their leadership in education, business, peace, and religion.[38] Once International House New York was completed, this Committee of Management, composed of prominent Americans of international outlook and influence, would become the Board of Managers of the House responsible for its operation and "programs of international service free of any religious, educational or political bias."[39]

The transition of the club to International House New York did not make an immediate public impact because the construction of a home center for foreign students was regarded as just another charitable act of Rockefeller, Jr. New York newspapers reported that Rockefeller built "a residential center for foreign students in the vicinity of Columbia University," "to be free from bias—religious, educational, and political," and women were eligible for residence, although they "will have their own separate entrance, elevator, and social rooms." The International House New York would facilitate "the activities of the Cosmopolitan Club and its unique place in the student life of New York."[40] Few people recognized that the new International House was created with the mission to serve as a center of a movement "that might profoundly affect the whole problem of international relations."[41]

Rockefeller was shrewd in soliciting the appearance of government officials at the official occasions of his new enterprise of international relations. On November 26, 1922, he invited his old friend, Secretary of State Charles E. Hughes, to speak at the cornerstone ceremony of International House New York.[42] Rockefeller knew too well that even Hughes came as his personal friend rather than in the capacity of secretary of state, his presence would nonetheless have profound political implications. He figured that so many foreign students were to be at the ceremony that the speech of the secretary of state would undoubtedly be reported in the newspapers of all the countries that the students represented. Furthermore, Rockefeller truly wished that the government would cooperate with private efforts to promote U.S. foreign relations through cultural understanding. He wrote Charles Hughes: "As these young men and women from the nations of the world are received with sympathy, interest and cordiality by the United States, they will naturally cherish a friendly feeling for our country, and from the positions of leadership which they will subsequently occupy in their own lands will be able to exercise a mighty influence looking toward the establishment of peace and goodwill among men throughout the world." Rockefeller explained that international goodwill developed through students would be "far better than her armies or battleships as a protection to the United States in the years to come," and the influence of international goodwill would be "vigorously active in promoting a better understanding of and a more sympathetic attitude toward our country." "The far-reaching influence of such a service is too obvious to require further amplification," he concluded.[43]

Rockefeller and Edmonds wanted a motto inscribed above the main entrance of International House New York to reflect the expectations, faith, and spirit of this new institution. Not far from the house was the Civil War hero Ulysses Grant's tomb, on which was engraved his simple words, "Let us have peace," spoken after the war. These four words offered an inspiration for Rockefeller, who reasoned that "where brotherhood prevails, peace must prevail."[44] He considered brotherhood an essential element of many qualities, such as understanding, loyalty, love, unselfishness, tolerance, and helpfulness as well as justice and goodwill. Although we have experienced World War II, the Cold War, and many other events of international violence, "That brotherhood may prevail" still remains today above the main entrance of International House New York.

In September 1924, International House New York opened as a residential, social, and recreational center for foreign and American students. It was a 13-story-tall building and provided residence for 525 graduate students with two-thirds foreign and one-third American.[45] The American students living in the house were carefully selected so that foreign students would meet the best American youth on a daily basis. Although the International House provided dormitories for men and women students, their residences were completely separated in the conventional pattern of college residence at the time. The women's dormitory of 125 rooms was on the west side of the building with a separate "ladies" entrance and elevator, and the men's dormitory of 400 rooms was in the center and east side with its own entrance and elevator.[46] The separation by walls of the dormitories and of the social and recreational rooms made International House three buildings under one roof. Although the men and women dormitories were separated, racial integration in International House appeared far more radically progressive than what the society at large was willing to accept. There were common recreational facilities to both men and women on the first two floors. They included an auditorium, a library, a cafeteria, music practice rooms, a gymnasium, and men's and women's social rooms.[47] Originally, a swimming pool was planned for the students, but it was never built. The Board of Trustees and the Board of Management, which were made up of "internationally minded" New York social and business progressive elite, felt it too shocking to have men and women of all races swim in the same pool. In the end, a pub was built on the site of the swimming pool.

The progressiveness of the International House was manifested in its aim at "the improvement of the social, intellectual, spiritual, and physical condition of the men and women students from any land, and without discrimination because of religion, nationality, race, color, or sex, who are studying in the colleges, universities, and professional schools of the City of New York."[48] As a non-profit, self-supporting institution, the administration of the house was carried out by the student council, the staff, and the director, whose family also lived in the house. Harry Edmonds was the first director of International House New York, continuing the work that he started more than a decade ago. Old programs such as Sunday suppers, national nights, home hospitality, and international forum continued while new ones were created to fulfill the mission "that brotherhood may prevail." New programs included a candlelight ceremony of international goodwill, group discussions, language tables, folk dances, athletic games, and the annual Halloween Festival. These social and recreational activities no doubt helped the students familiarize with each other's cultures, customs, and ways of life and broaden their horizons to understand other nations and peoples. The popular Halloween Festival and other programs conducted in American settings, however, permeated the life of the students with the subtle and direct influence of American culture.

International House New York was an experiment in human relations. Leaders of the International House Movement expected that if friendship among different races could be forged at the International House, it should work out in outside society. People living in International House New York included Muslims, Hindus, Buddhists, Confucianists, Roman and Greek Catholics, Protestants, Jews, and so on. The International House was virtually a miniature of the world with paid memberships. (See Table 3.2 for memberships) The house had explicit policies neither to impose a particular religion upon those of another faith nor to restrict any expression of particular religious beliefs, but Christian religion was always a key element in International House life. The Christian environment reflected not only the legacy of the old Cosmopolitan Club but also the impact of the Christian Student Movement active on American campuses at the time. Foreign students, although interested in discussing American democratic ideals and principles of liberty, resented being exploited for any religious purposes. Because of the emphasis on Christianity, some students questioned the sincerity of the house's religious policy. Subsequently, the governing board worked with the students and formulated a new religious policy that emphasized tolerance of all creeds as the principle of religious life at the house. With regard to individuals' religious beliefs, the house made clear that "students have the fullest freedom and independence and...whatever they arrive at is the result of their own independent thought and action."[49] Religious meetings under the auspices of different groups were welcome, but no religious propaganda or religious exploitation was permitted. The new policy also shifted to a more liberal attitude toward religious diversity when it stated that religion should not be insisted as solely Christian, although no conflict with the campus Christian Student Movement should be developed.

In the 1920s, Asians were a large group in International House New York, constituting about 34 percent of the residency. Chinese students were of such a dominant national group that the 1920s were labeled as the "decade

**Table 3.2**
**International House Memberships, 1924–1934\***

| Year | Students | Countries represented |
|------|----------|----------------------|
| 1924–1925 | 821 | 70 |
| 1925–1926 | 1035 | 66 |
| 1926–1927 | 1012 | 61 |
| 1927–1928 | 969 | 61 |
| 1928–1929 | 887 | 63 |
| 1929–1930 | 804 | 67 |
| 1930–1931 | 1012 | 72 |
| 1931–1932 | 1022 | 72 |
| 1933–1934 | 835 | 66 |

Sources: Compiled from Annual Reports of International House New York, 1924–1934.

\*The numbers included non-residents of International House.

of the Chinese" (see Tables 3.3 and 3.4). The Chinese students played an active role in building cultural connections between the East and the West. Their presentation of the classical Chinese play Hua Mu Lan, the story of a young woman disguised as a man to serve for her father in the army and making herself an army general, was most popular.[50] The 1920s also saw spontaneous hospitality of racial and inter-group activities. Racial prejudice and color sensitivity always existed, however, despite the amiable atmosphere in the International House. For example, one day a white American found himself next to a black in the bathroom; he left immediately, thinking that was too much. But internal struggles went on for a long time: Why did he come to the International House if he expected racial exclusion? His adjustment to racial integration and the acceptance of everyone as equal continued years later when he became the president of Fisk University and worked to improve this "splendid school for colored people in Tennessee."[51]

Students also frequently debated about Western imperialism while living in the International House. Hindus and British students discussed British imperialism in India although they disagreed on many issues. So did the Filipinos and American students about American imperialism in the Philippines. Despite cultural differences and political contentions, the residents of International House held an optimistic view of the mission of the International House Movement. One student wrote that International House successfully solved "its problems through its philosophy of strict

**Table 3.3**

**Leading Foreign Nationals Residing in I-House New York, 1925–1929**

| Year/ Countries | China | Canada | Japan | Philippines | Germany | Norway |
|---|---|---|---|---|---|---|
| 1925–1926 | 101 | 55 | 54 | 47 | 45 | 25 |
| 1926–1927 | 106 | 66 | 37 | 26 | 65 | 27 |
| 1927–1928 | 87 | 59 | 35 | 36 | 58 | 33 |
| 1928–1929 | 80 | 48 | 28 | 25 | 71 | 29 |

Sources: Compiled from Annual Reports of International House New York, 1925–1929.

**Table 3.4**

**International House New York Members by Regions, 1926–1929\***

| Year/ Regions | N. America | Europe | Asia | S. America | Australia | Africa |
|---|---|---|---|---|---|---|
| 1926–1927 | 394 | 335 | 230 | 39 | 11 | 3 |
| 1927–1928 | 384 | 325 | 227 | 26 | 10 | 3 |
| 1928–1929 | 338 | 290 | 211 | 30 | 13 | 5 |

Sources: Compiled from Annual Reports of International House New York, 1925–1929.

*The numbers included non-residents of International House New York.

independence and its cooperative organization of student advice and director's decision."[52]

But founders had high expectations for International House New York. Rockefeller, Jr. hoped that the mission of the International House Movement would extend each year in ever-widening circles, that other such houses would spring up in the international student communities of the world, and that all these centers would join hands with various endeavors to promote international brotherhood. In a biblical discourse, he described International House as the home of all nations, "shining forth as a beacon light to guide humanity into the safe harbor of world brotherhood, proclaiming to mankind the gospel of peace on earth and good will toward men."[53]

Foreign students studying in the United States became acquainted with American political ideals of democracy and freedom, but they also saw and experienced racial prejudices and other problems. As an intellectual sojourner, the student would carry the knowledge of both sides of American society and disseminate it in his or her native country. Leaders of the International House, however, would like foreign students to disseminate only the positive side of American society to promote friendly relations between Americans and other peoples. John D. Rockefeller, Jr. personally appealed to the students to remember the best of America. At the Candlelight Ceremony of 1926, Rockefeller asked the students: "Think of this, your foster land, as a friendly nation, and satisfied with nothing but the highest ideals and even inspired to large service of mankind." He continued, "Your stay has been of sufficient duration to have you see the best in America and in the American people." Rockefeller tried to convince the students that negative encounters should not obscure the essential kindness of American people: "I fancy there is nothing more disheartening than to come as a stranger to a great city like this, or any other great city. One must feel like the mariner on the ocean without fresh water…people everywhere and not a friendly face or glance, or word. And yet that does not represent the attitude of this great city, nor the attitude of this people. We, as Americans, are essentially friendly." He wanted the students to remember America as a religious country and Americans as a friendly people and people of ideals. He claimed that American businessmen were not just money-grabbers but had high ideals in regard to the relation of labor and capital. He wanted the students to remember "that an increasing number of Americans believed that labor and capital are friends, are partners, that neither can be most successful at the expense of the other, but only in cooperation with the other."[54]

In terms of international affairs, Rockefeller assured the students that "America is interested in the nations of the world and in the peoples of the world—deeply and profoundly interested, and she wants to be the friend of nations and of peoples."[55] When students asked why the United States refused to join the League of Nations, he explained that the United States did it in an act of "caution more than anything else." Despite their gratitude of his generosity in sponsoring the International House, the students were less convinced by Rockefeller's comments, which were not so candid about American society and politics. His emphasis on remembering the best of America demonstrated his strong desire that the students make positive contributions to the spread of goodwill between their countries and America and the building of good cultural, industrial, and commercial relations with Americans. He was trying, in his own way, to contribute to American diplomacy. He had sincere hopes that his efforts, as part of spreading American influence to the world through non-governmental institutions, would bring positive results to world peace.

## *THE EXTENTION OF INTERNATIONAL HOUSES*

News of International House New York spread around the world. Rockefeller, Jr. was swamped with requests to build similar houses in other American educational centers as well as in European metropolises like Geneva, Berlin, Paris, and London.[56] Harry Edmonds was enthusiastic about the spread of International Houses, but Rockefeller did not want to jump ahead before "the success of International House from a financial point of view" had been proven. He told Fosdick, "I am interested in the possibility of extending this work in which I so strongly believe, if it can be extended on an equally sound financial, social, and spiritual basis."[57] Rockefeller's hesitation was affected by a financial survey of International House New York, which showed a 5 percent deficit in the first year.[58] Rockefeller was not a "starry-eyed" idealist, although he had passion for his work. One of his closest associates once described him as follows: "He was a man of immense practicality, but he believed passionately in the power of the human race to progress, and with this affirmative, dynamic faith he sought for institutions by which this progress might be accelerated."[59] International House New York improved the next year by keeping a balanced budget. Given the fact that the house had no precedent to go by and was administered by a small staff headed by Edmonds, the operation of the house was quite an accomplishment.

The financial balance of International House New York gave Rockefeller confidence to build more international houses. In 1926, Rockefeller asked Fosdick and the building committee to work with him as the Committee on the Extension of International House. Harry Edmonds was commissioned to travel across the United States to make surveys of the needs and opportunities in other metropolitan areas of developing foreign student centers comparable to International House New York. As the first international house was built on the Atlantic Coast, the extension committee decided to build the second on the Pacific Coast and the third in the midland of America. Berkeley, CA and Chicago were chosen as the locales for the next two international houses—not only because they had large foreign student populations (see Table 3.5), but also because they were strategically important to the international understanding between Americans and other peoples.

### International House Berkeley

International House Berkeley had a unique and far-reaching role rather than functioning just as a residential center for foreign students to meet Americans on a daily basis. Because the Bay Area was the entrance point to the United States from Asia, International House Berkeley was to serve as a center for the promotion of goodwill and cooperation between Asians and Americans in a region where racial prejudices against Asians were particularly strong at the time. In a letter to President Robert Sproul of U. C. Berkeley, Rockefeller pointed out, "By bringing together in unfettered cooperation the educated young people of all lands, many of whom will in years to come be leaders in their several countries, and by giving them full opportunity for frank discussion on terms of equality, there is being performed, I believe, a service for the well-being of the world." Rockefeller continued that International House Berkeley, so close to the Golden Gate where much of the world's commerce and travel passed, would provide "both a community and an opportunity much fuller and richer" than could be otherwise obtained.[60]

International House was an idea from the East Coast. Concepts of both racial integration and co-educational residence appeared, however, too radical and eastern in California. There were concerns: "This idea out of New York; would it work *here*? Women *and* men in the same building? *All* races, too?"[61] Although Berkeley was an educational center, racial hostility toward non-whites was prevalent in the community. Views of women's education were also less liberal than in eastern states. One scholar pointed out that the Berkeley campus was less impacted by the Progressive Movement than those in New York and Chicago.[62] Ideas from the East Coast were often met with suspicion and resistance in California. When Edmonds first came to negotiate a site for the International House Berkeley, he was offered the north side of the campus—"an area ravaged by fire," he recalled. It was also the "back door" to the campus. Dissatisfied with the offer, Edmonds proposed a location on Piedmont Avenue, the home area of fraternities and sororities. Unlike the East Coast, foreign students and non-whites were excluded from fraternities and sororities at the University of California then. Foreign students, particularly Asians, lived in their semi-ghetto houses, isolated from campus life and American students.[63] Edmonds chose the location on Piedmont Avenue not because it was the "front door" of the campus but because he wanted to draw the isolated students into an international community and to provide them with easy access to campus life.

Edmonds and Rockefeller invited major administrative officials of the University of California to visit International House New York, who, after this obviously educational tour, became responsive and enthusiastic about the International House project in Berkeley. But several groups in the Bay Area remained resistant to the International House because it promoted racial integration and co-educational residence. They considered the International House morally unacceptable and institutionally threatening. Local YMCA secretaries and landlords, for fear of losing their constituency and business, refused to cooperate with the International House project.[64] Many Berkeley landlords protested against the construction of the International House for fear of an influx of foreigners. Antagonism reached the height when more than 800 people gathered in Berkeley to protest racial integration in the International House. They shouted that the

International House would cause Berkeley "to be overrun with blacks and Asians."[65] In addition, co-educational residence appeared "immoral" to local norms. Although International House Berkeley was built with a separate section for women students, it was still regarded as too radical to have men and women living in the same building. The university itself did not encourage co-educational residence, either. When International House Berkeley was completed and opened on August 18, 1930, it was the first co-educational residence west of Mississippi.[66]

International House Berkeley was built in the Mediterranean style and blended well with Californian scenery and climate. This eight-story residential center offered single rooms for 338 men and 115 women, primarily for graduate students, with social and recreational facilities similar to those of International House New York. The house was open to students of all nations in the Bay Area without restriction based on color, race, creed, or sex. The number of American students was set at 25 to 35 percent of the total residents in the house.[67] The property was titled to the university but was leased to International House Berkeley as a separate corporation legally independent of the university. The board of directors of this corporation, composed mostly of outstanding men and women in the state of California "who have the purpose and work of the House at heart," was responsible for the operation and fulfillment of its mission.[68] Allen Blaisdell, who had been a resident and staff member at International House New York, was made the first executive director of International House Berkeley. Standing on the West Coast, the International House assumed the mission of serving as a center to extend internationalism and to connect the West with the East.

### International House Chicago

Unlike U. C. Berkeley, the University of Chicago was eager to promote the building of an international house on its campus. It formed a special committee to cooperate with Rockefeller's Committee on the Extension of International House and even offered to place all its facilities at the command of the Extension Committee.[69] International House Chicago was supposed to be open to all foreign students studying at colleges and universities in the greater Chicago area. After conducting a survey, Edmonds recommended the Grant Park area, south of the Midway, in downtown Chicago as the location of International House

**Table 3.5**

**Foreign Students at Columbia, Berkeley, and Chicago, 1925–1935\***

| School/Year | 1925-26 | 1928-29 | 1930-31 | 1932-33 | 1934-35 |
|---|---|---|---|---|---|
| Univ. of Calif. (Bkly) | 544 | 651 | 799 | 563 | 582 |
| Columbia Univ. | 541 | 899 | 766 | 346 | 423 |
| Univ. of Chicago | 265 | 266 | 286 | 233 | 137 |

Sources: Compiled from IIE Annual Reports of the Director, 1926–1935.

*The three universities were among the top 10 schools with the largest foreign student population in the 1920s and 1930s..

Chicago. But Trevor Arnett, who was vice president of the University of Chicago before coming to work for the Rockefeller Foundation, suggested a site north of the Midway and east of the University, on which International House Chicago now stands. Arnett thought that since the International House was primarily for graduate students, that place was most desirable because it offered several advantages. First, it was in easy reach of the social and intellectual life of graduate work at the university, whereas living south of the Midway actually cut students off from university life. Secondly, it was close to the train station (convenient for transportation). Thirdly, the International House would architecturally complete the university skyline on the north side of the Midway.[70]

During the construction, International House Chicago did not encounter the same kind of resistance that Berkeley House did. But there were concerns that the International House would compete with the university and local community for housing and dining businesses.[71] Local restaurant operators therefore organized themselves to keep putting pressure on the university to make sure that the International House was not going to compete with their businesses, which the university gladly obliged. Moreover, the university wanted to have the exclusive rights of ownership of the International House.[72] But Rockefeller did not have such an inclination, despite his family's special relationship with the university. He wanted to keep International House Chicago independent from the university. His purpose of establishing International House Chicago was to offer "the education in international fellowship and understanding of the students of the world who are studying in Chicago and [its] vicinity." He wanted to use the International House "to promote international understanding and friendship on the part of the people of Chicago and of the Middle West toward other nations and cultures than our own."[73] The state law of Illinois, however, would not grant tax exempt status unless the International House was legally part of an educational institution.[74] In the end, Rockefeller agreed to entrust the property to the University of Chicago with the understanding that the International House would be governed by an independent board of governors.[75] Like in New York and California, Rockefeller encouraged that the house's Board of Governors select as members "private citizens who are specially interested in and able to further the welfare of such students and the cause of international understanding." He hoped that "representatives not only of the University of Chicago, but also of other institutions of higher learning in and near Chicago" would be enlisted to direct International House Chicago.[76] The emphasis on recruiting local citizens to participate in this special enterprise of international relations indicated the mission of the house as a center to expand internationalism in the heartland of America, where isolationist sentiments had a strong appeal.[77]

International House Chicago was an eight-story building of neo-Gothic style that fit in with the architectural features of the university. It opened in October 1932, providing 507 rooms in two separate residential wings for men and women, respectively. A total of 518 persons could be accommodated. In addition, International House Chicago, like its sister houses, contained a cafeteria, a library, gymnastic and social rooms, and a large auditorium seating up to 450 people. The initial residents were selected by the house based on their cultural "tolerance" and "intellectual curiosity." The management of International House Chicago believed that much of the success of "this experiment depends upon the type of people who lived in the House." From the experiences of the other two international houses, it was learned that cultural and social prejudices, hostility, and conflict might well accentuate "a thousand-fold by sheer proximity" if people did not open their minds to understand and appreciate different cultures and customs. Only those who were willing to live with people of different religious, political, and social beliefs—not for the comfort of better facilities but for the advantage of associating with and understanding of people of other cultures—would promote international living.[78] Although International House Chicago was designated as a department of the university, it was managed independently in administrative and financial matters. The university exercised little control over the house even though the house's first director, Bruce Dickson, was also the university's foreign student advisor.[79]

After the Berkeley and Chicago Houses, the Extension Committee planned to build more international houses in the United States and around the world. Places such as Boston, Philadelphia, Paris, and Tokyo were all under consideration. But many plans failed to materialize because of the Depression and increasing militarism in the world. International House Paris, which opened in 1936, was the only one that Rockefeller, Jr. successfully financed after the three International Houses in the United States. Instead of a residential home, International House Paris was a social and recreational center for students of all nations studying at the Cité Universitaire in Paris. The plan for an International House Boston proceeded but then was aborted. At great pains and expenses, Rockefeller bought a piece of land on the Charles River Esplanade of Cambridge in 1932 in the hopes of building another house for international students. But, the number of foreign students in Boston was decreasing during the Depression and the prospect of running a financially independent residential center appeared dim. In Philadelphia, the University of Pennsylvania Christian Association originally had an International Student House that dated back to 1918.[80] When International House New York was completed, leaders of the Philadelphia Christian Association came and visited it. They were very impressed with International House New York and asked Edmonds to talk with Rockefeller about a possible extension of International House to Philadelphia. Edmonds enthusiastically helped them write a report on the foreign student situation in Philadelphia. But Rockefeller was not favorably impressed with the report and did not make a commitment.[81] By the mid-1930s, the world was increasingly threatened by military aggressions in Asia and Europe. Rockefeller decided not to go ahead with any more international houses and disbanded the Extension Committee.[82]

## CHALLENGES OF THE EXPERIMENT

The three International Houses in America had similar educational and social programs, with Sunday Supper the central social and cultural activity, but each of the houses also had its own special major event of the year. In New York, it was the Halloween Festival; in Chicago, the International Night; and in Berkeley, the Folk Festival. Programs were open to resident and non-resident students alike. The annual Candlelight Ceremony at each International House, which took place at the end of the academic year, symbolized the mission of International Houses to the world. Each student with a kindled candle in hand pledged their determination to carry to the outer world the sense of fellowship they had forged during their stay at the International Houses. Although the three houses were related to each other in purpose and ideals, they were independent enterprises of their own, each governed by an independent board made up of prominent figures in local business, education, and public service.[83] There was little attempt to centralize the control of the three houses, although cooperation and coordination was encouraged for the common interest of strengthening their programs. The emphasis on independent management also illustrated Rockefeller's concept that International Houses carried special missions beyond those of established institutions and that the experiment of international living, once put into practice, should not be limited by established visions. International Houses were not endowed except for the site, the building, and the furnishings,[84] which characterized the philanthropic giving of the Rockefeller philanthropies (in other words, to get things started and let them go of their own accord).[85]

The 1930s were a difficult time that tested the mission of the International House Movement. Foreign student memberships at International Houses decreased as the Depression dragged on and imminent war clouds gathered. More than half of the residents in International House New York were American students since the mid-1930s.[86] In order to recruit more foreign students and preserve the international character of the house, the Student Council of International House New York suggested the increase of scholarships and the lowering of room rates and living expenses.[87] Hardly any of these suggestions were implemented because of the concerns about the financial status of the house.

Students also became pessimistic about the mission of International Houses. Problems of race relations and inter-group relations appeared to be more difficult to manage than in the optimistic 1920s. In International House New York, the problem of "social distance" of different racial groups "strikes at the very roots of House living." On the surface, residents lived and dined under one roof, and most of them talked to each other. But there existed European and non-European "cliques" and American and non-American divisions. The gap between American students and foreign students began to widen in the early 1930s. The House Board attempted to find solutions to the inter-group problems through a scientific study by the Committee on International Relations of the Council of Religious and Social Studies in 1935.[88] Although the committee made several proposals, problems of inter-group relations remained.[89] The aloofness of foreign students and the insulation between American and non-American groups were even reinforced by an "oversized American group" in the house in the late 1930s.[90] One foreign student wrote, "The Americans stand to lose by an indifferent attitude toward students from the East. This apparent lack of interest in other cultures may be due to the unusually large proportion of Americans in the House this year." An Indian student complained, "the average American student has a very shallow knowledge of our [Oriental] problems, political, social or economic...Those Americans who are imperialists are such because they possess, like some Europeans, a superiority complex which makes them believe that they have a mission to perform in civilizing nations which they consider to be backward. Their attitude toward missionary work is founded on a similar basis, which might aptly be termed 'religious imperialism.'" But one German student pointed out that the difference of students' opinions and ideas on "the perfection of the world in its present shape and particularly of the United States in its present organization...is the most valuable asset of International House, and their discussion will eventually benefit and not hurt the United States and other nations."[91]

While race and inter-group relations posed a major challenge to the mission of International Houses, tensions between nationalism and internationalism threatened to defeat the goal of the whole International House Movement. Assertions of nationalist sentiment within the setting of International Houses tended to be strong among students whose countries were engaged in wars against each other or in the anti-colonial movement of independence. For instance, nationalism was demonstrated by both Chinese and Japanese students in their reaction to Japan's invasion of China. Chinese students protested against Japan's brutal assault on China, but Japanese students (with a few exceptions) tried to defend the military invasion. Nationalism also united Indian students against the British rule in India and Filipino students against American occupation of their country. One student wrote, "The House helps bring about cultural and social understanding, but has little effect upon our personal political beliefs about the problems of our own countries."[92] Leaders of International Houses tried to mitigate tensions between national groups but achieved little as long as wars continued in various parts of the world.

Cultural and political tensions within International Houses in the 1930s led people to questioning: "Would the differences of race, religion, and culture prove insurmountable barriers to friendship and understanding?" Students' reactions to the mission of International Houses varied. In their letters to Rockefeller, Jr., there were expressions of deep gratitude and appreciation but there were also complaints about cliques in the houses and bad attitudes of staff toward non-member students. Some expressed doubts about the ideals of International Houses in "a world where man's greatest object of hatred is man," but others showed conviction that brotherhood *can* prevail because that was the only road to survival.

The International Houses faced the hardest days when World War II broke out. As a unique institution and an experiment of international living, the International Houses were put to test by the war. Both Berkeley and Chicago Houses were turned over to military use during the war. The Berkeley House was rented to the U.S. Navy in 1943 and was renamed after a war hero as "Callaghan Hall." Student residents of the house were relocated in fraternity houses.[93] In Chicago, half the house was occupied by Army and Navy trainees on the university campus. Ernest B. Price, director of International House Chicago, left to join the Office of the Coordinator of Information in 1942 at the call of the State Department.[94] International House Berkeley returned to normal civilian student life after three years of military occupation, and so did International House Chicago after two years of military service. The International House Movement revived after the war when large numbers of foreign students again came to the United States. The mission of International Houses survived but was adapted to the Cold War environment as more international houses and centers were being built in postwar America and Europe.[95] The International House Movement, originally conceived and developed in the 1920s as a new catalyst for world peace, has grown into a truly worldwide phenomenon with unique social and educational functions today. The International House Movement exemplified American philanthropy's attempts to spread American democratic ideals and to foster international goodwill. This effort illustrated the active participation of private institutions in international affairs and the expansion of American cultural influence in other nations when the United States government downplayed its role in international leadership. Private institutions sought the cultural approach to maintain world peace through friendly cultural and commercial relations. Such a thrust of private efforts also demonstrated the belief that non-governmental institutions could serve and accomplish what the government could or would not. John D. Rockefeller, Jr. and his associates knew too well the various economic and commercial disadvantages for the United States to withdraw into itself. They were aware that the United States, in order to keep its international stature to expand commerce and trade, "needed to vastly increase its contacts with and knowledge of the rest of the world" and "needed a new brand of leaders with global vision."[96] Foreign students in the United States appeared as one of the best resources to realize the vision of creating peaceful international relations through educating the future world leaders with American democratic values. The International House Movement illustrated a creative endeavor of the philanthropists and educators to conduct American diplomacy and to exert American leadership in the inter-war years.

Moreover, the optimistic views of human relations that guided the International House Movement in the 1920s helped construct a liberal vision of international relations as well as a progressive social order at a time when racial integration and co-educational residence were hardly acceptable in American society. Endeavors to promote international goodwill and understanding through the education of foreign students became, indeed, an attempt to integrate all races and genders on an equal footing. Although there was widespread resistance to racial integration and co-educational residency, the International Houses were able to overcome those challenges in the process of creating their own existence. Issues of race, gender, and religion that were at play in the heart of International House life transcended the narrow concerns of the education and welfare of foreign students. Hence, the International House Movement epitomized an experiment that tested both liberal internationalism and social progressivism.

## *NOTES*

1. John E. Harr and Peter Johnson, *The Rockefeller Century* (New York: Scribner's, 1988), 153–173.

2. George W. Gray, *Education on an International Scale* (New York: Harcourt, Brace and Company, 1941), 8.

3. Raymond Fosdick, *John D. Rockefeller, Jr.: A Portrait* (New York: Harper and Brothers, 1956), 391.

4. *Excerpts from the Memoirs of Harry Edmonds* (International House New York, 1983), 8–11; W. Sheridan Warrick, "International Houses and Centers," *The International Encyclopedia of Higher Education* 4, ed. Asa S. Knowles (San Francisco: Jossey-Bass, 1977).

5. The Cosmopolitan Club Movement, which started in 1907 across the country, included coed and single-sex clubs. In the case of the latter, men and women in the same educational institution had separate chapters. The New York club was coed. See Chapter 1 for the discussion of the Cosmopolitan Clubs Movement.

6. *Excerpts,* 12.

7. "Mr. Carnegie and the Foreign Students," folder 3290 titled "Money-Philanthropy, individual (Carnegie)," box 206, John R. Mott Papers, MG #45, Special Collections, Yale Divinity School Library.

8. Invitation cards of early 1920s, International House New York Archives.

9. Harry Edmonds to Robert W. Gumbel, 30 January 1922, folder 68, box 10, RG III 2G, Rockefeller Family Archives, RAC.

10. *Membership Handbook,* The Intercollegiate Cosmopolitan Club of the City of New York, 1923, 13, International House New York Archives.

11. Ibid., 6.

12. Fosdick, *John D. Rockefeller, Jr.,* 391–392.

13. *Excerpts,* 27–28.

14. Foreign students began to increase in the Midwest and the West Coast when universities in these areas increased and were strengthened.

15. Cleveland H. Dodge contributed $25,000; Frederick Osborn, $10,000; Cleveland E. Dodge, $5,000; John Pratt, $5,000; Sam Thorough, $500; and a balance advance of $14,500. Folder titled "Historical," drawer 1, International House New York Archives.

16. *Excerpts,* 28–30.

17. "John D. Rockefeller, Jr. to Build House for the Intercollegiate Cosmopolitan Club," News Release of Rockefeller, Jr.'s office, 16 October 1921, folder 68, box 10, RG III 2G, Rockefeller Family Archives, RAC.

18. Ibid.; John D. Rockefeller to Charles Hughes, 21 October 1922, folder 68, box 10, RG III 2G, Rockefeller Family Archives, RAC.

19. Fosdick to Rockefeller, 9 March 1921, folder 68, box 10, RG III 2G, Rockefeller Family Archives, RAC.

20. Ibid.

21. Fosdick to Rockefeller, 28 March 1921, box 10, Rockefeller Family Archives, RAC.

22. Ibid.

23. Fosdick to Rockefeller, Jr., 9 March 1921, folder 68, box 10, RG III 2G, Rockefeller Family Archives, RAC.

24. For campus separatism, see Lynn Gordon, *Gender and Higher Education in the Progressive Era* (New Haven, CT: Yale University Press, 1990). For American feminism in the 1920s, see J. Stanley Lemons, *The Woman Citizen: Social Feminism in the 1920s* (Urbana, IL: University of Illinois Press, 1973).

25. Fosdick to Rockefeller, 28 March 1921, box 10, Rockefeller Family Archives, RAC.

26. Wickliffe Rose was president of the General Education Board and the International Education Board, and Vincent was the president of the Rockefeller Foundation. Both were advisors of Rockefeller, Jr.

27. Fosdick to Rockefeller, 28 March 1921, box 10, Rockefeller Family Archives, RAC.

28. Frederick Osborn to Rockefeller, 27 April 1921, folder 68, box 10, RG III 2G, Rockefeller Family Archives, RAC.

29. Rockefeller, Jr. to Fosdick, 1 April 1921, folder 68, box 10, RG III 2G, Rockefeller Family Archives, RAC.

30. Frederick Osborn to Rockefeller, 27 April 1921, folder 68, box 10, RG III 2G, Rockefeller Family Archives, RAC.

31. Ibid.

32. Appendix to a letter of Frederick Osborn to Rockefeller, 27 April 1921, folder 68, box 10, RG III 2G, Rockefeller Family Archives, RAC.

33. Harry Edmonds to W. S. Richardson, 7 February 1922, folder 79, box 11, Educational Interests series, Rockefeller Family Archives, RAC.

34. Harry Edmonds to Rockefeller, 31 October 1921, folder 68, box 10, RG III 2G, Rockefeller Family Archives, RAC.

35. Ibid.

36. *Membership Handbook,* 5.

37. "Plan for the Cosmopolitan Club," 15 June 1921, folder 68, box 10, RD III 2G, Rockefeller Family Archives, RAC; Fosdick to Rockefeller, 12 May 1924, folder 68, box 10, RG III 2G, Rockefeller Family Archives, RAC.

38. Edmonds to Rockefeller, 21 March 1921, folder 68, box 10, RG III 2g, Rockefeller Family Archives, RAC.

39. "John D. Rockefeller, Jr. to Build House for the Intercollegiate Cosmopolitan Club," 16 October 1921, box 10, Rockefeller Family Archives, RAC.

40. "A Rockefeller Gift to Foreign Students," *The New York Times*, October 16, 1921, 3:1; *The New York Herald*, October 16, 1921, 10:1.

41. Rockefeller, Jr. to Charles Hughes, 21 October 1922, folder 68, box 10, RG III 2G, Rockefeller Family Archives, RAC.

42. For Charles Hughes and his role in American diplomacy, see Betty Glad, *Charles Evans Hughes and the Illusions of Innocence* (Urbana, IL: University of Illinois Press, 1966).

43. Rockefeller, Jr., to Charles Hughes, 21 October 1922, box 10, Rockefeller Family Archives, RAC.

44. "The Work of International House," 18 November 1923, Rockefeller, folder 68, box 10, RG III 2G, Rockefeller Family Archives, RAC.

45. The International House New York Yearbook of 1924–1925 reported memberships of 258 Europeans, 75 Near Easterners, 130 Chinese, 40 Hispanic, 100 Japanese, 24 Indians, 300 Americans, 100 British, and 45 Filippinos.

46. This separation of residence continued until the 1960s, when a new arrangement put men on the first three floors, women on the next three, and men on the remaining floors. Interestingly, the conversion was not triggered by some radical thought of co-residence; instead, it was caused by men's complaints that women had all the rooms with the best views of the Hudson, and women complained that their rooms were more expensive.

47. Fosdick to Rockefeller, 12 May 1924, folder 68, box 10, RG III 2G, Rockefeller Family Archives, RAC; and "Notes for Guides Taking Visitors on a Tour of the House," May 1978, folder 2, drawer 1, International House New York Archives.

48. "Certificate of Incorporation," folder titled "History," drawer 1, International House New York Archives; Rockefeller to International Students' Association of the City of New York, 21 September 1922, folder 74, box 11, Educational Interests series, Rockefeller Family Archives, RAC.

49. "The Religious Policy of International House," appendix to letter from Edmonds to Rockefeller, 9 August 1927, folder 68, box 10, RG III 2G, Rockefeller Family Archives, RAC.

50. Disney did a better job in popularizing the story in American society in the 1990s through the movie "Mulan," although it lost its Chinese authenticity.

51. Newspaper clippings, *The Woman Citizen,* International House New York Archives (January 1927).

52. *International House New York Yearbook* (1931), 8.

53. "The Work of International House," Rockefeller, Jr., 18 November 1923, folder 68, box 10, RG III 2G, Rockefeller Family Archives, RAC.

54. Candle Ceremony Address of John D. Rockefeller, Jr., 9 May 1926, folder 68, box 10, RG III 2G, Rockefeller Family Archives, RAC.

55. Ibid.

56. *Ninth Annual Report of the Director* (New York: IIE, 1928), 5–6.

57. Rockefeller to Fosdick, 19 April 1926, folder 84, box 12, Educational Interests series, RG 2, Rockefeller Family Archives, RAC.

58. Edmonds to Rockefeller, 29 May 1925, folder 84, box 12, Educational Interests series, RG 2, Rockefeller Family Archives, RAC.

59. "Tribute to John D. Rockefeller, Jr." by Raymond Fosdick at the 35th Anniversary Dinner of International House, New York, 2 May 1960, International House New York Archives.

60. Rockefeller to Robert Sproul (president of Berkeley), 29 September 1930, folder 109, box 17, Educational Interests series, Rockefeller Family Archives, RAC.

61. *Excerpts,* 35.

62. Lynn Gordon, *Gender and Higher Education,* Ch. 2 on Berkeley.

63. *International House Berkeley: An Informal History,* International House Berkeley (Berkeley, CA: 1990), 3.

64. Fosdick to Rockefeller, 26 September 1927, folder 84, box 12, Educational Interests series, RG 2, Rockefeller Family Archives, RAC.

65. *International House Berkeley: An Informal History,* 3.

66. Ibid.

67. Rockefeller to Sproul, 29 September 1930, Educational Interests series, Rockefeller Family Archives, RAC.

68. Ibid.

69. Max Mason, president of the University of Chicago, to Edmonds, 21 April 1927, folder 84, box 12, Educational Interests series, Rockefeller Family Archives, RAC.

70. Trevor Arnett to Fosdick, 3 June 1927, folder 113, box 18, Educational Interests series, Rockefeller Family Archives, RAC.

71. Raymond Kuby, "Memo on Establishment of the Board of Governors of the International House," 21 May 1968, International House Chicago Archives.

72. Max Mason, president of the University of Chicago, to Edmonds, 21 April 1927, folder 84, box 12, Educational Interests series, Rockefeller Family Archives, RAC.

73. Rockefeller to Board of Trustees, the University of Chicago, 16 March 1931, International House Chicago Archives.

74. "House of Chicago" (paper prepared for a meeting of the directors of International Houses in Sydney, Australia, February 8–9, 1988), International House Chicago Archives.

75. Since the inception of Berkeley and Chicago Houses, Fosdick had advised Rockefeller to vest the title of the property permanently in the board of trustees of the university under a deed of gift, which would define the purposes of the donor. He even suggested the transfer of the property of International House New York to Columbia University. See his letter to Rockefeller, September 26, 1927. But Rockefeller seemed to think differently. He liked to follow the pattern of International House New York—in other words, to arrange a holding company and a lease to guarantee the independence of the management of the House. Fosdick argued that the advantages of vesting the property to the university were, among other things, the elimination of taxation, the suspicion of the West Coast in regard to things coming out of the East Coast, and the possible embarrassment over the ownership of the property should the purposes for which the International Houses were established ever die out. Consequently, the title of the property of International House Berkeley was vested in the University of California, and so was the property of International House Chicago to the University of Chicago.

76. Rockefeller to Board of Trustees of the University of Chicago, 16 March, 1931, International House Chicago Archives.

77. On isolationism in the Midwest, see George Grassmuck, *Sectional Biases in Congress on Foreign Policy,* The Johns Hopkins University Studies in Historical and Political Science, LXVIII (Baltimore: The Johns Hopkins University Press, 1950).

78. "International House Looks Forward," Sunday Supper Speech by Ernest B. Price, director of International House Chicago, 15 October 1939, 4, folder 114, box 18, Educational Interests series, RG 2, Rockefeller Family Archives, RAC.

79. "International House of Chicago," (paper prepared for a meeting of the directors of International Houses in Sydney, Australia, February 8–9, 1988), International House Chicago Archives. The house director also served as foreign student advisor of the University of Chicago from the early days of the house until 1974, when the dual responsibility was separated.

80. "A Pictorial History of the Nation's First International Student Center," a document from International House Philadelphia, demonstrated that as early as 1908, a Presbyterian missionary named A. Waldo Stevenson and his wife extended home hospitality to foreign students in their apartment on Larchwood Avenue. As the number of students increased, the program was adopted by the University of Pennsylvania Christian Association in 1910. In 1918, the association acquired the Pott's mansion at 3905 Spruce St. as an International Student House "for the cultivation of friendly relations among students of the world." The house was a community center for more than 200 foreign students and offered residential space for 12 students. Elmer T. Thompson succeeded Stevenson as the director in 1925 and remained in that position until his death in 1950. Under his leadership, an independent organization of International House of Philadelphia was established in 1943 and thus ended its relationship with the Christian Association.

81. Edmonds' letter of May 29, 1925, indicated Rockefeller's unhappiness with Edmonds' personal involvement in the Philadelphia proposal. It was obvious that Rockefeller would like his Extension Committee rather than any individual to deal with any group in extending international houses. Edmonds to Rockefeller, 29 May 1925, folder 84, box 12, Educational Interests Series, RG 2, Rockefeller Family Archives, RAC.

82. *Excerpts*, 37.

83. In the past decades, International House New York had a number of remarkable individuals serve its leadership. Former government officials with a strong interest in diplomacy who assumed chairmanship of the Trustee Board of International House New York after their retirement from government office included Henry Stimson, George Marshall, John McCloy, Dwight Eisenhower, Henry Kissinger, Gerald Ford, and John Whitehead.

84. Rockefeller, Jr. contributed $8 million to build the three International Houses, with $3 million for International House New York, $1.8 million for International House Berkeley, and $3.2 million for International House Chicago. His total contribution to the three houses amounted to $15,852,000, with $6,810,000 for International House New York; $3,925,000 for International House Chicago; and $1,800,000 for International House Berkeley (*New York Herald Tribune*, May 12, 1960).

85. See Raymond B. Fosdick, *The Story of the Rockefeller Foundation*, and John E. Harretal, *The Rockefeller Century.*

86. *International House New York Yearbook* (1938).

87. "International House Today," *International House New York Yearbook* (1938), 11.

88. John Mott, Trevor Arnett, and Paul Monroe were on the board of the council.

89. "Report of Committee on International Relations," 17 March 1935, folder "Edmonds, 1928–1939," drawer 1, International House New York Archives. The report criticized the life of International House New York as institutional but not religious and strong in nationalism versus internationalism. In response, Edmonds refuted that the house provided a "home" spirit and feeling among its residents, that International House life was religious but liberal, and that although there were problems of nationalism, a "wholesome tradition of the general membership is in favor of internationalism." The committee made specific recommendations on educational programs to cover political, economic, religious, and emotional spheres as a method of bridging friendship and knowledge and as a way of breaking down "the present gaps that loomed between Americans and foreign students in the House."

90. "International House Today" *International House New York Yearbook* (1938), 10–11.

91. *International House New York Yearbook* (1934), 10–17.

92. Ibid.

93. *International House Berkeley, An Informal History* (1990), 5.

94. Ernest Price, "International House Chicago, Suggestions for the Maintenance of International House for the Duration of the War," 30 April 1942; Ernest Price to Walter T. Fisher, president of the Board of Governors of International House Chicago, 27 April 1942, folder 114, box 18, Educational Interests series, RG 2, Rockefeller Family Archives, RAC.

95. More than 60 International Houses and Centers, modeled after the International House New York, were built all over the world in the 1950s and 1960s. The Association of International Houses was established in the 1960s, which provided a forum where International Houses and Centers all over the world could meet and discuss their affairs.

96. David Rockefeller, "John J. McCloy Memorial Lecture," International House, New York, November 28, 1989.

# Chapter 4

## Educational Assistance for World Progress: Teachers College, Columbia University

American educators' involvement in spreading American culture was often inspired by their belief in education as the most effective means to bring social progress and modernization in societies. Since the latter half of the 19th century, American educators had been involved in assisting with foreign educational development and educating foreign students. For instance, American educators directly participated in the modernization of education in Asia. Some faculty members at Harvard University were instrumental in the development of instruction in 1890 at the newly founded Keio University in Japan.[1] The University of Massachusetts helped establish Hokkaido University in Japan in the 1870s.[2] Faculty from Yale and Columbia went to China to teach as well as to serve as experts for educational reforms. John Dewey, the American educator and philosopher, had an enduring influence on Chinese modern education through his lecturing in China and his mentoring of Chinese students at Columbia University.[3]

After World War I, international educational efforts became directly tied with intercultural understanding and world peace. Amidst the enthusiasm of private participation in international affairs in the 1920s,[4] American educators sought to contribute to world peace and progress through international educational assistance. Their influence increased in Asia, Latin America, the Middle East, and Africa by participating in the educational reforms in these

A different version of this chapter was published in *Comparative Education Review* 41, no. 4 (1997), 413–434, with the title "International Activism and Comparative Education: Pioneering Efforts of the International Institute of Teachers College, Columbia University." Copyright ©1997 by the Comparative and International Educational Society. All rights reserved.

areas and educating the students from these regions in the United States. With the establishment of an International Institute at Teachers College, Columbia University in 1923, Teachers College spearheaded the international activism of American educators. Faculty at Teachers College believed that there was a worldwide demand for democracy and that the United States could make a great contribution to it because of its lengthy experience in democratic education. Their confidence in education as a social panacea reinforced their belief that world democracy, the basis for world progress, could only be achieved through education. They also viewed foreign students as "an educational League of Nations of great value" whose American experience would help them better understand the principles of democracy.[5] In the 1920s–1930s, rendering direct educational assistance to reform foreign educational systems and training foreign students as educational leaders characterized the active role of American educators in expanding American cultural and educational influence to other countries. Their international work also stimulated the development of comparative education studies as an academic discipline in American universities. This chapter examines the exportation of American democratic ideals and educational practice to foreign governments during the inter-war years by American educators, especially the faculty at Teachers College, Columbia University. It discusses the accomplishments of their efforts and analyzes the broader meaning of promoting world progress and cultural internationalism through international educational assistance.

## FOREIGN STUDENTS AND THE INTERNATIONAL INSTITUTE OF TEACHERS COLLEGE—HOPE OF WORLD DEMOCRACY AND PROGRESS

Teachers College traditionally enjoyed a high enrollment of foreign students. The largest foreign groups of students at the college included those from Asia, Europe, Canada, and the Middle East. By 1920, more than 2,000 foreign students had studied there.[6] The number of foreign students increased rapidly in the 1920s. For instance, more than 250 students from 34 foreign countries were studying at Teachers College in 1922.[7] Many of them were graduate students of considerable professional accomplishment before attending Teachers College. They had a wide variety of experiences in teaching and administration; some of them had held important administrative positions in their home governments.[8] The students were influenced by American political ideals of democracy while studying here, and their interest in democratic principles and practices became all the more heightened when the demand for democracy grew among peoples of the world. The impact of the democratic education of Teachers College was well illustrated by the career of a Chinese student who attended the college in 1916 and later became a famous educator in China:

My sole purpose in this life is to create a democracy by education and not by military revolution. After seeing the serious defects of the sudden birth of our Republic I was convinced that no genuine republic could exist without a genuine public education…I shall go back to cooperate with other educators to organize an efficient system of public education for our people so that they, following the steps of the Americans, will be able to develop and maintain a genuine Democracy which is the only realisable [sic] utopia of justice and liberty.[9]

Reflecting the general demand of society, Columbia University emphasized "a greater educational contribution to the building of democratic citizenship" during those years. President Nicholas M. Butler of Columbia University urged educators to extend the goal of democratic citizenship into a broader educational ideal of world citizenship.[10] As foreign students at Teachers College were specially selected and many returned to positions of leadership and influence in their home countries, Teachers College faculty regarded the students as important assets for international understanding and world democracy. They believed that foreign students, upon completion of their studies, would effectively carry home their American experience and apply it to their own countries.

Related to the spreading of American democratic ideals, Teachers College was also committed to establishing "a better international understanding, a more definite sympathy, and a more effective cooperation" in the world through the education of foreign students.[11] Professors who were active in international affairs realized, however, that the curriculum had been organized with American students in mind who were familiar with American ideals, aims, and history and who were preparing to teach in the United States. Foreign students came from very different educational systems and would return to work under different social and cultural conditions. Many foreign students were unfamiliar, except in the most general way, with American sociopolitical culture and the institutional organization that gave American educational ideals and practices their particular meaning and significance. Moreover, few foreign students had opportunities to observe actual school practices in the United States, just as many never had a chance to visit an American home. The faculty felt that foreign students could not serve effectively as an educational "League of Nations" unless special provisions were made to help them make the most of their educational experience in the United States. Additionally, more than 100 American missionaries were studying at Teachers College for their work in foreign lands. Some faculty felt that their needs also called for special programs different from the regular offerings in pedagogy and school administration. In short, an educational enterprise geared toward the needs of foreign students and teachers was considered imperative if American education was to make a major impact on world democracy and human progress.

Paul Monroe, director of the School of Education at Teachers College, was a leading advocate for international education and world democracy. He had been actively involved in America's international cultural and educational activities. He was on the International Relations Committee of the American Council on Education and also sat on the China Medical Board. He was a trustee of the Institute of International Education and of the Institute of Social and Religious Research. In addition, he chaired the Board of Trustees of Peking Union Medical College and Shandong Christian University. Monroe believed that the American model of democratic education provided the basis to achieve the goals of world democracy.[12] He explained:

Nations come into contact with nations through commerce, through travel, through politics, through religion, through cultural activities and interests. Each of these has its advantages and disadvantages in connection with the development of international good will. But of them all, that contact which we call educational—i.e. the cultural and intellectual contact—is the one which has the fewest disadvantages and the greatest advantage, from the point of view of those who are interested in cultivating international understanding and good will.[13]

According to Monroe, one large factor for human progress was the transfer of cultural elements from one people to another, and students were the intermediaries of cultural transfer when they traveled to different societies. Foreign students in the United States showed a great interest in extracting from American experience what was most applicable to the problems of their homelands. Monroe believed, however, that the function of students in the "dissemination and unification of culture has not been clearly recognized" despite the fact that in recent years the transfer of Western culture—science and democracy—to Japan and China had been greatly facilitated by the students from these countries who had studied in the West.[14] The influence of Western education on these students was also manifested in their leadership roles in the revolutions that occurred in China as well as in Turkey.

Monroe traveled extensively and saw the rapid social and political changes in many countries, namely China, Japan, the Philippines, Turkey, Greece, Spain, and Eastern European countries. He saw nationalism arise with the drastic sociopolitical changes in these countries, which posed both opportunities and challenges to the establishment of a modern educational system. Monroe pointed out, "Modern education is shaped by four fundamental social forces: modern industry, natural sciences, Democracy and nationalism." There was a distinction between nationalism and nationality. People perceived nationalism as marked by a spirit of narrowness, exclusiveness, and patriotic emotion that identified all the interests and activities of a country with its political sovereignty. It was regarded as a threat of power rather than an expression of culture. Nationality, on the other hand, was regarded as an expression of a common culture—a common way of thinking, feeling, and acting about essential things by the masses of the people. Monroe believed that culture was an artificial product that could be manufactured. It was in this manufacturing of a culture that education became central. A national educational system usually provided two essential functions: one was to select and train a small number of persons with superior ability upon whom the conduct of society must depend (in other words, the education of leaders), and the other was to educate the masses of people.[15]

As an educational expert on the Far East and missionary education, Monroe showed tremendous interest in foreign students and missionary students. He had been in charge of foreign student affairs at Teachers College for more than 20 years. Similarly, foreign students looked to him as their advisor. For quite a while, Monroe had been contemplating a center for the professional training of foreign students. In order to get funding, he approached John D. Rockefeller, Jr., who had already shown great interest in the education of foreign students by sponsoring the International House Movement. Monroe tried to call Rockefeller's attention to the distinctive educational needs of foreign students in addition to their various and complicated problems of social adjustment. He explained that although the social life of foreign students was taken care of with the establishment of International Houses, the students needed the same kind of personal guidance and help in their intellectual and professional training. He believed that the creation of a professional training center for foreign students at Teachers College would supplement other efforts to ease their social and personal adjustment to the American environment.[16] Monroe told Rockefeller that he was interested in the professional training of foreign students "chiefly as a means of spreading and interpreting democracy, and of developing international understanding and fostering international good will."[17] He argued that in the modern world, "the educational processes of a democracy have become of supreme importance" for cultural and political purposes. Hence, "the foreign student of education has far more significance in the interchange of cultural achievements" than in the past.[18] He believed that with a shared knowledge of science and democracy, the foreign student was "in reality dedicating his life to the service of internationalism," and, in the case of Oriental students, "to the better understanding between the Orient and the Occident."[19] "We have one of the most profound instruments for accomplishing these ends right in our own hands here if we make use of it," Monroe wrote Rockefeller, Jr.

Later, Monroe submitted a formal proposal to Rockefeller, Jr. that included three major elements: 1) support for foreign students, 2) surveys and research, and 3) the training of missionaries. Monroe reasoned that in regard to meeting foreign students' needs, scholarships were essential in helping promising students with their studies. There were few scholarships at Teachers College, and tuition charges were extremely high for foreign students who either worked part-time jobs or relied on meager grants from their home governments. In addition, about 125 missionaries were studying at Teachers College in 1921–1922 and needed scholarships for missionary education, field training, and dormitory facilities as well.[20] Rockefeller found

Monroe's proposal "interesting and very significant." He suggested that Monroe hold a conference with his advisors—George Vincent, Raymond Fosdick, and Wickliffe Rose. The three advisors therefore formed an informal committee and investigated the plausibility of Monroe's proposal. They concluded that a training center for foreign students was a fundamentally sound idea, but they felt that the funding should more appropriately come from an agency of international education than from Rockefeller himself.[21] As for the proposed assistance to missionaries, the three advisors felt that it called for personal rather than institutional support and that if Rockefeller desired to make a contribution to education under missionary auspices, the proposed program was a valuable contribution. In short, Rockefeller's advisors tried to separate foreign student education from missionary education.

At this time, a new agency—the International Education Board (IEB)—was being formed by the Rockefeller Foundation to direct educational operations on an international scale. Wickliffe Rose, president of the General Education Board (GEB) who had extensive experience in directing international activities of the Rockefeller Foundation, assumed the presidency when the IEB was chartered in January 1923. Monroe's proposal was therefore transferred to the care of the IEB. This shift of sponsorship caused certain uneasiness on the part of Teachers College although Rockefeller, Jr. himself had shown strong personal interest in the proposal. Possibly to test the commitment of the IEB, William F. Russell, dean of the College of Education at the State University of Iowa and son of Dean James E. Russell of Teachers College, called Wickliffe Rose on November 29, 1922 for advice on whether he should take a position outside of New York now that Monroe had sent him a tentative invitation to enter "an international institute." Rose replied that Monroe had "sufficient guarantee to justify Doctor Russell in not commiting [sic] himself" elsewhere.[22] Hereafter, Rose held several conferences with James E. Russell and Paul Monroe in regard to the proposed institute. Dean James Russell then submitted to the IEB a formal proposal on behalf of Teachers College. Rose welcomed the proposed institute as "essential to the larger international plans" that the IEB was undertaking and believed that the two organizations would be mutually helpful.[23] In the meantime, Dean James Russell, to ensure the funding, requested a written statement from Raymond Fosdick that Rockefeller, Jr. would personally underwrite the project.[24] On February 8, 1923, trustees of the IEB approved the Teachers College's proposal of an international institute. They authorized a subsidy of $1 million for a 10-year period with no more than $100,000 each year.[25] Rockefeller, Jr. personally advanced the funds for this purpose.[26]

The International Institute was established as an integral part of Teachers College with Paul Monroe as director and William F. Russell as associate director.[27] Staff included Isaac L. Kandel, Thomas Alexander, George S. Counts, Lester M. Wilson, Milton C. Del Manzo, and Ruth Emily McMurry. The work of the institute aimed to achieve three purposes: 1) to give special advice and instruction to foreign students, 2) to bring American schools in touch with the best of foreign educational theory and practice, and 3) to render direct educational assistance to foreign countries upon invitation.[28] The institute took as its mission the expansion of American democratic education to other countries through foreign students and the assistance of the development of foreign countries, especially the modernization of "backward" countries, via education. The philosophy behind the institute's programs, in addition to its international concerns, derived from the progressive educational belief that education was the primary means of social progress. Educators at Teachers College drew an analogy between their program of assisting foreign countries and the reconstruction of the South after the Civil War. "Many countries in the world to-day curiously resemble the South of a generation ago," remarked William Russell. "We believe...we are at least in part performing the same function that Dr. Buttrick and the General Education Board performed in the United States." Buttrick selected "promising and well-connected young men, sent them away to secure training and new ideas," and assisted them in building schools in the South.[29] In other words, the institute saw itself as an educational base to extend American cultural and educational influence to other countries and applied the practical lessons drawn from the rehabilitation of the American South in such an international endeavor.

The International Institute began to offer a specially designed curriculum in 1923–1924 that included some special courses for foreign students and some general courses on comparative education, on education and nationalism, and on missionary education. The inclusion of courses on missionary education in the institute's curriculum suggested that leaders of the institute had incorporated the needs of missionary students in their educational agenda, although the institute was set up for the professional training of foreign students and international educational assistance. The courses were intended to help foreign students build a general foundation for further specialized studies, to discover their own special interests, and to select the appropriate courses that would meet their particular needs in the future. American students were not excluded from these courses. In fact, American students taking courses at the International Institute increased steadily from the late 1920s to the 1930s (see Table 4.3 for foreign students at Teachers College and the total enrollment at the International Institute).

The institute claimed that its work would place foreign students in an equal position with American students in regard to the regular courses offered by the college. Even with the special courses created, the fundamental principle was neither to segregate foreign students from their American counterparts nor to interfere with their specialization in any field of education. The institute emphasized that it had no intention to monopolize students from foreign countries, nor would its courses substitute for the regular courses of the college. Although foreign students usually spent their first year

under the supervision of the institute and devoted their time to the specially
designed courses, the whole university curriculum at Columbia was open to
them. The students were expected "not only to appreciate and evaluate
American and other educational systems but also to exercise discriminating
judgment rather than the imitative instinct in applying modern scientific
principles to their own particular sphere of professional service."[30]

Four courses were directly geared toward foreign students: Education
429–430, "Fundamental Course for Students and Teachers from Foreign
Lands"; Education 227–228, "Visitation and Observation of Schools and
School Practices"; Education 229–230, "American Institutions and Ideals";
and Education 272, "Rural and Village Education for Students from Foreign
Lands." Education 272 was specially designed to meet the needs of students
who would teach in foreign countries and who would deal particularly with
the educational problems of rural peoples in Asia, Africa, and South
America. It focused on topics such as the village as the center for education
and social work, the organization and administration of primary and high
schools in village centers, curriculum development, teacher training, and
adult education. Education 229–230 was at first taught by Stephen Duggan,
director of the newly founded IIE. He taught the institutional basis of
American life in a comparative perspective, which helped foreign students
better appreciate the differences between American institutions and the institutions of other countries.

Education 429–430 tackled the social, political, and other influences that
had contributed to the making of education in the United States. It was team
taught in the form of lectures and discussions by William Russell, Paul
Monroe, Isaac Kandel, and other faculty members—concentrating on topics
such as the aims and ideals of American education, the diversity of its education, the support and control of education, the organization of elementary,
secondary, and higher education, and the preparation and status of teachers.
It was an introductory course for foreign students to familiarize themselves
with prevailing American educational conditions and to illustrate the various
efforts made in the United States to adjust education to the needs of a
democracy.[31] However, doubt was expressed within the College administration as to the necessity of such a course as Education 429–430. But students'
enthusiasm for the course and the faculty's belief in its importance as an
essential preparation for foreign students finally convinced the administration.[32]

Education 227–228 was a complementary course to Education 429–430,
designed to initiate foreign students into American schools. Visitations to
schools also offered, in a more general sense, an opportunity for the students
to understand American culture better. The institute provided $10,000 a
year to conduct these field trips so that students could have firsthand experience studying the organization of American schools, their curricula, methods, and problems—concrete examples of what they were critically studying

in classrooms. For instance, a group of 36 students from 14 countries made a field trip to the Hampton Institute in Virginia. They inspected various departments and students' dormitories, visited Bible classes, attended church services, took part in the work of the school farm, and attended YMCA programs on campus.[33] It was not clear how the students reacted to the various components of the school programs, but they were encouraged to learn from the Southern experience what might be applicable to the situation of their home countries. In general, student visitations were concentrated in the South and on the East Coast, although they made a few trips to the Midwest. The students valued the opportunities to observe schools firsthand, to have direct contact with schools and students, and to get "a bird's-eye view of the origins and growth and the present tendencies" of American education.[34] Their visits of educational institutions in rural and urban settings included state departments of education, county school systems, black schools, normal schools, and colleges and universities. They also visited social institutions that performed an educational service such as children's courts, settlements, and clinics.[35] There was no doubt that such educational experiences shaped the students' visions of educational reforms of their own countries.

## SCHOLARSHIPS AND THE SPREAD OF AMERICAN EDUCATIONAL INFLUENCE

Many foreign students who studied at Teachers College received financial aid through scholarships and grants from the institute. A total of 742 scholarships and grants were awarded in the years 1923–1936 (see Table 4.1). In fact, the institute searched for the most promising candidates in foreign countries and then attracted them with generous scholarships or grants for a systematic professional training at Teachers College. The selection of promising students was not necessarily based on scholarly merits but on the potential influence those candidates might have on the governments and the educational development of their home countries once they finished their training. The importance of scholarships, therefore, was so obvious in successfully recruiting the most desired students from abroad.

The institute established two types of scholarships. One was the tuition scholarships, financed by 10 percent of the annual $100,000 funds from the IEB, and the other was Macy grants, provided by a fund of $20,000 each year for five years from V. Everit Macy, a trustee of Teachers College. Macy grants covered the total expenses of living, travel, and tuition. Grant recipients were nominated by the Ministries of Education of the respective countries to which the grants were assigned. Some nominees came from the staff of the Ministries of Education of those countries, who generally held important government positions. Professors of the International Institute usually participated in the nomination process during their visits to these countries.

*Making the World Like Us*

**Table 4.1**
**Scholarships and Grants, 1923–1936\***

| Academic Year | Tuition Scholarships | Macy Grants | Total |
| --- | --- | --- | --- |
| 1923–1924 | 44 | | 44 |
| 1924 (Summer) | 31 | | 31 |
| 1924–1925 | 43 | 7 | 50 |
| 1925–1926 | 58 | 18 | 76 |
| 1926–1927 | 68 | 28 | 96 |
| 1927–1928 | 54 | 24 | 78 |
| 1928–1929 | 45 | 17 | 62 |
| 1929–1930 | 52 | 17 | 69 |
| 1930–1931 | 48 | 22 | 70 |
| 1931–1932 | 56 | 38 | 94 |
| 1932–1933 | 31 | | 31 |
| 1933–1934 | 12 | | 12 |
| 1934–1935 | 12 | | 12 |
| 1935–1936 | 17 | | 17 |
| Total | 571 | 171 | 742 |

Sources: Compiled from "International Institute of Teachers College, Report of the Director," *Dean's Report,* Teachers College, 1924–1937, and cross-referenced with information from "Memorandum Concerning the International Institute of Teachers College," sent to Raymond Fosdick by William Russell, 1931.

*These grants include full and partial awards. Scholarships for summer sessions were sometimes included in the reports of the director.

In 1926, for example, while on a world tour of educational missions, Paul Monroe made visits to the capitals of Austria, Hungary, Czechoslovakia, and Germany to confer with the ministers of education of these countries about potential Macy grant recipients. In Prague, he had hoped to arrange for the coming of Dr. Francis Praus, Secretary of the Ministry of Foreign Affairs, who was also in charge of educational affairs with foreign countries. But Francis Praus was too ill to accept the offer, and the institute had to be content with a less prominent nominee.[36]

In the first 10 years of the International Institute, there were 2,393 foreign students at Teachers College—to whom 483 full tuition scholarships and

140 full Macy grants were awarded.[37] A tabulation of the Macy grants awarded to foreign students shows, however, that while the institute was interested in a wide variety of countries, it emphasized certain areas. China, Czechoslovakia, India, Germany, Scotland, and Russia were the major recipients of Macy grants (see Table 4.2). Similarly, students from these countries tended to receive more tuition scholarships. Between 1923 and 1928, the institute awarded 174 full tuition scholarships to foreign students, with 49 for Chinese, 11 for Indians, nine for Russians, eight for Turks, and seven for Germans. The total numbers of students from these nations were, respectively, 272 Chinese, 23 Indians, 50 Russians, 21 Turks, and 30 Germans during the same period.[38]

**Table 4.2**
**Distribution of Full Macy Grants to Various Countries, 1925–1932**

| Regions | 1925 | 1926 | 1927 | 1928 | 1929 | 1930 | 1931 | 1932 | Total |
|---|---|---|---|---|---|---|---|---|---|
| Africa | | | | | | | 1 | | 1 |
| Australia | | 1 | 1 | | | | | | 2 |
| Austria | | | | 1 | | | | | 1 |
| Brazil | | | | 1 | 1 | | 1 | | 3 |
| Bulgaria | | | 2 | 1 | 1 | | | 1 | 5 |
| Chile | | | | 1 | 2 | | | | 3 |
| China | 1 | 1 | 2 | 1 | 1 | 2 | 1 | | 9 |
| Czechoslovakia | | | 1 | 1 | 1 | 2 | 2 | 2 | 9 |
| Denmark | | | | | | 1 | | | 1 |
| Ecuador | | | | | | | 1 | | 1 |
| Egypt | | 1 | | | | | | 1 | 2 |
| England | | | 1 | 1 | | | | | 2 |
| Estonia | | | | | | 1 | | | 1 |
| France | | | | 1 | 1 | 1 | 1 | 1 | 5 |
| Germany | 1 | | 3 | 2 | 1 | 2 | | 1 | 10 |
| Haiti | | | 1 | 1 | 2 | | | | 4 |
| Hungary | | 1 | 2 | 1 | | | 1 | | 5 |
| India | 1 | 2 | 4 | 1 | 1 | 2 | 1 | 1 | 13 |
| Iraq | 1 | | | 2 | | 1 | 1 | 1 | 6 |

| Regions | 1925 | 1926 | 1927 | 1928 | 1929 | 1930 | 1931 | 1932 | Total |
|---|---|---|---|---|---|---|---|---|---|
| Italy | | | | 1 | 1 | 1 | | | 3 |
| Japan | | 1 | 1 | 1 | | 1 | | | 4 |
| Korea | | | | | | | 1 | | 1 |
| Mexico | | | | | 1 | | | | 1 |
| New Zealand | | 1 | | | | | | 1 | 2 |
| Palestine | | 1 | 1 | | | | | 1 | 3 |
| Persia | 1 | 1 | | | | | 1 | 1 | 4 |
| Poland | | 1 | 1 | 1 | | 1 | | | 4 |
| Puerto Rico | | 1 | 2 | 1 | 1 | | | 1 | 6 |
| Romania | | | | | 1 | | | | 1 |
| Russia | 1 | 2 | 1 | 1 | 1 | 1 | | | 7 |
| Scotland | | 1 | 1 | 1 | 2 | 1 | 1 | 1 | 8 |
| Spain | | | 1 | | | | | | 1 |
| Sweden | | | | | | | 1 | | 1 |
| Switzerland | | 1 | | | 1 | | 1 | 1 | 4 |
| Turkey | 1 | 2 | 2 | 1 | | | | | 6 |
| Yugoslavia | | | | | 1 | | | | 1 |
| Total 36 | 7 | 18 | 28 | 24 | 17 | 17 | 14 | 15 | 140 |

Sources: Compiled from "International Institute of Teachers College, Report of the Director," *Dean's Report,* Teachers College, 1925–1932.

The policy to award scholarships at the institute was not strictly based on "merits and needs." Rather, it was made on the basis of strategic considerations of expanding American influence to foreign countries and the need for American education to have personal contact with educational leaders in these countries. In the original proposal to the Rockefeller Foundation, Teachers College stated that distribution of scholarships was to be limited "to students certain to occupy positions of leadership in their own countries."[39] Again, in a 1932 memo to Del Manzo (provost of Teachers College) regarding the selections and nominations for scholarships, Paul Monroe recommended the "preferred treatment to a few of these because of the strategic position of their work and because of the contacts which we may not have but wish to build up."[40] It was the hope of Teachers College that those who received scholarships would, upon completion of their work, be employed in the public education systems of their own countries.[41]

The institute evidently targeted the education of foreign elite so that they would carry back American democratic education with greater and more immediate impact upon their own societies. Although American educators had left their imprint on educational development on almost every continent, East Asia and the Middle East were the two areas where the influence of American educators was most strongly felt in the 1920s–1930s. These two regions, which were undergoing "cultural renaissance" in the early decades of the 20th century, appealed to modern educators with peculiar interest.[42] Revolutionary changes in East Asia, especially in China, involved significant participation of American educational efforts. The "renaissance movement" that swept the entire Arab world and the religious disturbance and revolutions that produced new governments in that region enticed American educators to participate in rebuilding educational systems in that ancient culture. Moreover, as in East Asia, American philanthropic and religious organizations had established some important educational institutions in the Middle East in earlier decades, which provided American educators with existing contacts and foundations to build upon.

In the 1920s, the international work of Teachers College was concentrated more in the Pacific area than in any other place. Of the foreign students at Teachers College, fully 25 percent came from China and nearly 50 percent from Asian countries.[43] The investment of the college in these students seemed to have yielded good results. Many former students assumed prominent positions in the educational systems of their own countries. They worked in the ministries of education, state boards of education, or served as presidents, deans, professors, directors of educational research, principals of schools, and heads of missionary institutions. By the end of the 1920s, more than 200 Chinese graduates of Teachers College had taken positions in Chinese higher educational institutions—governmental, private, or missionary. On his visit to China in 1926, Paul Monroe found himself working with a former student, Dr. P. W. Kwo, who was the first Chinese to receive a doctorate at Teachers College and was now head of the newly established China-America Institute.[44]

The American influence on the educational development of the Middle East increased conspicuously in the 1930s as Arab students at Teachers College returned home and took important positions in their own educational systems. On a visit to Iraq in 1930, Monroe met several of his former students: one was secretary to the king, another was the inspector of the Basra district, two others were principals of normal training schools, and another was a leading teacher in the higher normal school. All five were former Macy grant recipients and were now leaders in the kingdom's school system.[45] In Iran (then Persia), a former student at Teachers College, Seddigh A'alam, convinced the minister of education and the minister of court that one solution to the educational problems in their country was to establish throughout the empire a system of American secular schools, which he presented as "far in advance of the French system."[46]

In the meantime, faculty members of Teachers College directly participated in foreign educational development by serving as educational experts
and by sitting on boards of foreign educational institutions or bi-national
organizations in different countries. Monroe was most active in this respect.
He was deeply involved in the educational reform in China in the 1920s,
where belief in democracy and science as a social panacea began to exert a
dominant influence on the thinking of Chinese intellectuals. In 1924, when
the U.S. government released to China the remainder of the Boxer
Indemnity funds, Monroe played an important part in the daily work of the
China Foundation for the Promotion of Education and Culture as well as in
its inception and organization. Under the authorization of both the United
States and Chinese governments, he worked out a plan acceptable to both
parties for the use of the returned indemnity. He focused the returned
money on student fellowships, the building of a National Library, and the
strengthening of science education in China—especially the production of
science teachers and the establishment of laboratories at middle schools and
colleges. Of the 15 trustees of the China Foundation, five were Americans,
including John Dewey and Paul Monroe.[47]

When the institute emphasized the work in the Middle East in the 1930s,
Monroe was heavily involved in the educational development of that region
by serving as advisor to the Near East College Association of six colleges. At
the invitation of the trustees of Robert College and the Constantinople
Women's College, and with the approval of Teachers College, Monroe
became the president of the aforementioned two educational institutions in
Turkey in 1932. He served in that capacity for three years while devoting
half of his time as director of the International Institute of Teachers
College.[48] Monroe strongly believed that his service in the Middle East
would enhance the influence and prestige of American education there.

The influence of American educational ideas and practices abroad was
realized not only through the education of foreign students and direct faculty
participation in foreign educational development but also through the extensive surveys and research of foreign educational conditions by the faculty of
Teachers College. There were basically two types of investigations of foreign
educational conditions. One was the investigation for the purpose of increasing the knowledge of foreign systems, and the other was the survey of existing educational conditions in order to carry out reforms. Such educational
investigation and assistance were often made at the invitation of foreign governments and sponsored by American philanthropies.[49] American educators
conducted surveys in countries like China, the Philippines, Mexico, Puerto
Rico, Chile, Argentina, Uruguay, Brazil, Czechoslovakia, Poland, Africa
(including women's conditions there), and the Middle East. As a result, their
recommendations exerted major impact on educational reforms in such different countries as the Philippines in 1925, China in 1925, Puerto Rico in
1926, and Iraq in 1932.[50]

The institute also took a great interest in the educational changes in the new Soviet Russia by accepting and educating its students and conducting research on Soviet educational and cultural reform programs. George Counts made frequent visits to Soviet Russia and wrote extensively about its educational reforms in the 1920s and 1930s. In reference to these activities with Soviet Russia, Paul Monroe claimed, "The Institute is no respector [sic] of political forms as our interest is in education only."[51]

Moreover, the institute worked with international organizations on educational issues. For instance, it examined the work of the Near East Relief and made educational policy suggestions to the organization as to how to take care of the 60,000 orphans and 40,000 dependent children under its supervision. The institute also investigated the conditions and needs of schools for American children in China, Japan, Korea, India, and Europe at the request of the Institute for Social and Religious Research.[52] Additionally, the institute cooperated with the IIE in receiving foreign education commissions and leaders. When Stephen Duggan, director of the IIE, was on a world trip in 1925, William Russell of the institute served as acting director of the IIE.[53]

## RESEARCH ON INTERNATIONAL AND COMPARATIVE EDUCATION

To increase the knowledge of educational developments in other countries and to disseminate American ideas of education, faculty members of the institute attended international conferences on education and conducted research abroad. They visited foreign educational authorities and inspected foreign schools to familiarize themselves with new practices. Their educational investigations and studies covered dozens of countries in Asia, the Middle East, Latin America, Africa, and Europe. The research activity of the faculty resulted in a large quantity of publications dealing with foreign and comparative education, which included *China: A Nation in Evolution* by Paul Monroe; *The Reform of Secondary Education in France* and *French Elementary Courses of Study* by Isaac Kandel; *The Soviet Challenge to America* and *A Ford Crosses Russia* by George Counts; *The Reorganization of Education in Prussia* by Isaac Kandel and Thomas Alexander; *The New Education in the German Republic* by Thomas Alexander and Beryl Parker; two collections of *Essays in Comparative Education* by Paul Monroe and by Isaac Kandel, respectively; and *Guidebook to Some European School Systems.*[54]

The institute began publishing *The Educational Yearbook* in 1923 with Isaac Kandel as the editor. *The Yearbook*, which was the first of its kind, played a crucial role in the exchange of information on international and comparative education throughout the world—especially during a time when literature on comparative education and foreign educational developments was extremely limited. Studies of foreign educational conditions by the staff of the institute were often first published in *The Yearbook.* Some volumes of *The Yearbook* treated educational issues in specific regions; others treated selected topics such as church-state relations in education, rural education, adult education, missionary education, and so on.[55] *The Yearbook* also contributed enormously to the dissemination of American ideas and practices of democratic education in other countries. The annual publication of *The Yearbook* lasted for 21 years from 1924 to 1944.[56] As a pioneer in the field, *The Educational Yearbook* had a wide circulation in educational institutions abroad as well as at home. It was also instrumental in the creation of the next comparative education journal, *Year Book of Education,* in London in 1932. Also important to the increase of knowledge of foreign and comparative education was the creation of the International Institute Library. Its outstanding collections on worldwide education were the best at the time for research on foreign and comparative education.

The unique contribution of the International Institute to the educational profession was attributed not only to its accomplishments abroad but also to its achievements at home. Through professional training, lecturing, and publications of research, the institute broadened the approach of education scholarship by developing comparative education studies as an academic discipline in American universities. Comparative education courses were offered at the International Institute and attracted large numbers of students, both foreign and American. In the 1930s, when economic depression and increased international tensions caused a significant decline of foreign students in this country as well as at Teachers College (see Figure 4.1), American students considerably outnumbered foreign students in taking courses at the institute (see Table 4.3 for comparison). Monroe reported, "Some of the courses attracting the largest attendance offered by the staff of the Institute are those in which the attendance is almost wholly of American students. Chief among such courses are those relating to foreign educational systems, to modern schools in European countries, and to nationalism."[57] American students who specialized in comparative education also made research trips to European countries.[58]

As a result, interest in the international aspects of education grew throughout American schools of education. This growth was demonstrated in the expansion of comparative education courses and the increased interest of American educators in courses and materials related to comparative education.[59] Many of the pioneers in comparative education, who primarily focused their attention on American and European educational systems, were trained at Teachers College. Faculty members of the International Institute also went to different universities to lecture on comparative education. For instance, Isaac Kandel was a guest professor on comparative education at the University of California, The Johns Hopkins University, and the University of Pennsylvania. Thomas Alexander taught American education at the University of Berlin. Paul Monroe co-edited the first periodical devoted to comparative and international education, the *International Review of Education*. In addition, foreign students played an important role in promoting comparative

**Figure 4.1**

## Foreign Student Increase at Teachers College and in the United States, 1923–1938

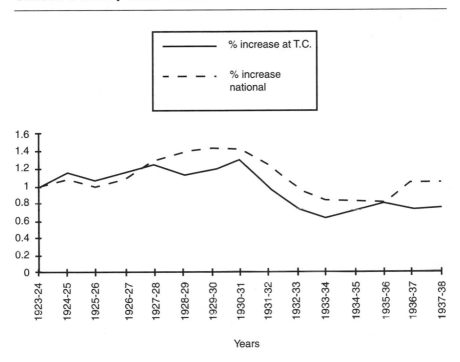

Years

Sources: National statistics of foreign students were gathered from the *Annual Report of the Director of the Institute of International Education*, New York, 1928–1940; statistics of foreign students at Teachers College were compiled from *Dean's Report*, Teachers College, 1924–1936, and from "Report of the International Institute of Teachers College to the Rockefeller Foundation," January, 1939.

**Table 4.3**

## Foreign Students (T.C.), Scholarships and Total Enrollment (International Institute), 1923–1938

| Year | Foreign Students | Countries Represented | Scholarships | Macy Grants | Total Enrolled |
|---|---|---|---|---|---|
| 1923–1924 | 265 | 42 | $9,138 | | 253 |
| 1924–1925 | 309 | 49 | 12,724 | | 275 |
| 1925–1926 | 280 | 49 | 10,585 | $1,320 | 237 |
| 1926–1927 | 302 | 44 | 13,785 | 25,940 | 457 |
| 1927–1928 | 328 | 53 | 12,250 | 31,510 | 459 |
| 1928–1929 | 296 | 54 | 9,750 | 17,530 | 763 |
| 1929–1930 | 311 | 46 | 10,005 | 20,180 | 729 |
| 1930–1931 | 343 | 53 | 10,000 | 19,783 | 747 |
| 1931–1932 | 260 | 49 | 10,970.21 | 14,621.61 | 1202 |
| 1932–1933 | 197 | 40 | 7,451 | | 701 |
| 1933–1934 | 166 | 37 | 1,460 | | 523 |
| 1934–1935 | 191 | 38 | 1,560 | | 361 |
| 1935–1936 | 211 | 38 | 2,870* | | 327 |
| 1936–1937 | 194 | 38 | 3,650* | | 238 |
| 1937–1938 | 199 | 35 | 10,237.50* | | 273 |
| Total | 3852 | | $126,435.71 | $130,884.61 | 7545 |

Sources: This table is integrated from tables attached to the "Report of the International Institute of Teachers College to the Rockefeller Foundation, January, 1939."

*After 1934–1935 scholarships to foreign students were made from Teachers College Scholarship funds, including Dean's Scholarships, as indicated from 1935–1936 to 1937–1938 in the previous table.

education in the United States. They instructed American teachers and students through informal conversations, class discussions, and speeches to student bodies—including those of the schools that they visited during their field trips. Many foreign students achieved remarkable success as lecturers on comparative education.[60]

## THE FUTURE OF THE INTERNATIONAL INSTITUTE: DIFFERENT VIEWS

In view of the remarkable accomplishment of the institute, Paul Monroe hoped that the original 10-year grant of the IEB would become a permanent endowment. In a report about the first five years of the institute, Monroe indicated such a desire to the leaders of the IEB. Monroe also asked Rockefeller, Jr. personally to "investigate the work of the Institute with a view to its permanent endowment as a substitute for the continuance of the subsidy."[61] Rockefeller instructed that the request for endowment should be reviewed by the original committee of Raymond Fosdick, Wickliffe Rose, and George Vincent and that permanent financing should be considered before the 10-year grant expired.[62] Wickliffe Rose thought it advisable to have the situation of the institute thoroughly examined before the IEB took any action on the question of further endowment.[63]

Trevor Arnett, who was an official at the Rockefeller Foundation after years of work at the University of Chicago, was assigned to examine the work of the institute. He visited some classes and held extended conferences with Paul Monroe, William F. Russell (who became the dean of Teachers College in 1927), and members of the faculty. On March 15, 1928 he sent Raymond Fosdick a 13-page memorandum on the functions of the institute. Arnett had a different view of how international educational assistance should be promoted. His recommendations subsequently made a decisive difference for the future of the institute. In short, Arnett summarized the institute as having five major functions: 1) making special provision for the foreign students so as to enable them to profit from American education; 2) giving instruction and guidance to American students who were concerned with education in other lands; 3) supervising studies and investigations undertaken in European countries by American students; 4) investigating foreign educational conditions as a means of rendering assistance and increasing knowledge; and 5) acting as a channel of international exchange of educational contacts to serve the cause of international understanding and goodwill.

Arnett concluded that all these functions were useful and were worthily performed, but he questioned whether they were so special as to warrant the creation of a separate institution to perform them. In his opinion, only the first function was the most needed: the unique situation of foreign students called for special treatment and orientation to American educational practices and customs. The remaining functions, however, could be properly exercised by the regular faculty and schools of education of large universities—particularly those at which foreign students enrolled in large numbers. He argued that the preliminary courses for foreign students might be advantageously offered as part of the regular university curriculum rather than via a special agency like the International Institute. His inspection of the courses at the institute also showed that all the courses were chiefly for American students except for three—two on American education and one on American institutions and ideals—that were geared toward foreign students.[64]

While Arnett acknowledged the contribution of the work of the International Institute, he posed a serious question for the Rockefeller philanthropic officers: Should any grant of the IEB be confined to one institution rather than to all institutions properly qualified, wherever located? "Is there not danger of the promulgation of one type of theory and method if these activities are restricted to the Faculty of one institution?" he asked. He argued that when foreign students were encouraged to come to Teachers College because of available scholarships and other aid, there was danger that they might receive a too narrow and one-sided perspective. If these students were enabled to select any qualified institution, they would in all probability carry back to their home countries a broader view of the American educational system. "Would it not be better," he suggested, "to make its [IEB] grants available to any institution which at the moment might be in a position to carry them successfully and profit by the expenditure?" This question, he thought, "applied with most propriety to grants from the International Education Board" and "with almost equal force to gifts from Mr. Rockefeller [Jr.]." Also, "Any donor whose special interests centered in one institution and who felt moved to promote the welfare of foreign students might appropriately restrict his gifts for this purpose to that institution."[65]

In regard to the permanency of the institute, Arnett thought that there were grave doubts as to the permanent need of making special provision for foreign students other than fellowships to enable them to study in America, which should be available at all qualified universities. Arnett argued that although it was most helpful for foreign students to receive special treatment for orientation, the amount of special attention and its duration should be as brief as possible. Foreign students, he felt, should be required early on to become a part of the regular routine, "for only in this way will they really get into the spirit of our institutions and become self reliant." He estimated that as "Oriental nations" (which then needed the most assistance) became better educated, the foreign students seeking education in this country would not need special attention other than language assistance. In his view, special provision to foreign students would generally work better by detailing certain members of the regular faculty to supply special guidance and instruction to them. When the need diminished or ceased, the special arrangement could readily be terminated. Therefore, he concluded, it was unwise to endow the International Institute in perpetuity because there were serious doubts as to the permanency of the need.[66]

Abraham Flexner, director of Educational Surveys of IEB, read both Monroe's report and Arnett's memo on the functions of the institute. He concluded that by the end of the grant, "steps should be taken to decentralize the work of the Institute and to encourage all the better schools of education to participate in the work now centralized in the International Institute."[67] In addition, Wickliffe Rose was not inclined to have the grant renewed at the time of its expiration.[68] Monroe's request for permanent endowment of the institute was thus rejected.

But Teachers College would not give up easily. In May 1931, Dean William F. Russell of Teachers College presented to the General Education Board (IEB ceased to exist as an operating agency after the reorganization of the Rockefeller Boards in 1928) a request for new funding of the institute. At the invitation of Raymond Fosdick, Trevor Arnett and David Stevens met with Dean Russell to review the work of the institute. The new group of foundation officers had little interest in making a new grant, but at the suggestion of Fosdick, the trustees of the GEB came to an agreement that a grant of $150,000 would be authorized to the institute on a tapering basis for a period of five years, beginning on the date when the original grant expired.[69] Leaders of the GEB told Dean William Russell that the International Institute "was not the type of enterprise which the Board would enter de novo."[70] The purpose of the five-year grant was to enable the institute to adjust its affairs to the new financial situation and to give Teachers College adequate time to seek new support elsewhere for the institute. Officers of the GEB thought that with the original 10-year grant and a subsequent contribution for a five-year period, the Rockefeller Foundation fulfilled its responsibility to the institute. This decision, however, did not mean that the Rockefeller Foundation abandoned its interest in sponsoring international cultural understanding. In fact, the Rockefeller philanthropy showed a special interest in the study of non-western languages and cultures by launching a series of summer institutes in 1933–1934 at universities such as Harvard, Columbia, and Cornell for the instruction of the languages and cultures of Japan, China, and Russia. It also made grants to the universities of Washington, California, Stanford, Yale, and Chicago as well as the Library of Congress to obtain books on the history, literature, and philosophy of Oriental civilization and the Slavic culture.[71]

But the final five-year grant to the institute of Teachers College came at the moment when student attendance at the institute reached its peak (see Table 4.3). The reduction of financial resources severely curtailed the research work and the scholarships of the institute, which coincided with the decline of the foreign student population (see Figure 4.1) occasioned by worldwide economic depression and the worsening conditions of international relations in the 1930s. Although the institute continued its instruction and research in international and comparative education, its momentum significantly sagged. The administration of Teachers College was ready to give up the institute after the unsuccessful attempt to obtain continued sponsorship from the Rockefeller Foundation. But Paul Monroe warned that it was "very short-sighted and uneconomical to scrap all of this at the first sign of financial difficulty ahead…if we at this time consented to the dismantling of the Institute it could never be re-established with anything like its present prestige."[72] He suggested that it would be better to accept the financial analysis of the situation and leave the future to take care of itself. In 1938, when the terminal five-year grant expired, the institute went out of existence just before World War II and on the eve of a full-scale postwar international education movement in the United States.

The education of foreign students and faculty involvement with international educational operations, however, did not stop with the demise of the International Institute. Foreign student enrollment at Teachers College remained around 200 before World War II (although it dropped to around 120 during the war years) and skyrocketed to about 400 immediately after the war.[73] Four faculty members of Teachers College, Lester M. Wilson, Ruth E. McMurry, Harriet Hayes, and Walter Hager, acted as an advisory committee to give foreign students guidance. When two of them left Teachers College in 1942, Kandel and three other professors were appointed to serve on the committee. As part of their responsibility, the committee advised foreign students on their selected programs of studies during the registration and suggested changes in their programs whenever they felt the need. The committee strongly recommended foreign students to take comparative education as their major field in the first year of study, during which their advisors would have sufficient time to work out an academic orientation program for them. Many students were not well prepared for highly specialized or advanced courses in the beginning. But as soon as the student was qualified and had identified a more definite field of specialization, a declaration of his or her major would be made.[74]

In 1942, some faculty at Teachers College tried to revive the defunct International Institute in anticipation of a postwar surge of foreign student enrollment in American universities. It was speculated that the United States would assume a more important role than ever before in international educational affairs. Isaac Kandel made a presentation on "The Place of the International Institute of Teachers College, Columbia University as an International Center for the Study of Education." He argued that the International Institute of Teachers College was concerned not only with the education of foreign students but also with the broadening grasp of educational theories and practices for American students.[75] These broader functions would be fundamental to America's involvement in foreign educational development; however, the effort of the faculty did not result in anything substantial to re-establish the institute.

In the meantime, Teachers College began cooperating with the U.S. government on educational projects abroad during the war. After WWII, Teachers College started sending teams of educators to Afghanistan, India, Kenya, and Peru on behalf of the government and philanthropic foundations to assist with the development of those countries.[76] Clarence Linton was key to the Teachers College's programs and contract in Afghanistan. He left Teachers College in 1942 to join the war effort, working for the government. After the war, he returned to Teachers College but remained actively involved in the educational projects of the government and connected Teachers College with those projects. As a professor of education, he had been an advisor and chairman of student guidance at Teachers College.[77] He played an important role in the formation of the National Association for Foreign Student Affairs (NAFSA) and served as the first president when it was established in 1948.[78] These continued efforts of Teachers College in international assistance and foreign student education reflected a tradition of the college but also indicated a departure as the college began a long association with the government in educational operations abroad during the Cold War. Educators of Teachers College were extremely active in U.S. educational assistance to Africa in the 1960s, where they even dubbed themselves as "educationaries." The professional training of foreign students and the direct participation in educational reforms of other countries by American educators no doubt facilitated the dissemination of American political and social ideals of democracy as well as its educational theories and practices. Through the educational programs at Teachers College, foreign students were indoctrinated with the ideals of democratic education as a social panacea—and many tried to apply their acquired knowledge to their own countries. The close association of the institute with many foreign governments also exerted a far-reaching impact of the United States in foreign countries.

The work of Teachers College faculty illustrated the unique role of educational institutions in shaping U.S. foreign relations. The impact of American educational and cultural influence was most notable and profound in East Asia and the Near East during the interwar years because of the International Institute. Intellectual cooperation in educational reforms for democracy and human progress characterized the rhetoric of the faculty of Teachers College and the educational leaders of various countries. The international activities of the institute and its educational influence abroad contributed significantly to the cultural relations of the United States with other countries.

Despite its relatively short existence, the institute had a far-reaching impact on educational development at home, as well. The international educational activities of the institute and its prolific production of scholarly research and collection of materials on other countries' educational systems aroused growing interest in foreign educational developments and in the field of comparative education among American educators. The development of comparative education as an academic discipline in American schools of education enhanced the international scope of work of American educators. These various educational efforts laid solid groundwork for the worldwide international education operations during the Cold War.

## *NOTES*

1. *The Autobiography of Fukuzawa Yukichi,* trans. Eiichi Kiyooka (Tokyo: Hokuseido Press, 1960), 363; Martin Bronfenbrenner, *Academic Encounter: The American University in Japan and Korea* (New York: Free Press of Glencoe, 1961), 22.

2. Robert S. Schantes, *Japanese and Americans: A Century of Cultural Relations* (New York: Harper, 1955), 55.

3. John Dewey spent two years in China in 1919–1921, delivering more than 60 major lectures and meeting with educational leaders. Many of his Chinese students at Columbia were leading educators in China. He was awarded an honorary Ph.D. at the National Peking University and was referred to as the "Second Confucius" at the presentation. See Douglas Smith, "An Impact Analysis of John Dewey and His China Experience," (paper presented at the 1995 Shanghai International Symposium on "Important Issues in Sino-American People's Friendly Exchanges Since the 19ᵗʰ Century.") See also Barry Keenan, *The Dewey Experiment in China* (Cambridge, MA: Harvard University Press, 1977); T. C. Ou, *Dewey's Influence on China's Efforts for Modernization* (Jamaica, NY: Center of Asian Studies at St. Johns University, 1978); Hu Shi, "John Dewey in China," *Philosophy and Culture—East and West: Philosophy in Practical Perspective* (Honolulu, HI: University of Hawaii Press, 1962).

4. For private participation in international affairs, see Emily S. Rosenberg, *Spreading the American Dream* (New York: Hill and Wang, 1982).

5. *Teachers College Bulletin* (May 12, 1923), 4.

6. "Foreign Student Advisor," RG 25, Special Collections, the Milbank Library, Teachers College, Columbia University (T. C. Special Collections).

7. "International Institute of Teachers College, Report of the Director," *Dean's Report* (Teachers College, 1924), 55–57.

8. Ibid.

9. Wen Tsing Tao to Dean J. E. Russell, 16 February 1916, folder 755D, "Livingston Scholars, 1915–1916," series 10, RG 6, James Earl Russell Papers, T. C. Special Collections. Wen Tsing Tao was known as Tao Xingzhi in China. His educational thought significantly contributed to China's modern education.

10. Lawrence Cremin et al., *A History of Teachers College, Columbia University* (New York: Columbia University Press, 1954), 76.

11. Ibid., 3–4.

12. Monroe's ideas about world democracy were well expressed in his 1918 volume, *The American Spirit: A Basis for World Democracy*, 1918, box 1a, RG 28, Monroe Papers, T. C. Special Collections.

13. Folder titled "Speech of 1924," box 6B, RG 28, Monroe Papers, T. C. Special Collections.

14. Paul Monroe, "The Cross-Fertilization of Culture: The Function of International Education," *News Bulletin* (Honolulu, HI: Institute of Pacific Relations, February 1928), 1–2.

15. Paul Monroe, "Education and Nationalism," folder titled "Speeches and Papers, 1926–1936," box 6B, RG 28, Monroe Papers, T. C. Special Collections.

16. "Proposal to the Rockefeller Foundation," folder titled "International Institute Correspondence, Projects, Proposals, 1920s," box 6a, RG 28, Paul Monroe Papers, T. C. Special Collections.

17. Paul Monroe to John D. Rockefeller, Jr., 7 April, 1922, folder titled "Columbia University, Teachers College, International Institute," box 60, Educational Interests series, RG 2, Rockefeller Family Archives, RAC.

18. Ibid.

19. "Proposal to the Rockefeller Foundation," Monroe Papers.

20. "Memorandum on International Institute of Teachers College," 7 October 1931, folder 280, box 19, series 1, International Education Board, RAC.

21. Raymond B. Fosdick, Wickliffe Rose, and George E. Vincent to John D. Rockefeller, Jr., 6 November 1922, folder titled "Columbia University, Teachers College, International Institute," box 60, Educational Interests series, FG 2, Rockfeller Family Archives, RAC.

22. "Memorandum on International Institute of Teachers College," 7 October 1931, International Education Board, RAC.

23. George W. Gray, *Education on an International Scale, A History of the International Education Board* (New York: Harcourt, Brace and Company, 1941), 85–86.

24. James Russell to Raymond Fosdick, 10 January 1923, and Fosdick to James Russell, 13 January 1923, folder 275, box 19, series 1, International Education Board, RAC.

25. Wickliffe Rose to Dean James Russell, 8 February 1923, folder 275, box 19, series 1, International Education Board, RAC.

26. "Memorandum on International Institute of Teachers College," 7 October 1931, International Education Board, RAC.

27. William Russell succeeded his father as dean of the Teachers College in 1927.

28. "Report of the International Institute of Teachers College to the Rockefeller Foundation," January 1939, 1–2, folder titled "International Institute, General Education Board (2)," box 39, RG 6, W. F. Russell Papers, T. C. Special Collections.

29. William F. Russell, "Memorandum Concerning the International Institute of Teachers College," 25 May 1931, 13, folder 280, box 19, series 1, International Education Board, RAC.

30. "Courses for Students and Teachers from Other Lands" (*Teachers College Bulletin,* May 12, 1923), 6–7.

31. Ibid., 7–9.

32. Paul Monroe to Dean William Russell, 11 January 1932, folder titled "Monroe (2)," box 46, RG 6, William Russell Papers, T. C. Special Collections.

33. William Anthony Aery to Wallace Buttrick, 13 June 1923, folder 275, box 19, series 1, International Education Board, RAC.

34. Foreign students to the president of the General Education Board, 29 May 1926, folder 276, box 19, series 1, International Education Board, RAC.

35. William F. Russell, "Memorandum Concerning the International Institute of Teachers College," 25 May 1931, 3, International Education Board, RAC; "International Institute of Teachers College, Report of the Director," *Dean's Report* (Teacher's College, 1924), 59–60.

36. Monroe to Dean James Russell on the Atlantic, n.d., folder titled "Columbia University, Teachers College, International Institute," box 60, Educational Interests series, RG 2, Rockefeller Family Archives, RAC.

37. Folder titled "International Institute Reports," box 6a, RG 28, Paul Monroe Papers, T. C. Special Collections.

38. Folder titled "International Institute—Scholarships," box 40, RG 6, William F. Russell Papers, T. C. Special Collections.

39. "Proposal to the Rockefeller Foundation," Monroe Papers.

40. Monroe to Dr. Del Manzo, 14 January 1932, folder titled "International Institute (Correspondence)," box 39, RG 6, W. F. Russell Papers, T. C. Special Collections.

41. Folder titled "International Institute Scholarships," box 40, RG 6, W. F. Russell Papers, T. C. Special Collections.

42. "International Institute of Teachers College, Report of the Director," *Dean's Report* (Teacher's College, 1930), 52–53; *Dean's Report,* (Teacher's College, 1924), 62–63.

43. Monroe, "The Cross-Fertilization of Culture," 6.

44. Monroe to Dean James Russell, n.d., on the Atlantic, Rockefeller Family Archives, RAC.

45. "International Institute of Teachers College, Report of the Director," *Dean's Report* (Teachers College, 1930), 53.

46. Charles C. Hart to the secretary of state, Washington, D. C., 27 April 1931, 3, folder 112, box 101, series 1, General Education Board, RAC.

47. Monroe to Dean James Russell, n.d., on the Atlantic, Rockefeller Family Archives, RAC; "International Institute of Teachers College; Report of the Director," *Dean's Report* (Teacher's College, 1925), 43–44.

48. "International Institute of Teachers College, Report of the Director," *Dean's Report* (Teachers College, 1932 and 1933).

49. Teachers College professors often used surveys as scientific tools to investigate educational problems. School surveys were a favorite technique to spread progressive ideas in America. See David Tyack, *The One Best System* (Cambridge, MA: Harvard University Press, 1974), 191–194.

50. "International Institute of Teachers College, Report of the Director," *Dean's Report* (Teachers College, 1924–1933).

51. Monroe, "The Cross-Fertilization of Culture," 4.

52. "International Institute of Teachers College, Report of the Director," *Dean's Report* (Teachers College, 1924), 62.

53. "International Institute of Teachers College, Report of the Director," *Dean's Report* (Teachers College, 1925), 45.

54. "International Institute of Teachers College, Report of the Director," *Dean's Report* (Teachers College, 1924–1933).

55. George Z. F. Bereday had a good summary of the contents of *The Educational Yearbooks.* See his book, *Comparative Method in Education* (New York: Holt, Rinehart and Winston, 1964), 233–236.

56. When the 10-year grant from the IEB came to an end, Kandel wrote the Rockefeller Foundation to request support to continue the *Yearbook,* but no grant came through. In the end, the Carnegie Corporation provided Teachers College with a grant of $10,000, which kept *The Yearbook* going for a few more years. (See correspondence between Isaac Kandel and Edmund E. Day, 15, 19, 28 May 1936, and memo, 30 September 1936, folder 912, box 101, sub-series 1, series 1, General Education Board, RAC; Box 42, RG 6, William F. Russell Papers, T. C. Special Collections.

57. "International Institute of Teachers College, Report of the Director," *Dean's Report* (Teachers College, 1930), 51.

58. "International Institute of Teachers College, Report of the Director," *Dean's Report* (Teachers College, 1934), 68.

59. "International Institute of Teachers College, Report of the Director" (1934), 67–68. Also see E. H. Epstein, "Comparative and International Education: Overview and Historical Development," *The International Encyclopedia of Education* 2, 2d ed., eds. Torsten Hus and T. Neville Postlethwaite (New York: Pergamon, 1994), 918–923.

60. "International Institute of Teachers College, Report of the Director," *Dean's Report* (Teachers College, 1930), 52.

61. Monroe to Rockefeller, Jr., 11 April 1927, folder titled "Columbia University, Teachers College, International Institute," box 60, Educational Interests series, RG 2, Rockefeller Family Archives, RAC.

62. "Memorandum on International Institute of Teachers College," 7 October 1931, folder 280, box 19, series 1, International Education Board, RAC.

63. W. Rose to R. Fosdick, 4 May 1927, folder 278, box 19, series 1, International Education Board, RAC.

64. Trevor Arnett to Raymond Fosdick, 15 March 1928, 9, folder 279, box 19, series 1, International Education Board, RAC.

65. Ibid., 10–11.

66. Ibid., 12.

67. Abraham Flexner to Trevor Arnett, memo, 27 February 1928, folder 279, box 19, series 1, International Education Board, RAC.

68. "Memorandum on International Institute of Teachers College," 7 October 1931, International Education Board, RAC.

69. "International Institute of Education," memo of David H. Stevens, n.d., folder 280, box 19, series 1, International Education Board, RAC.

70. "Re: International Institute," memo of Trevor Arnett, 5 November 1931, folder 280, box 19, series 1, International Education Board, RAC.

71. Raymond B. Fosdick, *The Story of the Rockefeller Foundation* (New York: Harper and Brothers Publishers, 1952), 249, 251.

72. Monroe to Dean Russell, 12 January 1932, folder titled "Monroe (2)," box 46, RG 6, William F. Russell Papers, T. C. Special Collections.

73. Folder titled "Foreign Students (2)," box 2, RG 6, William F. Russell Papers, T. C. Special Collections.

74. Folder titled "Committee on Foreign Students," box 14, RG 6, William F. Russell Papers, T. C. Special Collections.

75. Folder titled "International Institute (correspondence)," box 39, RG 6, William F. Russell Papers, T. C. Special Collections.

76. Bereday, *Comparative Method in Education,* 186.

77. Folder titled "Linton, Clarence," box 43, RG 6, William F. Russell Papers, T. C. Special Collections.

78. We will discuss NAFSA in following chapters.

# Part II

---

## After World War II

# Chapter 5

## Changes in Government Cultural Policy and the Realignment of Private Forces in Worldwide Educational Exchange

While private institutions such as religious organizations, philanthropic foundations, and educational institutions were the key players in pushing America's cultural influence to various parts of the world in the early decades of the 20th century, the U.S. government maintained primarily a stand of "laissez-faire" or "noninvolvement" in this field. But in the 1930s, in the face of an increasing challenge of European cultural expansion (especially that of German cultural influence) in Latin America, Washington began to realize the importance of cultural diplomacy in international power politics. President Franklin Roosevelt initiated a new policy toward Latin America, the "Good Neighbor Policy," of which cultural relations constituted a prominent part. In a radical departure from its tradition, the U.S. government began to sponsor educational exchanges with foreign countries—in this case, Latin American countries. Congress passed laws to give the legislative mandate to provide funds for cultural relations programs. The cultural exchange programs with Latin America eventually became a prelude to the government's worldwide commitment to educational and cultural exchanges after World War II. Cultural programs played a crucial role in the Cold War propaganda.[1] With the government playing a leading role in guiding and encouraging international cultural exchanges, a wide variety of new programs of educational exchange were developed.[2] Government initiatives significantly impacted the participation of private groups in international cultural and educational affairs and their relations with the government.

## CULTURAL RELATIONS WITH LATIN AMERICA— A PRELUDE TO WORLDWIDE EDUCATIONAL EXCHANGES

Despite the fact that the United States joined the Pan American Union in 1890 and sent representatives to inter-American conferences afterward, it sponsored few cultural activities with Latin America before 1930. In contrast, European governments—Germany, Britain, France, and Italy—had extensive cultural exchanges with Latin American countries.[3] Germany was particularly active in expanding its cultural influence in Latin America. Three-fourths of the 900 foreign schools in Latin America were German. More German than American publications existed in the libraries of Latin American countries. Moreover, there were active educational exchanges of students and professors between Germany and Latin American countries.[4] Washington considered the cultural activities of European powers in the Western Hemisphere a serious encroachment on "America's sphere of influence" and a challenge to the Monroe Doctrine. In the cultural battle to extend influence and prestige, the traditional U.S. "dollar diplomacy" proved inadequate. Washington needed cultural diplomacy to counteract European penetration and to retain U.S. dominant influence in the Western Hemisphere.

### Legislative Mandate

Before the initiation of the "Good Neighbor Policy," President Herbert Hoover had toured South America in 1929, and his visit generated an increased interest of cultural exchange with Latin America by U.S. private organizations.[5] In 1936, President Franklin Roosevelt called for a special Inter-American Conference for the Maintenance of Peace at Buenos Aires to discuss urgent matters among American Republics. Secretary of State Cordell Hull headed a delegation to the conference and proposed the "facilitation by government action of the exchange of students and teachers."[6] As a result, an agreement was signed by all participants at the conference for the exchange of students, professors, and teachers. Congress approved the agreement in 1937, and two new agencies—the Division of Cultural Relations in the Department of State and the Interdepartmental Committee for Scientific and Cultural Cooperation—were established in 1938 to carry out cultural relations programs with Latin America. The State Department was designated to carry out the cultural relations programs with Latin America in cooperation with other U.S. government agencies. In 1939, Congress passed Public Law 355, authorizing the President "to render closer and more effective relationship between American republics."[7] The law remained the chief mandate for the government's educational, cultural, and technical assistance activities until the passage of the United States Information and Educational

Exchange Act (known as the Smith-Mundt Act) in 1948. In order to accelerate the defense of the Western Hemisphere during World War II, an Office of the Coordinator of Inter-American Affairs was established in 1940 and was headed by the energetic Nelson Rockefeller to coordinate technical, commercial, and informational programs with Latin America.[8]

The change of government policy and the creation of new agencies within the structure of the federal government directly linked cultural exchanges with American foreign policy purposes and national interests. Starting in 1939–1940, student exchanges with Latin American countries under U.S. government sponsorship began with modest travel grants approved by Congress. In the following years, Congress authorized a variety of maintenance and travel grants for Latin American students to come and study in the United States. This was the first time since the Chinese Boxer Indemnity Remission that the U.S. government had appropriated money to support educational exchanges. Moreover, the U.S. government, for the first time in its history, appointed cultural relations attachés to its embassies in Latin American countries in 1940. Such appointments, which were later used worldwide, initiated a new function of the American embassies. Cultural affairs became increasingly "an irrevocable component of American foreign policy." Philip Coombs, former assistant secretary of state for Educational and Cultural Affairs, characterized educational and cultural relations as "the human side" of foreign policy, as they focused on people, ideas and values, understanding and attitudes, and skills and knowledge. Educational and cultural activities, therefore, became a fourth dimension of foreign policy that was interwoven with the more traditional dimensions of American diplomacy—political, economic, and military.[9]

## Recruiting Expertise from the Private Sector

Although the State Department was authorized to conduct cultural exchange programs, it had little experience or expertise in the operation of the programs. In the face of urgent needs to effectively implement the cultural aspect of the "Good Neighbor Policy," Secretary of State Cordell Hull decided to draw on the expertise of the private sector by appointing leading members of professional organizations to form an advisory committee for the Division of Cultural Relations of the State Department. IIE Director Stephen Duggan was named the chairman of the advisory committee while presidents of national research councils, officials of major educational institutions and professional organizations, and the commissioner of the U.S. Office of Education served as the regular members on the committee, which operated from 1938 to 1946 as a policy recommendation body to the State Department.[10] From the very beginning, the committee members advised that government cultural programs should be conducted through private agencies already operating in the field of educational exchange. There were two main advantages, in their opinion, to entrust government projects to private administration. First, it could retain the goodwill that had been developed by America's private institutions in Latin America; and second, it would raise fewer suspicions about the political purposes behind the government programs. They made these recommendations with the assumption that the activities of the private organizations were not in conflict with the overall government foreign policy purposes.[11] In addition, cooperation between government agencies and private institutions would mitigate fears within American educational circles of possible government interference and control.

Four major private organizations were immediately recruited for their professional expertise by the State Department: the American Council of Learned Societies, the American Library Association, the American Council on Education, and the IIE. Previously, the State Department had basically ignored the IIE when it represented the United States in conducting educational exchanges with many foreign countries all the years since the end of WWI. But the IIE now became the State Department's major contractor to implement government cultural programs with Latin America. Because the IIE had conducted student exchange programs with Latin American countries before the advent of the "Good Neighbor Policy," it was entrusted under government contract to administer government grants for the maintenance and travel of Latin American students. The IIE was also entrusted with the administration of the Roosevelt Fellowships funded by the Office of the Coordinator of Inter-American Affairs. The Roosevelt Fellowships provided one fellowship for each Latin American country for their scholars to come and study in American higher educational institutions.[12]

Moreover, the government solicited universities and individuals experienced with foreign student affairs for the successful handling of educational exchanges. J. Raleigh Nelson, director of the University International Center for Foreign Students at the University of Michigan, was a pioneering foreign student advisor. He wrote the State Department and Stephen Duggan, expressing his willingness and that of his university to cooperate in every way to carry out exchanges with Latin America. Nelson emphasized the importance of hospitality programs in the overall educational exchange and illustrated his point with his own experience. Once, he entertained in his parents' house a Dr. Ramerez Brown, a government minister of Nicaragua who had strong anti-American sentiments. But the visit to an American home left Brown with good personal feelings toward Americans, which Nelson felt was instrumental in tempering Brown's anti-American sentiments.[13] At his suggestion, the State Department opened reception centers in Washington, D.C., New York, Miami, and San Francisco to welcome distinguished foreign visitors. Even the White House offered receptions to foreign students.

In 1936, Eleanor Roosevelt began to invite foreign students to an annual tea at the White House. She was also a frequent speaker at foreign student gatherings and remained actively interested in international educational affairs during her lifetime.[14]

## National Defense during the War and Exchange with Latin America

The political meaning associated with the education of Latin American students in the United States highlighted the needs for effective guidance and orientation of foreign students to American society if cultural exchanges were to achieve the expected effect for foreign policy objectives. With the encouragement of the State Department and the Office of the Coordinator for Inter-American Affairs, the IIE formed the Advisory Committee on the Adjustment of Foreign Students in 1940 as a central forum to coordinate and improve the supervision of foreign students (Latin American students especially) in American colleges and universities. Edgar J. Fisher, the IIE Assistant Director who had extensive educational experiences abroad, served as the chair while the leaders of International Houses and foreign student advisors of several universities and colleges served as committee members.[15]

Major problems that Latin American students (and foreign students in general) encountered in America included social adjustments, academic orientation, and financial difficulty. In order to solve the financial problems of Latin American students, the Advisory Committee of the IIE suggested that a distribution of responsibility be balanced out, with colleges and universities offering tuition scholarships, the Division of Cultural Relations of the State Department providing travel grants, and the Office of the Coordinator for Inter-American Affairs assisting with the maintenance of these students.[16] Many American colleges and universities cooperated by increasing tuition scholarships for Latin American students while the government, philanthropic foundations, and business corporations offered travel and maintenance grants. The result was significant. In 1939–1940, 6 percent of Latin American students received tuition waivers from American colleges and universities; but by 1944, such assistance had increased fourfold with nearly 25 percent of Latin American students receiving tuition scholarships.[17] The support to Latin American students and scholars was regarded as part of the "total efforts for war," because exchange programs with Latin America were expected to play a positive role in Pan-American defense during World War II. Even the work of the IIE was gradually dominated by Latin American exchange activities, with the number of Latin American students increasing dramatically (see Table 5.1). In contrast, the number of European students dropped significantly because of the war (see the comparison in Table 5.1).

**Table 5.1**

## Latin American Exchange Persons with IIE Sponsorship, 1941–1946

| Countries | 1941–1942 | 1942–1943 | 1943–1944 | 1944–1945 | 1945–1946 |
|---|---|---|---|---|---|
| Argentina | 13 | 20 | 21 | 24 | 41 |
| Bolivia | 1 | 12 | 10 | 9 | 10 |
| Brazil | 41 | 53 | 41 | 58 | 87 |
| Chile | 36 | 38 | 30 | 34 | 38 |
| Colombia | 10 | 21 | 30 | 59 | 40 |
| Costa Rica | 13 | 23 | 28 | 32 | 24 |
| Cuba | 2 | 14 | 22 | 17 | 19 |
| Dominican Republic | 1 | 1 | 3 | 5 | 6 |
| Ecuador | 6 | 11 | 16 | 19 | 15 |
| El Salvador | | 1 | 7 | 7 | 3 |
| Guatemala | 5 | 4 | 11 | 10 | 9 |
| Haiti | 2 | 6 | 10 | 13 | 12 |
| Honduras | 3 | 2 | 5 | 10 | 8 |
| Mexico | 10 | 31 | 28 | 23 | 21 |
| Nicaragua | 1 | 4 | 8 | 9 | 13 |
| Panama | 7 | 8 | 18 | 23 | 15 |
| Paraguay | 1 | 3 | 6 | 6 | 11 |
| Peru | 17 | 24 | 48 | 43 | 37 |
| Uruguay | 6 | 9 | 8 | 11 | 18 |
| Venezuela | 4 | 5 | 11 | 12 | 10 |
| Total Latin America | 179 | 290 | 361 | 424 | 437 |
| Total Europe & others | 140 | 71 | 55 | 53 | 115 |

Sources: IIE annual reports, 1941–1945, appendices.

## *FROM LATIN AMERICAN STUDENTS TO ALL FOREIGN STUDENTS—THE CLEVELAND CONFERENCE*

The rapid increase of Latin American students on American campuses and the interest of the government in educational exchange programs suddenly made foreign student problems a pressing issue for university administrators. Problems of Latin American students were, in fact, typical of foreign students. In addition to financial difficulties, foreign students also had problems with admission and classification, adjustment to curricula and degree requirements, English language proficiency for academic and non-academic needs, housing, and health insurance.[18] University admission officers were usually baffled by foreign credentials due to their lack of knowledge of foreign educational systems. Educators and administrators found many Latin American students having difficulty speaking English, taking notes in class, and using libraries. Besides, there were war-related student problems, such as the drafting of foreign students and the evacuation of Japanese-American students. Strangely, there was little exchange between colleges and universities concerning how to deal with these problems although pressures for expanding educational exchange kept coming from the federal government and the IIE. In seeking help, many universities directed their questions to the IIE, the most experienced professional organization in educational exchange. Apparently, universities and colleges faced the same challenge in regard to foreign students. In an effort to find solutions to the problems common on campuses, the Advisory Committee on the Adjustment of Foreign Students called for a national conference of foreign student advisors under the auspices of IIE and in cooperation with the State Department, the Office of the Coordinator for Inter-American Affairs, and the U.S. Office of Education. More than 100 university and college administrators and various organizational representatives attended the first national conference on foreign student affairs in Cleveland, Ohio in April 1942. The problems of Latin American students were given special attention because of the particular interest in Pan Americanism during the war. Financial sponsorship for Latin American students was a major concern, because universities were pressured to create more scholarships for increasing numbers of Latin American students. University administrators were not happy about the pressure to admit more Latin American students with scholarships, and they pointed out that it was a fallacy to believe that tuition did not cost the educational institution any money. They urged that a stable source to finance the Latin American scholarship program be found outside of educational institutions.[19]

The Cleveland conference also addressed other issues concerning all foreign students, such as Selective Service Regulations, the evacuation of

Japanese-American students from the West Coast, and the need for funds and work opportunities for stranded students from China, the Middle East, and European countries. The conference served as a turning point for foreign student education in the United States, as the government obviously was concerned with the whole spectrum of foreign student education in relation to American national security. Educational exchange programs played an important role in the total war efforts of information and propaganda. Successful handling of foreign student problems had a direct bearing on national defense. Although the exchange programs with Latin America were particularly intertwined with the "Good Neighbor Policy," Pan-American defense, and U.S. national security during the war, the importance of all foreign students in international relations was emphasized at the Cleveland Conference: "[T]hese young men and women, as they return to their respective countries, come to occupy rather important positions, positions of influence...they become the interpreters of ourselves to their own people. That is an indication of the importance of our task."[20]

## THE IMPORTANCE OF FOREIGN STUDENT ADVISING

Needless to say, a successful operation of educational exchange requires special administrative attention to the education of foreign students. One of the major objectives of the Cleveland conference was to promote the appointment of foreign student advisors on individual campuses. Before 1940, only 13 universities had officially appointed foreign student advisors (see Table 5.2). Most of those who had been appointed were foreign language professors or faculty/administration members whose professional and personal experience had something to do with foreign cultures. Advising foreign students was their extra responsibility or a part-time job.

The State Department and the IIE strongly recommended an adequate time allotment and office space for foreign student advisors. Edgar Fisher of the IIE emphasized the necessity and importance of having foreign student advisors on campuses. He argued that the advising of foreign students was "a field of activities through which our colleges and universities can make increasingly outstanding contributions toward a more tolerant and happy world." He pointed out that foreign students "are cultural ambassadors representing varying and valid national cultures, which, as our own, should be preserved in their finest expressions."[21] Resonating the work strategy of Christian missionary leaders in the early decades, Fisher pointed out that foreign students could interpret their cultures to American students while they were studying in America and learning about American culture and way of life. He emphasized that the students needed advising to adjust to American systems and customs to better understand America and its people.

There were three major areas in which a foreign student badly needed help: academic adjustment, social adjustment, and U.S. immigration regulations.

**Table 5.2**

**Years of Appointments of Foreign Student Advisors by Universities**

| University | Year |
| --- | --- |
| University of Illinois | 1908 |
| The University of Michigan | 1911 |
| American University | 1929 |
| George Washington University | 1929 |
| Temple University | 1930 |
| University of Florida | 1930 |
| University of Chicago | 1930 |
| University of Cincinnati | 1935 |
| Louisiana State University | 1936 |
| Cornell University | 1936 |
| Oklahoma State University | 1937 |
| The University of Texas | 1938 |
| University of Utah | 1940 |

Sources: *NAFSA newsletter*, May 1962, 4.

Fisher did not think that the Office of Student Affairs at universities could adequately perform those services because the work required special knowledge. The foreign student advisor was expected to act as a friend and a guide in helping the students adjust academically and socially. He or she must know the students' cultural backgrounds to correctly estimate their needs and problems. The advisor also needed to determine the academic courses best suitable to the students in terms of their English proficiency and their specialty. Moreover, the advisor must be well informed of U.S. immigration regulations and restrictions regarding foreign students.

According to Fisher, a foreign student advisor could make contributions at three different levels. First, *at an individual level,* foreign students would be better integrated into university communities through the help of the foreign student advisor. American students would at the same time benefit by having opportunities to learn cultures different from their own and by developing "tolerance and understanding" through such experiences. Second, *at an institutional level,* universities would benefit by saving the time of other officials and making foreign student advising more efficient and centralized.

And third, *at a national level*, government agencies and private organizations would be capable of communicating directly with one official instead of several about issues affecting foreign students. Fisher summarized, "The interests of all—students, faculty, and institutions themselves—are best served by having a counselor of foreign students, officially appointed by the authorities of the college or university." "Such a position is amply justified by broadened horizons of the American students, and the increased reputation of the university in other countries."[22] Universities seemed to respond positively to the call for appointing foreign student advisors. In 1943, a year after the Cleveland conference, the number of foreign student advisors had increased from 40 to 285 in the entire United States.[23]

In the midst of growing attention to foreign student advising, the IIE created a Counsel and Guidance Center (later the Counseling Office) to handle the needs of foreign students (primarily Latin American students) during the war. The Counseling Office administered U.S. government loans and grants for Latin American students and offered services to foreign student advisors concerning issues of immigration, income tax regulations, and types of visas. Moreover, it sent a field secretary to interview Latin American students to find out their specific problems with adjusting to the American society and their evaluation of courses and exchange programs as a whole. The field secretary also evaluated community reactions toward foreign students in terms of how many local organizations were involved in and what hospitality programs were created for foreign student education.[24]

The Counseling Office cooperated with various organizations to provide a wide variety of assistance to foreign students, such as transportation, vocational advice, the administration of emergency funds, securing opportunities for part-time employment, special hospitality during vacations, and the placement of foreign students as counselors in summer camps and as instructors at summer schools or foreign language institutes. The Counseling Office, with the assistance of local "Y" units and churches, also helped traveling foreign students get in touch with American families in different cities and towns to increase the contact between Americans and foreign students.[25] Meanwhile, the IIE continued the Orientation Conference for incoming students at International House New York, where the IIE-sponsored students were shown around New York City and were invited to Sunday suppers in American homes.

## CULTURAL EXCHANGE WORLDWIDE IN THE COLD WAR

Educational exchanges with Latin America became a prelude to the U.S. government's commitment to postwar worldwide cultural exchanges. The U.S. government had increasingly expanded its exchange programs during the war with East Asia and the Middle East, where American private institutions had long been involved in local educational development. The U.S. government initiated educational and cultural exchanges with China, India, Afghanistan, Iran, Egypt, Ethiopia, Turkey, Lebanon, and Liberia under the President's Emergency Fund. In addition, the government provided financial support to American-founded schools in these areas.[26] After the war, governmental exchange programs continued and accelerated with the advent of the Cold War. 1946 saw the passage of the Fulbright Act, which authorized the State Department to enter into agreements with foreign governments to conduct academic exchanges.[27] In 1948, government commitment to educational and cultural exchanges reached a new height with the passage of the United States Information and Educational Exchange Act (known as the Smith-Mundt Act), which authorized annual congressional appropriation to fund educational and cultural exchange programs worldwide.

Opinion varied within Congress, however, as to the value of educational and cultural programs. When WWII was coming to an end, questions were raised about whether wartime information and educational exchange programs (part of war propaganda) should be continued. In testimony before the House Foreign Affairs Committee in October 1945, Assistant Secretary of the Department of State, William Benton, contended that foreign relations had ceased to be government-to-government contacts.[28] He pointed out that "peoples of the world are exercising an ever larger influence upon decisions of foreign policy." He asserted that the United States had an obligation to give a "full and fair picture" of its way of life and its foreign policies to peoples abroad. He not only confirmed the necessity of cultural exchange but also strongly recommended that all "cultural relations" programs should not be a miscellany of goodwill activities but should be designed "to support United States foreign policy in its long range sense and to serve as an arm of that policy."[29]

When Senator J. William Fulbright introduced a bill to use U.S. credits in foreign currencies to finance academic exchanges in September 1945,[30] he made a similar argument that exchange expenditures should be made under regulations "to conform to American foreign policy and promote better relations between the respective governments."[31] The advancement of human knowledge among peoples of the world was not the major concern of Senator Fulbright. Given the dominant position of the United States in international affairs after the war, "it became vital to the national security to understand the minds of people in other societies and to have American aspirations and problems understood by others."[32] With these premises, the Fulbright Act was passed in 1946 without exciting any strong opposition in Congress, although some Congressmen remained dubious about the value of educational exchange to U.S. national interest. But when the Smith-Mundt bill was introduced in 1946 proposing the expansion of educational exchanges worldwide, it encountered, however, strong opposition in Congress. Opponents of the bill charged that the exchange of students and teachers would let down immigration bars and open American schools "to Communists and agitators." The proponents adhered to the need of countering "the bitter Soviet propaganda attacks on the United States." Before the bill was passed, a joint Senate-House committee made trips to 22 European countries in 1946–1947 to investigate the necessity of information and educational exchange programs. The committee returned with a report that stressed the dangers of Soviet propaganda and strongly supported the bill.[33] As a result, Congress passed the Smith-Mundt Act (Information and Educational Exchange Act), which "carefully and deliberately determined that a program of educational exchange shall become an essential part of the conduct of this nation's foreign affairs."[34] Under the Smith-Mundt Act, educational and cultural exchanges were expected to contribute to the goals of making the world understand the United States. Hence, an emphasis on a unilateral approach was adopted in American exchange programs.

Moreover, the United States actively exerted its influence on educational and intellectual cooperation in the postwar world through its role in UNESCO.[35] Such an assertion of leadership offered a sharp contrast to the government's attitude toward the League of Nations and international intellectual cooperation after World War I. Furthermore, the Marshall Plan, which was launched in 1948 with a strong emphasis on economic aid to Europe, undertook large overseas operations in both technical training and information exchange. President Truman's Point Four of sharing American technical know-how with the "underdeveloped" nations also led to the creation of a plethora of exchange programs.[36] The stress on technical and economic aid to war-devastated Europe and the "underdeveloped" countries helped extend American educational exchange programs to every corner of the world and brought tens of thousands of foreign technical and industrial trainees to the United States.

Government initiatives gave rise to new meanings to the international educational exchange activities. In what was emphasized as a policy of "Total Diplomacy" in the Cold War, economic aid and technical assistance were intertwined with military purposes and served as an instrument of mutual defense to oppose the spread of Communism. Whether a military alliance or a student exchange, it was all considered as fulfillment of American leadership of the "free world" in confrontation with the Soviet-led "Communist world." The strategy of international educational exchange thus began to shift to a unilateral approach to exporting American culture and American know-how, although "mutual understanding" remained the watchword. With the advent of the Cold War, the word "exchange" actually meant the export of American values, the projection of the great success of the American system, and the influence on the thinking of foreign trainees and students. Hundreds of thousands of foreign nationals were brought to the United States as students to experience American democratic institutions and values, whereas Americans were sent abroad as experts to spread

American technical know-how and way of life. The Cold War was not only the confrontation between two different political systems but also the battle between two cultures. Educational "exchange" served the purpose of channeling political propaganda to "win the hearts and minds of men" in this confrontation. Many departments and agencies of the federal government, such as State, Justice, Labor, Defense, Health, Education and Welfare, Interior, Agriculture, Commerce, the Mutual Security Agency, and the Technical Cooperation Administration, participated in the "exchange" programs.

## EFFORTS TO SEPARATE EDUCATIONAL EXCHANGE FROM POLITICAL PROPAGANDA

The immediate political objectives of the Cold War obviously shaped government cultural exchange programs, and therefore, the direction of international educational exchange as a whole. The government weighed each undertaking of exchange in terms of political impact and foreign policy purposes. The Cold War intensified after the outbreak of the Korean War. The National Security Council included international information and educational exchange among the "United States programs for national defense" to be integrated with the military and economic programs.[37] The government launched a "Campaign of Truth" in 1950, urging "the intensified use of radio and films, a significant increase in the numbers of foreign students to the United States, and support of the United Nations…to stimulate and guide the efforts of multitudes of individual citizens in furtherance of the national information and educational programs." It also demanded that "the international propagation of the democratic creed be made an instrument of supreme national policy."[38]

Private institutions, sometimes not fully informed of the goals of those programs, were urged to do what the government wanted them to do. Educators were often confused over government policies on exchanges and complained about the lack of coherence in the goals of government programs. The Advisory Commission on Educational Exchange also pointed out that there was a lack of agreement on the objectives of cultural exchange. It listed four different interpretations of the purpose of exchange programs: (1) to transplant American methods and techniques to other countries in order to "Americanize" them; (2) to acquaint other nations with the accomplishments of the United States in fine arts and scholarship to impress them with our cultural achievements; (3) to help other countries meet their problems of education to be guided mainly by local needs; and (4) a special form of the information program of the State Department.[39]

While the government's principal interest in expanding educational exchange was to achieve short-term political objectives, educators were more interested in the long-term educational goals. When the government emphasized political propaganda (part of the "Campaign of Truth" in the 1950s) in the name of combating the "aggression of Communism," it provoked a negative reaction among American educators and other interested groups in the private sector. Educators favored long-term cultural exchanges for mutual benefit and a minimum of overt propaganda. They criticized the government for making educational and cultural exchanges politically patronizing. In their minds, the primary objective of exchange should be educational and not propaganda. They recommended that educational and cultural exchanges should be honest, calm, intellectually mature, and direct toward raising an appreciation of the fundamental attitudes and values of different peoples.[40]

Educators attempted to separate educational exchange from information programs (overt propaganda). In 1947, when the Smith-Mundt Act was under fervent debate, a group of educators led by Ben M. Cherrington[41] of the University of Denver and George Zook of the American Council on Education condemned the "mixing" of information and educational exchange. They recommended a complete organizational and administrative separation of the two programs. To those educators who had been involved in educational exchange long before the government stepped in to take the lead, information was for "international power politics"—an instrument "to implement diplomatic policies of the Department of State"—whereas educational and cultural exchanges were "nonpolitical" for the mutual benefit of exchange countries. They argued that the American tradition favored the divorce of educational activities from the control of the federal government. The government role, especially that of the State Department, "should be to stimulate, facilitate, and coordinate" educational exchange. In addition, they worried that if educational and cultural activities were not separated from political propaganda, citizens of other nations might see them as new forms of American cultural imperialism. Many professional organizations, such as the Association of American Colleges, the National Educational Association, the American Council of Learned Societies, the American Council on Education, and the Institute of International Education, fully supported the recommendation of such a separation.[42]

The CFRFS, the oldest organization on behalf of foreign student affairs in the United States, also criticized the government's integration of information and educational exchange for political purposes. Leaders of church boards, Foreign Mission Conferences and Boards, the YMCA and YWCA, and other Christian organizations worried that the government might exert too much control over American education and that the program of cultural relations might be misused to support the government's political agenda. They resented that the Division of Science, Education, and Art (of the "Y" World Service) was pressured to interfere in postwar education programs "by preparing special textbooks for use throughout Europe and by training teams of American teachers to re-educate Europe." At the 1946 Consultation Conference, Oliver

Caldwell of the State Department's Division of Exchange of Persons told the delegates of various Christian organizations that the U.S. government wished to create friendships "not through mass exchange of people but by the right kind of exchange" for foreign policy objectives. Some Christian leaders responded that they "have not seen fit to cooperate in this program."[43]

Even the IIE, now a major government contractor for exchange programs, was disturbed by the 1946 Sargeant Report of the State Department, which suggested that student exchanges should be used to "implement" United States foreign policy.[44] Laurence Duggan, who succeeded his father as the director of the IIE in late 1946, wrote Assistant Secretary of State William Benton, expressing the IIE's concerns that student exchange programs were used for political propaganda purposes.[45] Laurence Duggan emphasized that student fellowships "must not be a means whereby our government hopes to influence foreign students in the United States in favor of particular policies and programs." He reiterated the IIE's traditional policy of promoting international understanding through educational exchanges. But he acknowledged that there was nothing wrong in hoping that foreign students might develop appreciation, sympathy, and even active support for certain American foreign policy objectives.

How effective was the educators' attempt to separate educational exchange from political propaganda (information programs)? Not very, as some scholars noted. With the Cold War dominating international relations and shaping American domestic politics, "educational exchange was massively overshadowed by the information program and reduced, administratively, to a 'media service' thereof. Information received the major share of the budget and the bulk of attention."[46] The impact of the educators' protest only resulted in the nominal separation of information from educational exchange, as mandated by the Smith-Mundt Act. Accordingly, the Office of Educational Exchange of the State Department established two divisions— one was the Division of Libraries and Institutes for information exchange and the other was the Division of International Exchange of Persons for educational exchange. In reality, the two divisions worked as two arms of a cultural war of political propaganda.

## THE REALIGNMENT OF PRIVATE ORGANIZATIONS IN EDUCATIONAL EXCHANGE

The government's role in expanding educational and cultural exchanges worldwide fundamentally changed the position of private organizations in the field and led to the reconfiguration of those private forces. Under the auspices of the IIE and the State Department, three national conferences of foreign student advisors and college administrators were held in 1946–1948 to achieve effective cooperation among colleges and universities, professional organizations, and the government in the new frontier of worldwide educational exchange.

Those conferences, which were also attended by representatives of the U.S. government, foreign governments, and bi-national and international organizations, aimed at improving exchange programs and foreign student advising on campuses. But there was tension between the government pressure for universities to accept more foreign students and universities' limited capacity to do so. Participants of the conferences tried to reach a consensus about admission policy regarding foreign students. Herschel Brickell, chief of the Division of International Exchange of Persons of the State Department, emphasized the importance of educational exchange in U.S. foreign relations. He tried to persuade university officials: "The vast potentialities of good that may come from an exchange of students" had been demonstrated by the programs with Latin America and the exchange with China, where more than half of the Nationalist government officials had received American education. Brickell pointed out, "we stand now on the brink of the extension of this program to all countries of the world." The government "has a part to play in the future of cultural relations of every character," and it was setting aside a considerable sum of money for educational exchange. In an effort to estimate effectively foreign students' English proficiency, the State Department was to subsidize the College Entrance Examination Board to develop a standard universal English test, which would be applied abroad to all candidates for study in the United States.[47]

University officials expressed that no quota should be imposed upon the admission of foreign students and that individual schools should deal with the situation according to their own specific circumstances. For instance, some state universities had to cut down the admission of foreign undergraduate students because of pressing domestic demands but kept their graduate schools open to foreign students. Other schools like the Massachusetts Institute of Technology (MIT) had to limit foreign students to 100 in 1946 (that was the quota) because of various domestic demands to train military officers. University officials requested that the IIE extend its services to those foreign students who were not sponsored by the government but who constituted the majority of the foreign student population. They also emphasized the need for a clearinghouse to disseminate statistical information on all foreign students.[48]

In addition to enlisting university cooperation, the State Department also suggested the federation of organizations that were engaged in foreign student affairs in order to avoid duplication and to strengthen their service. When many agencies were involved in promoting cultural relations between the United States and other countries, there was inevitable competition and duplication of work. Many agencies interpreted the suggestion as a call for restructuring private organizations into specialized agencies while maintaining mutual interdependence. At this time, a group of foreign student advisors proposed to form a national association of their own, which was the first step toward professionalization. The promotion of the expansion of exchange programs had actually helped create a "new business" of international education in which foreign student advisors were indispensable. But there was debate on the necessity of such an association of foreign student advisors. Some people argued that the IIE had been doing the job. Why not let them continue? Others felt that the IIE had too much work for a relatively small staff and that a national organization would professionally strengthen the foreign student advisor's status in academic institutions and in the community. Still others believed "that a peer network, rather than a strong central agency, was the route to take in tying foreign student advisors and others together to educate each other and strengthen their own programs."[49] The State Department favored the creation of such an association and believed that it would help improve foreign student advising and therefore the effectiveness of exchanges. George Allen, assistant secretary of the State Department, asked how should "this association as a group give effective support to the Department of State in developing a long-view program of student exchange under the GI Bill of Rights, the Fulbright Act and the Smith-Mundt Act?" He emphasized that foreign students "will have great influence on the future of the world. Most of these students will return to positions of responsible leadership in their own countries and the impressions of the United States which they take back are considered…to be even more significant than the technical knowledge and skills which they acquire."[50]

The belief that student exchanges would help advance world peace remained a rallying force among foreign student advisors. Allen Blaisdell of International House Berkeley sounded very much like Harry Edmonds in the 1920s when he appealed at the 1950 Conference on International Educational Exchanges: "A peaceful world cannot be built out of peoples dominated by the prejudices and preconceptions of isolation and the inertia of ignorance. It will be built, if built at all, by men and women trained in the professions essential to human welfare, and who, while so being trained, become experienced in the difficult art of cooperation." Educational exchange was considered a long-term enterprise for "free and extensive" interaction between peoples in "formal and informal processes" for the "amelioration of world conditions."[51] In the Cold War, the pursuit of peace meant the fight against Communism, and "amelioration of world conditions" meant the containment of Communism. When military actions were deterred by mutual fear of total destruction by the nuclear weapons, the flow of ideas became crucial in Cold War propaganda to "win the hearts and minds." In Allen Blaisdell's words, "Ideas are also weapons—weapons which can be utilized only by educational exchange. The free mind and free flow of ideas and knowledge among peoples provide such powerful weapons for peace that only when we review the progress of mankind itself can we measure their potentialities."[52]

The National Association of Foreign Student Advisors (NAFSA, later changed to the National Association for Foreign Student Affairs) was founded at the 1948 Conference on International Student Exchanges in Ann Arbor, Michigan "to develop a dynamic international cultural relations program, particularly through student exchanges."[53] Clarence Linton, Foreign Student Advisor at Teachers College, Columbia University, served as the first president, and Allen Blaisdell, Foreign Student Advisor and Director of International House Berkeley, served as vice president.[54] As a professional organization of "foreign student advisers, teachers of English as a foreign language, Fulbright counselors" and others representing government agencies, national, bi-national, and international organizations, NAFSA aimed at marshaling "the interest and resources of all institutions, organizations, and individuals concerned with student exchange programs" and sought close working relationships with the U.S. government to develop policies and procedures of international educational exchange.[55]

In the face of the rising profession of foreign student advisors, CFRFS and the IIE began to adjust by redefining their proper roles in the expansion of educational exchange. CFRFS responded with program adaptation to find its own niche in the changing environment. CFRFS leaders reasoned, "Since the government is primarily responsible for foreign relations, and the colleges and universities are primarily for education, other agencies should find their primary opportunity elsewhere."[56] "Where lies now the distinctive function of our Committee?" asked Anson P. Stokes, chairman of the administrative board of CFRFS.

With the IIE acting as the major government contractor and the newly founded NAFSA taking over the advising of foreign students, CFRFS leaders did not feel easy about their own organization's position in the field, which "led some to wonder if initiative has passed permanently from the Committee to others."[57] Foreign student services had been the focus of CFRFS work during the past 40 years. To redefine the special role of CFRFS in educational exchange, some suggested that the unique responsibility of CFRFS was to strengthen students' religious lives while others such as the IIE and NAFSA were concerned with foreign students' academic and social adjustments. But how much should CFRFS get involved in the students' religious choices? CFRFS was originally established with the fundamental principle of contacting and helping all foreign students regardless of their religious beliefs.

John Benjamin Schmoker, who became the general secretary of CFRFS in 1947, was a charismatic leader with an extensive background in educational, religious, and community services. In defining the role of CFRFS in postwar educational exchange, Schmoker pointed out, "[a]s a Christian agency we…seek to interpret our religious institutions, and to give the experience and training that will be helpful to the student when he returns to his home country." He emphasized, "It is the personalized service we offer."[58] Therefore, CFRFS concentrated on its traditional programs of port-of-entry service and community programs while it moved to strengthen campus-community cooperation. Port-of-entry service was one of the most popular programs among foreign students. Thousands of CFRFS associates met foreign students at ports of entry and helped them with their temporary housing, baggage, and transportation. As many colleges and universities did not have foreign student advisors, CFRFS shared its experience with the volunteer faculty at local campuses to solve foreign students' problems. CFRFS also trained individuals and groups in local communities to work cooperatively with campus personnel in broadening opportunities for foreign students to meet Americans and to visit local industries. CFRFS urged the acceptance of foreign students "into campus groupings as part of the American student total educational experience." In the meantime, community programs shifted to emphasize local visits related to the specialty of the students, because many postwar foreign students came to America for technical and industrial training. CFRFS leaders felt that traditional social gatherings at Sunday dinners and civic club talks, "desirable and satisfying as they may be," were "not the kind of meaningful experiences" for the foreign students in postwar America. Instead, they encouraged local communities to offer specialized experiences for foreign students by coordinating community programs with the students' education programs. For instance, foreign students of agriculture would spend weekends on farms or meet with 4-H clubs, and students of engineering would visit local business companies and participate in community projects.[59] In short, CFRFS smartly adapted its programs along with the political purposes of the Marshall Plan and Truman's Point Four.

Similarly, the IIE also underwent a restructuring to meet the new demand of services. Through cooperation with professional associations, industrial corporations, and the government, the IIE was now *the* leading institution providing professional services for both the private and public sectors in the field of educational exchange. This growth of influence and stature of the IIE was seen "as the source of much of the Institute's strength as well as the source of many of its difficulties, particularly in its relationship with other organizations."[60] There was pressure for the IIE to collaborate with other organizations. The IIE was asked to formalize its relationship with professional organizations by officially designating their representatives for its foreign student programs. Moreover, under the direction of Harry H. Pierson, formerly chief of the Division of International Exchange of Persons of the State Department, the IIE was to expand services to exchanges with underdeveloped countries and colonial areas and to offer assistance to non-government sponsored students who comprised more than four-fifths of the entire foreign student population. The Carnegie Corporation and the Rockefeller Foundation equally shared the IIE's expansion cost of $300,000 for 1947–1949.[61]

## POSTWAR FOREIGN STUDENTS

Postwar government policies encouraged the flow of foreign students to the

United States and thus began a "new era" of international education in U.S. history. The emphasis on reaching "the underprivileged" and promoting "better understanding of the United States among the peoples of the world" helped bring more students, scholars, and trainees from developing countries. The composition of foreign students, therefore, changed significantly. Undergraduate foreign students became increasingly the majority in postwar America. In addition, the number of special students, short-term visitors, and technical trainees rapidly increased, which diversified the foreign student population.

After World War II, the number of foreign students jumped from 7,542 in 1944–1945 to 26,759 in 1948–1949.[62] By 1953, more than 34,000 foreign students from 130 countries were studying at 1,460 American colleges and universities. More than half (54 percent) of them were undergraduate students, and only 30 percent were graduate students—the rest were either defined as "special students" or students with no academic status (visiting students/scholars on short-term exchange programs).[63] Humanities and engineering disciplines attracted the largest percentage of foreign students, each claiming 20 percent. Social sciences attracted 14 percent, the natural sciences 12 percent, and medicine and business administration 9 percent each. The great majority of foreign engineering students were undergraduates (71 percent), whereas a considerable portion of those in natural and social sciences (52 percent and 45 percent, respectively) were graduate students. Women made up less than a quarter of the total foreign student population, although the ratio of women to men differed significantly depending on the country of origin. For example, Filippino students had the highest ratio of women to men (44 percent), whereas Indians and Iranians had the lowest (14 percent and 11 percent, respectively).[64]

The representation of foreign students from major regions of the world also shifted after World War II (see Table 5.3). The number of Asian and European students increased dramatically, whereas Latin American students—who constituted about half of the foreign student population during the war—decelerated as the U.S. government shifted its attention to Europe and Asia in the early stages of the Cold War. Not until 1955 did the Fulbright exchange program begin with Latin American countries, although the IIE and other private institutions continued to encourage Latin American student exchanges.

Most foreign students were self-supportive (relying on their own or on family sources) for their study in the United States, although many European students came on exchange programs with financial support. In the 1950–1951 academic year, only 5.4 percent of all foreign students received full or partial support from the U.S. government, 4.2 percent received home government aid, and about 13.2 percent received scholarships from American colleges and universities.[65] In 1952–1953, about 11 percent of foreign students received U.S. government aid, 6 percent relied on home gov-

**Table 5.3**

**Foreign Students in the United States by World Regions, 1915–1953**

| Areas/ Years | 1915– 1916 | 1918– 1919 | 1935– 1936 | 1945– 1946 | 1949– 1950 | 1952– 1953 |
|---|---|---|---|---|---|---|
| Canada | 379 | 647 | 1075 | 1636 | 4508 | 4637 |
| Latin America | 630 | 1096 | 844 | 3864 | 6632 | 7705 |
| Europe | 1030 | 2921 | 1332 | 1806 | 5863 | 8130 |
| Asia | 1656 | 2324 | 3293 | 2325 | 9590 | 11986 |
| Africa | 81 | 101 | 83 | 88 | 945 | 1125 |
| Undesig- nated | 14 | 20 | | 56 | 176 | 213 |
| Total | 3790 | 7209 | 6627 | 9775 | 27714 | 33796 |

Sources: *The Unofficial Ambassadors* (annual report of the Committee on Friendly Relations among Foreign Students, 1953), 36.

ernment support, and 25 percent came on scholarships from universities and private organizations. All in all, 40 percent of the foreign students received aid either from private or public sources, whereas 60 percent were entirely self-supporting.[66] Europeans and Africans received the largest proportion of government support because many of them came on government-sponsored programs. Foreign students tended to concentrate at certain universities. In the early 1950s, about 47 percent of them enrolled in the top 25 universities—and more than half (54.5 percent) went to New York, California, Massachusetts, Michigan, Illinois, and Pennsylvania (Table 5.4).[67] But the students gradually spread out all over the United States.

The U.S. government sought to expand educational exchanges even as the domestic deluge of GIs and postwar high school graduates had already swamped American campuses. The congestion of the students in American higher educational institutions generated enormous demands for major changes in curricula as well as in administrative services. How many more foreign students would be admitted into American colleges and universities? The government was eager to enlist the full cooperation of colleges and universities to "furnish as generously as possible" opportunities for foreign students. Letters were sent to heads of universities by the IIE and the State Department, emphasizing the importance of educational exchange to serve American national interests. All educational institutions were expected to play their part in meeting the needs of foreign students and to help

**Table 5.4**

## States with Largest Foreign Student Population, 1950

| States | Student numbers | Percent of total foreign students |
|---|---|---|
| New York | 5,452 | 18.3 |
| California | 3,592 | 12.0 |
| Massachusetts | 2,187 | 7.3 |
| Michigan | 1,959 | 6.6 |
| Illinois | 1,778 | 6.0 |
| Pennsylvania | 1,295 | 4.3 |

Sources: *Education for One World* (New York: IIE, 1950–1951), 18.

generate "a greater and freer international flow of students." But there were complaints about the pressure of admitting more foreign students. Some university administrators were overwhelmed with frustration: "It is like asking to put three in a bed when we already have four!"[68]

## STUDENT AID AND COLD WAR POLITICS

While increasing numbers of foreign students kept coming, thousands from Asia, Eastern Europe, and the Middle East became stranded in the United States in the late 1940s and early 1950s because of political and economic commotion in their home countries. Financial difficulties adversely affected the lives of foreign students and educational exchange in general. A 1949 NAFSA survey showed that students from the following countries were in urgent financial need: China, India, Korea, Canada, Greece, Norway, Palestine and Israel, the Netherlands, France, Germany, the United Kingdom, Czechoslovakia, Peru, Mexico, Poland, Brazil, the Philippines, and Turkey.[69] Millions of dollars were needed to assist those students if student exchanges were to be successfully carried out as the State Department wished. Chinese students faced the most severe financial crisis. Political and economic crises in China led to the collapse of its finance system.[70] In 1948, when the Chinese Nationalist government eliminated the favorable exchange rate for its students abroad, thousands of Chinese students in the United States were thrown into financial despair. According to the January 1949 report of the U.S. National Student Association, some Chinese students virtually were starving while continuing their studies.

About 3,800 Chinese students were enrolled in American colleges and universities in the late 1940s. The severity of their problems made their needs particularly urgent in university communities. A survey at the University of

Minnesota showed that 60 Chinese students on campus needed immediate loans and scholarships from $45 to $450 in order to finish their academic year. Chinese students who wanted to return to China did not have the transportation money.[71] Large universities, such as Indiana, Michigan, and Minnesota, provided emergency aid through local resources. But as foreign students from many other countries also needed help, universities were burdened and frustrated at seeking support to help the stranded students when local resources were exhausted.

As the difficulties on individual campuses mounted, foreign student advisors and NAFSA leaders were urged to work out national solutions. Allen Blaisdell of NAFSA argued that "the solution required a mobilization of national resources and an even spread of responsibility." He pointed out that the task for NAFSA was "to develop a kind of instrument or instruments through which the dissociated institutions of American education can become vocal and influential on a national plane" at this critical moment of international education.[72] NAFSA president Clarence Linton discussed with the State Department and the U.S. Advisory Commission on Educational Exchange ways to extend emergency aid to foreign students. Universities and organizations such as the Greater New York Council for Foreign Students, the English-Speaking Union, and the China Institute in America—in addition to CFRFS, the IIE, and NAFSA—appealed to the government for emergency funds for foreign students, particularly Chinese students.

There was a general trend to tighten up provisions for foreign students while expanding student exchange, however. Educators were not happy that Congress did not increase financial support for educational exchanges after the passage of the Smith-Mundt Act. They pointed out that educational exchange programs still operated at the same financial level as before the act. Congress was more interested in the propaganda function of cultural exchange than in the educational goals. Rhetorically, international education was very much promoted, but financially the government was slow and reluctant to provide support. Educators urged the government to take more financial responsibility to support educational exchange. But William Johnstone, Jr., director of the Office of Educational Exchange of the State Department, told universities to exhaust whatever resources available before directing their demands to the government. "The Department of State is directed by the Smith-Mundt Act to conduct a program which is supplementary to the efforts of the private organizations," he explained. The government was committed to making good use of the private sector in operating programs that were integral to American foreign policy. Johnstone optimistically estimated that the available resources were great as an increasing number of countries were joining exchange programs with the United States.[73] The State Department encouraged universities to seek assistance for foreign students from the private sector—foundations, professional associations, business corporations, civic groups, communities, and individuals.[74]

Private groups and individual Americans showed impressive generosity by extending assistance to foreign students. Rotary clubs, Kiwanis clubs, garden clubs, business and professional women's clubs, Jewish organizations, churches, and many other groups were especially helpful by sending out checks of various amounts to stranded students. Rotary International set up programs of international student fellowships.[75] The sympathetic response of local communities could hardly solve the serious problems at campuses with large foreign student groups. Hence, foreign student advisors and community leaders began to mobilize local groups to write their legislators about the support of stranded students. In the case of Chinese students, they described this effort of support as combating the influence of "Communists." The University of Washington and the China Club in Seattle sent letters and pamphlets to other educational institutions as a way of campaigning to "earnestly urge and recommend that Congress take cognizance of this economic situation confronting said Chinese students and set in motion the machinery necessary to bring the much needed financial assistance to them."[76] Under the pressure of educational and private groups, the government allocated $500,000 from the Economic Cooperation Administration (ECA) to assist Chinese students in technical fields. The aid, however, could help only a small number of the specifically categorized Chinese students.

But in 1949, Congress appropriated $4 million (from ECA funds) as the Expanded Chinese Emergency Aid Program to cover the tuition, stipend, and trans-Pacific transportation for Chinese students.[77] Chinese students were also permitted to remain in the United States for three years while seeking employment.[78] This generous assistance, which came after the Chinese Communists won the Civil War and established a new government in China, clearly demonstrated how the Cold War politics swayed the action of Congress. In this context, the political implication of assisting stranded Chinese students was amplified and interpreted as a strong protest against "Communist aggression." Because of the political importance of the Aid Program for Chinese Students, Congress rejected the proposal by the IIE and NAFSA that the grants be administered by private agencies. Instead, Congress requested the State Department to directly administer the Expanded Aid Program.[79] Chinese students had to apply through designated representatives of higher educational institutions for the aid. Not all Chinese students received assistance from the Expanded Aid Program, however, because the aid was selectively given under the guidance of the State Department.

Desperate as they were for financial assistance, Chinese students had concerns about the Aid Program and whether it would attempt to buy their political loyalty. The political situation in China greatly influenced Chinese students in the United States. After the war against Japanese invasion, the Civil War continued between the Nationalists and the Communists. The

Chinese Student Christian Association (CSCA), which represented Chinese students in North America, called for a coalition government with agrarian reform in China and the cessation of American military aid to the Nationalists during the Chinese Civil War.[80] Moreover, Chinese students expressed great optimism in the new China when the corrupt Chiang Kai-shek's Nationalist government lost power to the Communists.[81] The students' strong commitment to a new China was interpreted by some Americans as Communist-inspired conspiracy and as support for Communism. Those political complications seriously damaged the relationship between the Chinese students and the Americans who had long worked with them.[82]

Meanwhile, NAFSA sought to formulate a general policy on emergency aid to foreign students by cooperating with the State Department and the U.S. Advisory Commission on Educational Exchange. The State Department agreed that the policy and practice regarding Chinese students' emergency aid would be used as the criteria for emergency assistance to foreign students in general. Government aid could only help solve the emergency need of a limited number of students, however. The majority of foreign students had to find remunerative work to alleviate their financial difficulties.[83] The State Department, the Immigration and Naturalization Service (INS), the American Council on Education, and NAFSA continued negotiations in an effort to reach a consensus on the approval of students' applications for change of status and permission to work. Consequently, the INS notified foreign student advisors that section 4 (e) students (those who held student visas) were permitted to accept employment during the 1952 summer vacation, "provided a responsible school official certifies that the student needs the employment in order to maintain himself to meet the necessary school expenses."[84]

## DIVISION OF LABOR

In the new national thrust of worldwide educational exchange, several key organizations completed the process of redefining their special roles in educational exchange in the first few years of the Cold War. By the early 1950s, there was a clear "division of labor" among the three major national organizations, with NAFSA focusing on foreign student affairs, the IIE concentrating on government exchange programs (mostly Fulbright and other government-sponsored exchanges), and CFRFS offering the port-of-entry service and community programs. In introducing foreign students and trainees to the great accomplishments of the United States, CFRFS leaders believed that community programs should be carefully planned and skillfully guided to provide foreign students with practical experience in American industrial, agricultural, and commercial enterprises as a supplement to their academic training. In their opinion, only when campus and community experiences were integrated could foreign students have "the total educational experiences" in America. General Secretary Schmoker of CFRFS began to serve as the secretary of NAFSA in 1950. His dual responsibility led him to view CFRFS as part of NAFSA. He pointed out that national and local activities of CFRFS must be in step with the carefully formulated educational plans of NAFSA. CFRFS did not presume to have the final word on programs of local orientation but intended to share its experience with local campuses as a partner. Schmoker urged CFRFS associates to plan and execute their programs in cooperation with foreign student advisors and the responsible faculty committees.[85]

CFRFS established central offices in big cities to supervise community programs. In 1948, the Greater New York Council for Foreign Students was formed to coordinate the 26 agencies that were directly engaged in foreign student affairs in the New York metropolitan area. In Cleveland, there was the Council of World Affairs, and in Seattle, there was the Foundation for International Understanding Through Students. Such localized, central organizations were also established in Chicago, Pittsburgh, and Philadelphia. These efforts aimed at a greater integration of college and community programs. Moreover, many cities and universities opened international houses/centers. Foreign students were placed in those houses before they were integrated into regular student dorms for fear that they might get isolated in the beginning.[86]

NAFSA was expected to tackle the most immediate issues of foreign students that challenged the exchange programs, which included English proficiency, cultural orientation, and immigration regulations. English language ability and cultural familiarity were essential for foreign students to adjust to American educational institutions. Therefore, teaching English as a second language was emphasized as an integral part of foreign student advisors' responsibilities. Foreign students were advised to take English as a credit course to improve their language proficiency. Classroom skills such as note taking and composition as well as oral-aural comprehension were stressed in language training classes. In terms of cultural orientation, universities were urged to emulate the practices and ideas that the IIE and the State Department had used in their orientation programs for their sponsored exchange persons.[87] It was suggested that foreign students be given an orientation kit to inform them of the institution and the community in which they were going to live. Some universities started to experiment with a full-week orientation program for foreign students before registration day (which eventually became the standard practice for foreign student orientation on American campuses). In addition, foreign students were encouraged to participate in special summer courses or pre-campus orientation to reduce their initial difficulties. Since there were only 15 such summer courses offered throughout the United States in the early 1950s, only a small portion of foreign students could attend. The foreign student advisor had to organize the orientation on either an individual or group basis.[88]

Personal counseling was particularly stressed in foreign student advising. Foreign student advisors were urged to maintain an open door policy and to make themselves available beyond the scheduled counseling hours. They were encouraged to act "as a listener, as a confidant, and as a friend" because "security and a sense of adequacy on the part of the foreign student is essential to adjustment and to good work habits." The advisors were also reminded to behave not like a police officer but as a counselor and to take objective methods in making available all the facilities of the institution and community to deal with different situations of foreign students. It was regarded as particularly important that the advisors maintain a close relationship with the Student Health Service and Mental Health Clinic. They were to discover the needs of new foreign students by contacting their fellow foreign students, American students, and faculty and community members who were associated with foreign student programs. Such an active role by the advisor was believed to help prevent serious problems.

Although there was no requirement that advisors be familiar with many languages, the advisors were encouraged to have skills to develop a natural rapport with foreign students. They were supposed to know the different cultures of the students and handle their problems properly and efficiently. In fact, students generally did not have serious "cultural shock" but daily "troubles." For instance, once a foreign student at a university on the West Coast was upset because he could not find a dark suit for a dance party. His foreign student advisor thought that he was overreacting to American culture and needed a special treatment. When he referred the student to a psychiatrist, the student replied: "But I don't need a psychiatrist. I just need a dark suit." A good advisor should be able to tell the nature of a student problem lest he himself get "hypersensitive."[89]

The most pressing technical problem for foreign student advisors, however, was the immigration laws and regulations that affected foreign students. Because knowledge of the laws and regulations was essential for adequate foreign student advising, NAFSA prepared handbooks for foreign student advisors that gave good instructions on how to help foreign students understand the regulations effectively. New regulations on visas and immigration status concerning foreign students and exchange persons were frequently modified as various exchange programs were created under the Fulbright Act, the Smith-Mundt Act, Truman's Point Four, and the Marshall Plan. Congress also made changes in the 1924 Immigration Act to adjust to race relations in post-WWII American society. Constant changes in government laws and regulations often caused confusion among foreign student advisors and other concerned persons. In cooperation with the Greater New York Council for Foreign Students, NAFSA tried to clarify the situation by informing foreign student advisors about the latest changes in immigration regulations and visas through handbooks, pamphlets, and newsletters. Donald Kerr, NAFSA

Immigration Committee chair and foreign student advisor at Cornell University, and Celestine Mott, executive secretary of the Greater New York Council for Foreign Students and the former acting director of International House New York, both contributed much to the interpretive analysis of immigration laws and regulations for foreign student advisors. Their books, *The F.S.A. and the U.S.A.: Pitfalls and Red Tape Affecting Foreign Students Elucidated in One Not-So-Easy Lesson* (by Kerr) and *The Immigration Act of 1952: An Analysis of Provisions Affecting Foreign Students and Other Educational Personnel* (by Mott), helped foreign student advisors comprehend the complicated immigration issues.

Immigration regulations directly influenced the experiences of foreign students in the United States. In 1949, NAFSA's Committee on Immigration Problems recommended to the U.S. Senate Judiciary Committee 13 points of change in immigration regulations. Both NAFSA and the IIE emphasized the importance of improving immigration regulations in regard to educational exchange. Consequently, several immigration procedures were simplified through negotiation with and the cooperation of the INS. For instance, foreign students did not have to apply to the INS but to their foreign student advisors for summer work permission.[90] They did not have to apply to the INS for permission to transfer from one institution to another during summer sessions. Colleges and universities were given more responsibility in determining the *bona fide* foreign students and weeding out the unqualified ones. Under the new policies, the INS also waived the required $500 bond fee for the *bona fide* student and his family, thus putting to an end this unpopular practice since the early 1920s. Moreover, the INS started to furnish foreign students with printed instructions of immigration issues upon their arrival in the United States.[91] In short, a whole set of policies and regulations were made to facilitate the student exchange programs and the treatment of foreign students/scholars.

The IIE was significantly transformed along with the expansion of international educational exchange after the war. Its new president, Kenneth Holland, was a man of extensive experiences with both public and private organizations of cultural affairs.[92] He was formerly the assistant director of the Office of International Information and Cultural Affairs of the State Department. IIE staff had also grown to more than 150 by 1950, administering more than 2,000 exchange fellowships with a budget of $600,000. Besides services to American colleges and universities, the IIE had contracts with the U.S. government, foreign governments, UNESCO, and binational educational foundations. The IIE was responsible for a large number of scholarships provided by the U.S. government, foreign governments, industrial corporations, and organizations outside the academic realm. Hence, IIE-related scholarships increased significantly. In 1952, IIE scholarship recipients constituted about 13 percent of the entire foreign student population (3,154 out of 30,462), whereas in the 1930–1931 academic year IIE scholarship recipients made up only 1.8 percent of the foreign student population.[93] The IIE's contracts with the U.S. government to administer Latin American programs, Fulbright Programs, Smith-Mundt programs, and the Army "reorientation" programs[94] constituted the bulk of IIE educational exchanges, bringing in an income of $183,730 in 1949. In contrast, services to other agencies only brought in an income of $18,920.[95] Services to universities dropped to less than 10 percent of IIE operations. Government funds and programs enabled the IIE to expand into a uniquely important organization but at the same time made it vulnerable to changes in government policy and less in control of its own destiny. To a great extent, the very existence of the IIE depended on government exchange programs. Although the IIE still remained a non-profit private institution, its responsibility for a wide range of government-sponsored programs indicated that the IIE had become primarily an operating agency for the government.[96]

Although the government passed laws to authorize cultural and educational exchanges with funding and politicians constantly offered supporting rhetoric, the government continued to rely extensively on private resources for the implementation of international cultural and educational activities. Indeed, the government called for "maximum utilization" of existing institutions in the United States and countries that participated in exchange programs. The U.S. Advisory Commission on Educational Exchange stated in its report to Congress on December 9, 1949: "Even if the government had the necessary resources it would still be desirable that private groups do the bulk of the work in this field. Understanding cannot be fostered on a purely governmental level."[97] With the government taking new initiatives, private organizations were pushed to readjust to the new demands in postwar educational exchanges. Key organizations such as NAFSA, the IIE, and CFRFS were restructured to serve special functions in "this new business" of international education. They cooperated with the government to coordinate programs and serve as the extended arms of government cultural diplomacy. While private resources were indispensable for the realization of government programs, government's support and promotion accelerated the expansion of cultural and educational exchanges and the professionalization of foreign student advising. Moreover, government exchange programs inevitably relied on university resources and personnel for their implementation, but government leadership in pushing the expansion of exchanges also led to the fast increase of international programs on American campuses. The working relations between the government and those professional organizations and educational institutions shed new light on the growing interdependence of the private and public sectors in the "total diplomacy" of the Cold War.

The role of the U.S. government in encouraging the expansion of educational and cultural exchanges greatly increased the political implications of international educational activities. Moreover, government policies shaped the scale and scope of educational exchange. As one international education officer pointed out, "Government program exercises a controlling influence over the exchange field and in a sense determines its character as well as its size and scope."[98] World War II was the watershed that made international educational and cultural exchanges increasingly an irrevocable component of U.S. foreign policy. The government constructed a new cultural diplomacy to fight the Cold War. Educational exchanges, which were first designed as an important instrument to counter Soviet propaganda, took on their own force and evolved into the propaganda media to project the great success of the American system. As technical assistance and educational exchanges were integrated with economic and military aid, the spread of American technology and culture in the world contributed to the achievement of the "total diplomacy" in the Cold War. All of these indicated a new departure of American foreign policy.

## NOTES

1. For the role of culture in the Cold War, see Walter L. Hixson, *Parting the Curtain* (New York: St. Martin's Griffin, 1997); Volker R. Berghahn, *America and the Intellectual Cold Wars in Europe* (Princeton, NJ: Princeton University Press, 2001).

2. The term "educational exchange" was often used as a synonym of cultural relations. Such interchangeable usage first appeared in the Information and Educational Act of 1948 (the Smith-Mundt Act). For its history, see Walter Johnson and Francis J. Colligan, *The Fulbright Program: A History* (Chicago: The University of Chicago Press, 1965), 19, 21f.

3. See Ruth E. McMurry and Muna Lee, *The Cultural Approach—Another Way in International Relations* (Chapel Hill, NC: University of North Carolina Press, 1947).

4. Cummins Speakman, *International Exchange in Education* (New York: The Center for Applied Research in Education, 1966), 31–32.

5. See Chapter 2 for the shift of attention to Latin America by the IIE and other private organizations.

6. For more information about Inter-American Conferences, see J. Manuel Espinosa, *The Inter-American Beginnings of U.S. Cultural Diplomacy, 1936–1948* (Washington, D.C.: State Department, Bureau of Educational and Cultural Affairs, History Studies, U.S. Government Printing Office, 1976); Francis J. Colligan, "Twenty Years After: Two Decades of Government-Sponsored Cultural Relations," *The U.S. Department of State Bulletin* 39, (1958).

7. *Monthly Catalog of the United States Public Documents* (Washington, D.C., 1939), 1137.

8. Francis J. Colligan, "Twenty Years After: Two Decades of Government-Sponsored Cultural Relations;" J. Manuel Espinosa, *Landmarks in the History of the Cultural Relations Programs of the Department of State, 1938–1936* (CU Collections, Department of Special Collections, University of Arkansas Libraries). The bulk of cultural activities of the Office of the Coordinator of Inter-American Affairs was transferred to the Division of Cultural Relations in 1943. The Office of the Coordinator and the Office of War Information were combined with the Division of Cultural Relations to form the Office of International Information and Cultural Affairs in 1946. For the relations between the division and the Office of the Coordinator, see Frank Ninkovich, *The Diplomacy of Ideas* (Cambridge: Cambridge University Press, 1981), 35–50.

9. Philip Coombs, *The Fourth Dimension of Foreign Policy: Educational and Cultural Affairs* (New York: Harper and Row, 1964), 6–7, 17.

10. Organizations represented on the committee included the IIE, the Association of American Colleges, the Association of American Universities, the National Association of State Universities in the United States, and the Association of Urban Universities (Minutes of the General Advisory Committee, 19 June 1941, 8–9, CU Collections, box 24, University of Arkansas Libraries); J. Manuel Espinosa, *Landmarks*, 1.

11. *Twenty-Fifth Annual Report of the Director* (New York: IIE, October 1, 1944), 10–11.

12. *Twenty-Second Annual Report of the Director* (New York: IIE, October 1, 1941), 5.

13. R. Nelson to Stephen Duggan, February 18, 1938; and memo of R. Nelson to the Department of State, 11 April 1938, CU Collections, box 24, Department of Special Collections, University of Arkansas Libraries.

14. *The Unofficial Ambassadors* (CFRFS, 1941), 7; *The Unofficial Ambassadors* (CFRFS, 1942), 10–11.

15. *Twenty-Third Annual Report of the Director* (New York: IIE, October 1, 1942), 8; *Twenty-Fourth Annual Report of the Director* (New York: IIE, October 1, 1943), 11–12; Report of the Conference of Foreign Student Advisers, Cleveland, OH: April 28, 29, and 30, 1942 (New York: IIE, 1942), ii. Sitting on the committee in 1941–1942 included John L. Mott (son of John R. Mott) from International House New York and seven foreign student advisors—Rollin S. Atwood from the University of Florida, Gladys Bryson from Smith College, Ben M. Cherrington from the University of Denver, Charles W. Hackett from the University of Texas, Charles B. Lipman from the University of California, Martin R. P. McGuire from Catholic University, and J. Raleigh Nelson from the University of Michigan.

16. Minutes of the General Advisory Committee, 19 June, 1941, 13, CU Collections, box 24, Department of Special Collections, University of Arkansas Libraries.

17. Harry H. Pierson, "Are We Ready for the Postwar Foreign Students?" *The Educational Record* (April 1945), 100. Many Latin American students came on their own and not on government fellowships.

18. Ibid.; Minutes of the Advisory Committee on the Adjustment of Foreign Students, 14–15 December 1944, CU Collections, box 24, Department of Special Collections, University of Arkansas Libraries.

19. Report of the Conference of Foreign Student Advisers (IIE, 1942).

20. Ibid., 2–3.

21. Edgar J. Fisher, *Counseling the Foreign Student*, IIE Pamphlet series, no. 5 (New York: IIE, March 1943), 7.

22. Ibid., 8–13.

23. Ibid., 14–24.

24. "Statement of the Functions of the Counseling Office of IIE Established According to Terms of Agreement between the Government and IIE," IIE document, n.d., CU Collections, box 24, Department of Special Collections, University of Arkansas Libraries.

25. *Twenty-Fourth Annual Report of the Director* (IIE, 1943), 12.

26. Isaac Kandel, *The Impact of the War upon American Education* (Chapel Hill, NC: University of North Carolina, 1948), 262; J. Manuel Espinosa, *Landmarks*, 3.

27. For details about Fulbright programs, see Johnson and Colligan, *The Fulbright Program*.

28. H. R. 4368, a bill "to extend and broaden the existing programs for the interchange of persons, knowledge, and skills between the people of the United States and the peoples of other nations."

29. *The U.S. Department of State Bulletin* 13 (Washington, D.C., July–December 1945), 589–593.

30. Many foreign countries purchased U.S. surplus property that had been left on their territory after the war. This property included military supplies and other items necessary for rebuilding their war-devastated countries. Those countries could repay the United States in dollars only (at the risk of upsetting their own and international economies), which would be a disaster that nobody wanted to see—especially in light of post-World War I experiences. Senator Fulbright proposed that those countries use U.S. credits in foreign currencies to finance educational exchange as payment for their purchases.

31. Charles Thomson and Walter H. C. Laves, *Cultural Relations and U.S. Foreign Policy* (Bloomington, IN: Indiana University Press, 1963), 61.

32. Johnson and Colligan, *The Fulbright Program,* 9.

33. Thomson and Laves, *Cultural Relations and U.S. Foreign Policy,* 66.

34. *First Semi-Annual Report of U.S. Advisory Commission on Educational Exchange* (Washington, D.C., February 1949), 4.

35. Ninkovich, *The Diplomacy of Ideas,* Chapters 4 and 5.

36. In his inaugural address in January 1949, President Truman spoke of four courses of action in international relations by the United States: support of the United Nations, programs for world economic recovery, the strengthening of freedom-loving nations against the dangers of Communist aggression, and lastly, Point Four, "a bold new program for making the benefits of our scientific advances and industrial progress available for the improvement and growth of under-developed areas." (See "Inaugural Address of the President," *The U.S. Department of State Bulletin* 20, January 30, 1949, 125.

37. *Sixth Semiannual Report of the United States Advisory Commission on Information,* 82nd Cong., 2nd sess., 1952, H. Doc. 526, 2.

38. Thomson and Laves, *Cultural Relations and U.S. Foreign Policy,* 78–80. A bipartisan resolution calling for a "worldwide Marshall Plan in the field of ideas" was sponsored by twelve senators based on a proposal by Assistant Secretary of State Edward Barrett in March 1950. In April 1950, President Truman underlined the essence of the proposal in a speech to the American Society of Newspaper Editors, urging a worldwide "Campaign of Truth."

39. *Third Semiannual Report of the United States Advisory Commission on Educational Exchange Activities,* 81st Cong., 2nd sess., 1950, H. Doc. 556, 6.

40. Thomson and Laves, *Cultural Relations,* 96; *Education for One World* (New York: IIE, 1953–1954), 17.

41. Cherrington was the director of the Social Foundation Institute at the University of Denver. He served as the first chief of the Division of Cultural Relations of the State Department in 1938–1940 when the government embarked on education exchange with Latin America.

42. Ben M. Cherrington, "Ten Years After," *Association of American Colleges Bulletin* 34, no. 4 (December 1948), 507–509, 520.

43. Report of the Bronxville Consultation Conference, June 14–15, 1944, *The Unofficial Ambassadors* (annual report of the Committee on Friendly Relations Among Foreign Students, 1944), 11; "Summary of the Sessions of Consultation Conference, Committee on Friendly Relations among Foreign Students, Bethlehem, PA, October 8–9, 1946," 1946, 3–4, folder titled "Everett Stowe Folder," CFRFS box #3, YMCA Archives.

44. The State Department appointed Howland Sargeant, a lawyer with a background in educational administration, to investigate the IIE's administration of student exchanges in September 1946. After interviews with many concerned persons, Sargeant came up with a 35-page report

officially known as "The United States Program for the Exchange of Students and Industrial Trainees." For details about the report, see Stephen Mark Halpern, "Institute of International Education: A History" (Ph.D. diss., Columbia University, 1969), 185–190.

45. Before coming to the IIE, Laurence Duggan was chief of the Division of Cultural Relations with Latin America of the Department of State.

46. Thomson and Laves, *Cultural Relations,* 72.

47. Ibid., 27–28. This test became the inception of TOEFL.

48. With government subsidies, the IIE began a special survey of Latin American students in 1943. The Committee on Friendly Relations Among Foreign Students had been conducting statistical surveys of foreign students annually since 1915 but did not proceed with elaborate statistical analyses. Beginning in 1945, CFRFS and the IIE agreed to jointly conduct a foreign student census. Their joint effort resulted in the publication of *Education for One World.* A national annual census of foreign students was conducted by the IIE from 1954 onward and was published in *Open Doors.* In a letter to IIE Vice President Donald Shank on December 21, 1955, Benjamin Schmoker officially acknowledged the transfer of foreign student data collection from CFRFS to the IIE and pointed out that the census conducted by CFRFS from 1915 to 1955 "has enabled the American public to be aware of the significance and breadth of the program and has supplied scholars with data for research programs." Ford Foundation Archives, PA 54–63.

49. Lee Zeigler, *NAFSA: Forty Years* (Washington, D.C.: National Association for Foreign Student Affairs, 1998), 2–3; George Hall of the IIE to Kenneth Holland of the Office of International Information and Cultural Affairs, the Department of State, 24 February 1947, CU Collections, box 24, Department of Special Collections, University of Arkansas Libraries.

50. IIE news release, 4 May 1948, box 10, file 9, NAFSA Archives; "Suggested Questions for Conference at Ann Arbor," box 10, file 3, conference documents, NAFSA Archives.

51. Report of the Conference on International Educational Exchanges, Congress Hotel, Chicago, IL (March 22–25, 1950), 9.

52. Ibid., 10.

53. IIE news release, 11 March 1948, box 10, file 9, NAFSA Archives.

54. *Conference on International Student Exchanges,* Ann Arbor, MI: May 10–12, 1948, IIE News Bulletin (1948).

55. "Brief Summary of Accomplishments of NAFSA During the First Year to June 1, 1949," 1, NAFSA Archives.

56. "Report of the Bronxville Consultation Conference, June 14–15, 1944," *The Unofficial Ambassadors* (CFRFS, 1944), 8.

57. Report to the Administrative Board of the Work of the Committee on Friendly Relations Among Foreign Students, 1 February 1941, CFRFS box #7, YMCA Archives.

58. *The Unofficial Ambassadors* (CFRFS, 1948), 3–5.

59. Ibid., 5–7.

60. *Twenty-Eighth Annual Report of the Director* (New York: IIE, October 1, 1947), 14.

61. Ibid., 14–16.

62. *Thirtieth Annual Report of the Director* (New York: IIE, October 1, 1949), 133.

63. There were regional differences. More than 60 percent of students from Latin America and Canada were undergraduates, while 60 percent of Indian students were graduates. European countries had almost an equal division between graduate and undergraduate students.

64. *Education for One World* (New York: IIE, 1954), 6–13.

65. *Education for One World* (New York: IIE, 1951), 33.

66. *Education for One World* (New York: IIE, 1952–1953), 16–17. There was an overlap in the percentages because one student obtained financial aid from several sources. Statistics on financial assistance were not complete because a significant percent (approximately 20 to 25 percent) of foreign students did not provide the information.

67. "Some Current Trends in the Student Migration from Abroad," Everett Stowe Folder, CFRFS box #3, YMCA Archives; *Education for One World* (1951), 18.

68. *Report of Conference of College and University Administrators and Foreign Student Advisors,* Chicago, IL: April 29–May 1, 1946 (New York: IIE, 1946), 91.

69. NAFSA Association file, NAFSA Archives, 1:A.

70. In China, inflation skyrocketed with prices rising 85,000 times within six months in 1948. See John K. Fairbank, *China: A New History* (Cambridge, MA: Harvard University Press, 1992), 334.

71. "Chinese Student Emergency Aid Fund," a report to NAFSA from Theodore C. Blegan, chairman of the Committee on Foreign Students, University of Minnesota, 14 December 1948, NAFSA Association file 1:A, NAFSA Archives.

72. *Special Report: The National Association of Foreign Student Advisers Annual Meeting,* Wade Park Manor, Cleveland, OH (March 28–30, 1949), 10.

73. Ibid., 9–24.

74. The State Department stated that it would be prepared to consider the provision of federal funds only on a strictly emergency basis. The U.S. Advisory Commission on Educational Exchange recommended that the State Department utilize Economic Cooperation Administration (ECA) funds as an emergency measure for the relief of Chinese students who were pursuing studies in technical fields, to which the State Department generally agreed.

75. *Special Report: The National Association for Foreign Student Advisers,* 12.

76. "Resolution adopted by the Board of Trustees of the China Club of Seattle, May 13, 1949;" "Letter by James Davis, Foreign Student Adviser, University of Washington, June 7, 1949;" "Minutes of China Institute, June 16, 1949;" CSCA 1949 folder, YMCA Archives.

77. The Program of Emergency Aid to Chinese Students and Scholars, 1949–1955 (81st Cong., Public Law 327) and Public Law 535, was administered under the State Department's exchange program. The total number of grantees during this period was 7,725, breaking down as 266 in 1948–1949; 2,400 in 1949–1950; 2,894 in 1950–1951; 1,355 in 1951–1952; 560 in 1952–1953; 196 in 1953–1954; and 54 in 1954–1955. See J. Manuel Espinosa, *Landmarks,* 5.

78. The Immigration and Naturalization Service called for interviews under oath of Chinese students who requested an extension of visas. NAFSA leaders were concerned with the type of questions asked and the psychological effect upon the students. Minutes of the Board of Directors, 16–17 October 1950, NAFSA 1:6, NAFSA Archives.

79. Memo, W. C. Johnstone to Chester Davis, 27 February 1951, Ford Foundation Archives, PA51–29, 6.

80. CSCA news release, 21 June 1948, CSCA folder 1948, YMCA Archives.

81. Ruth Haines, Report to J. Benjamin Schmoker, general secretary, "Committee on Friendly Relations," Everett Stowe Folder, CFRFS box #3, YMCA Archives.

82. In 1951, the Committee on Friendly Relations among Foreign Students ceased its relationship with the Chinese Student Christian Association, which was then dissolved.

83. *NAFSA Newsletter* (December 1952), 11.

84. *NAFSA Newsletter* (May 1952), 6.

85. *The Unofficial Ambassadors* (CFRFS, 1959), 3–5.

86. *The Unofficial Ambassadors* (CFRFS, 1951), 9; Benjamin Schmoker, "America Welcomes Foreign Students," *The Record: International Exchange* 6, no. 5 (Washington, D.C.: The Department of State, September–October 1950), 8–9.

87. Since 1949, the IIE had been administering an orientation program for the Department of State and the U.S. Army. Some colleges and universities also offered orientations, which primarily were programs of intensive English courses to prepare foreign students for their study in American universities. In the early 1950s, the IIE had about 20 orientation centers located on college campuses. The centers received foreign students on exchange programs under the Smith-Mundt Act. They also provided orientation for German, Japanese, and Ryukyuan exchangees under the U.S. Army contracts and grantees of the Ford Foundation programs from Greece, Turkey, Iran, Iraq, Egypt, India, and Pakistan. The orientation program of English language courses was later enlarged and incorporated into a full program that included the study of American history, economics, literature, and government. Such a program was designed to prepare foreign students for their academic and social experiences in the United States. It introduced the students to American life and customs, improved the students' abilities to use English, and familiarized them with the academic and administrative procedures in American universities. After the orientation, students were sent to the universities for academic training. Additionally, in order to give the students an opportunity to become acquainted with American daily life and to make friends with Americans, the IIE cooperated with the organization called Experiment in International Living by bringing exchangees into American homes as live-in guests for a month. See Virginia Slaughter, "Orientation Program—1952" (Report of the IIE Foreign Student Department Presentation to Regional Office Workshop, 6 October 1952, Ford Foundation Archives, PA52–103.

88. *Report of the Conference on International Educational Exchanges, Denver, Colorado,* April 11–14, 1951, 25–26, 29; *Report of the Conference on International Educational Exchanges, Michigan State College, East Lansing, Michigan,* April 23–26, 1952, 38–40.

89. *Report of the Conference on International Educational Exchanges, Denver, Colorado,* April 11–14, 1951, 27–28; *NAFSA Newsletter* (September 1952), 1.

90. On the issue of permission to work, government policy changed frequently and often posed restrictions on foreign students. It was a constant issue confronting the government and the educational organizations on behalf of foreign students.

91. "Report of NAFSA Committee on Immigration Problems for the Year 1948–1949," box 10, file 9, NAFSA Archives.

92. Laurence Duggan died unexpectedly in 1948. He became the director of the IIE after his father, Stephen Duggan, retired in 1946. Stephen Duggan, who was the first director of the IIE, died in August 1950 after 30 years of hard labor for the development of international education.

93. Cora Du Bois, *Foreign Students and Higher Education in the United States* (Washington, D.C.: American Council on Education, 1956), 207.

94. The Department of the Army operated a series of "reorientation" exchange programs with former enemy nations, namely Germany, Austria, and Japan, by bringing tens of thousands of selected students and leaders from these occupied territories to the United States to experience American democratic institutions and values. The IIE helped place these exchangees on fellowships in American colleges and universities.

95. *Thirtieth Annual Report of the Director* (New York: IIE, October 1, 1949), 7, 20.

96. Although the IIE was responsible for many government exchange programs, especially student exchanges, it tried to assert its fundamental philosophy that had been guiding its educational exchange programs from the very beginning. When the government combined political propaganda with educational exchanges, the IIE made its opposition clear. It expressed willingness to cooperate with the government, although it still wanted to "safeguard" educational activities from political propaganda. For details, see Halpern, "Institute of International Education," Chapter VII.

97. Johnson and Colligan, *The Fulbright Program,* 34–36.

98. Melvin Fox, "Report on Exchange of Persons Activities of the Ford Foundation," January 1953, Ford Foundation Archives, Report #001567.

# Chapter 6

## Philanthropy in Cold War Cultural Diplomacy: The Ford Foundation and the New Profession of International Education

Postwar America witnessed a wider range of philanthropic participation in international educational exchange. Old giants such as the Rockefeller and Carnegie philanthropies continued to emphasize cultural understanding by sponsoring programs of international studies and area studies. The Carnegie Corporation contributed more than $4 million to support international and area studies in 15 major American universities between 1947–1952.[1] But the newcomer, the Ford Foundation, played a unique role in the postwar national thrust of exporting American culture in the world. The Ford Foundation, together with the Carnegie, the Rockefeller, and other philanthropic foundations, sponsored conferences and research on international relations and educational exchange in the 1950s–1960s. More importantly, the Ford Foundation, in cooperation with the State Department, played a vital role in shaping the development of the new profession of international education through providing financial support to key organizations such as NAFSA, the IIE, and CFRFS to strengthen the national operations of educational exchange and foreign student/scholar affairs.[2] The long-term grants from the Ford Foundation to the IIE and NAFSA especially helped the institutional expansion of these two organizations, the professionalization of foreign student advisors, and the national movement of setting up international education offices on American campuses. As a result, a national bureaucratic infrastructure of international education was established by the late 1960s.

## THE FORD FOUNDATION: EXCHANGE PROGRAMS
## AS A MEANS TO AN END

As part of the new national drive to promote educational exchange for Cold War "total diplomacy," the Ford Foundation operated a variety of international exchanges in both academic and non-academic areas with unprecedented momentum in the 1950s–1960s. After the 1949–1950 restructuring, the Ford Foundation emerged as the largest American philanthropy with redefined interest in both international and domestic matters. The Board of Trustees decided "that the resources of the Foundation should be devoted to programs for the advancement of peace, education, the behavioral sciences, democratic institutions and economic stability" in the world. These goals were further categorized into five major areas: Area I—peace, Area II—democracy, Area III—the advancement of economic well-being, Area IV—education, and Area V—knowledge of human behavior.[3] Specific programs such as Overseas Development, Overseas Training and Research, International Affairs, and the Exchange of Persons were developed to achieve the objectives of Area I. The Exchange of Persons programs were supposed to complement other programs "to foster international understanding, maintain world peace, and combat communist threats to the western world by strengthening politically and economically the position of the free world, particularly the uncommitted developing countries."[4]

The Ford Foundation regarded exchange programs as means rather than ends in themselves. As far as the Ford Foundation was concerned, exchanges were primarily a means to world peace defined in Cold War perspectives and "accordingly, the Foundation's exchange program will be planned and conducted in the light of the ends the Foundation seeks to further through it."[5] Paul Hoffman, who previously directed programs of the Marshall Plan in Europe, served as the president of the Ford Foundation in the early 1950s. Hoffman also had experience in the American corporate world, as he was president of the Studebaker Corporation before he was chosen by President Truman to head the Economic Cooperation Administration (ECA) to implement the Marshall Plan.[6] In several of his reports to the trustees of the Ford Foundation in 1951, Paul Hoffman repeatedly stated that exchange programs were an important means "of strengthening the free world and of promoting international understanding."[7] These emphases of the Ford Foundation's international exchange programs demonstrated Hoffman's interpretation of the competition between the United States and the Soviet Union. They also indicated, as one scholar mentioned, his "firsthand impression of the Cold War confrontation with the Soviet Union" acquired when he was in Western Europe directing programs of the Marshall Plan.[8] Hoffman shaped the Ford Foundation's policy on exchange programs that continued throughout the 1950s–1960s although the presidency of the Ford Foundation changed hands several times.

Officials at the Ford Foundation defined three basic objectives of the exchange programs. First, the programs were to strengthen the free world and "create conditions that would make enduring peace possible." In this context, the Ford Foundation believed that Asia, the Middle East, and Europe were areas "more critical than others because they are under greatest pressure from the Soviet Union." Attention should be focused on "areas of tension wherein the acceptance of America is deteriorating and needs improvement." Hence, India, Pakistan, and the Near East immediately became the major concerns of the Ford Foundation because they "represented the soft under-belly of the European-Asian continent" and because "that was the place the Foundation ought to start its effort."[9]

Second, the exchange programs were expected to meet the democratization needs of a particular foreign country defined by the Ford Foundation. As Ford Foundation documents indicated, "The Foundation is not interested in the needs of all countries, or even in all the needs of any one country. . . . The Foundation is concerned with the democratic evolution of each country, as a free and responsible member of the world community . . . the Foundation must determine for itself what it regards as the important needs of a particular country . . . towards Foundation objectives and the conditions of peace."[10] Fully aware of imposing its own agenda on other countries, Ford Foundation officials nevertheless acknowledged that opportunities for cooperation with a particular country could exist only if the Ford Foundation's view of the country's needs somewhat fit with that country's own perception of its needs.

Third, the exchange programs emphasized the bringing to the United States of foreign "leaders" in every field who could exert immediate impact on public opinions about the United States rather than long-range improvement in attitudes in their home countries. The Ford Foundation gave short-term travel grants to foreign leaders who were "concerned with day-to-day development of public opinion." Non-academic exchanges in business, media, farm, and labor were given priority over academics—except for those intellectuals who occupied influential positions. Consequently, the Ford Foundation targeted the exchange programs of foreign community leaders and public opinion shapers by bringing to the United States selected foreign journalists, businessmen, scientists, artists, agricultural specialists, and religious leaders.

Moreover, the Ford Foundation did not support "exchanges of undergraduates or of persons at even lower educational levels except where specific, clearly defined technical training was to be provided with a reasonable assurance of strategic job opportunities for the trainee on his return home."[11] All of these specific deliberations aimed to gain the maximum public impact of the exchange persons in foreign countries. Anxious to make sure to choose the right types of individuals for the exchange, Ford Foundation officials

Making the World Like Us

approached social scientists at American universities for scientific guidance in determining the right kind of candidates with the promising potential to achieve the best results expected of exchanges.[12]

In their work of developing exchange programs, Ford Foundation officials began to question the old assumption that the educational exchange of bringing foreign nationals to the United States, in and of itself, was the way to promote international understanding and world democracy. They understood that the idea of promoting international understanding through education originally implied a broad Christian missionary sense of bringing people together spiritually and intellectually in order to dispel ignorance and develop goodwill. They pointed out that such an idea embodied the self-assured but "unproved assumption that first-hand acquaintance with the United States would give rise to an appreciation of its democratic institutions." Moreover, the assumption that exchanges promote international understanding "was based on the view that interpersonal relations were the basis of international relations, and that goodwill among individuals should therefore be fostered."[13] These opinions apparently derived from the officials' review of American past experience in international educational activity. The officials were not comfortable that the old assumptions continued to characterize the new national movement of educational exchange, especially when the international environment of politics had completely changed in the Cold War. Moreover, problems arising from exchange programs in the early 1950s had triggered a decline of foreign nationals' favorable opinion of the United States. In this context, Ford Foundation officials warned that it could not be taken for granted "that bringing a foreigner here will [automatically] put him on our side." They argued that it was probably true that the exchange person who visited the United States would leave feeling that he or she "knew" more about America, but that it was dubious if "he will 'understand' us better, in any sympathetic sense." Prejudices might very well be intensified by unsatisfactory experiences.[14] At an IIE conference in November 1951, Mark Starr, an IIE trustee, pointed out, "Some of our guests have left with a chip on the shoulder and a phobia against the United States and all it stands for." Cora Du Bois, IIE research director, also mentioned, "A recent study by Norman Kiell on Indian students in the United States…showed a marked decrease in favorable opinion about us after four to forty months in this country."

Carl Spaeth of the Ford Foundation questioned the effectiveness of a direct approach that emphasized to the exchange persons that they were brought here to increase their understanding of the United States. He argued, "Understanding will not be developed most effectively by seeking to impart it directly." He warned, "In addition to psychological resistances to anything resembling indoctrination, one may ask whether strangers ever become good friends by stating to each other that they believe in friendship and want to associate for that purpose."[15] If mere transplanting and direct approach were not enough, what should be added to render exchange experiences more effective in serving the Ford Foundation objectives as well as U.S. foreign policy purposes?

The Ford Foundation therefore re-examined the methods that were commonly used to achieve exchange objectives and requested social scientists to evaluate educational exchange to find out how well the exchange programs contributed to the increase of international understanding, such as favorable attitudes toward the United States. But social scientists replied that "the evaluation of the effectiveness of programs in this field was very difficult, if not impossible" because international understanding was an intangible goal. They calculated that if any exchange person left the United States with a greater "understanding" of the desired sort, it was probably the byproduct of a successful visit for other purposes. Nonetheless, they suggested that concrete objectives of exchanges should be defined and delivered in order to achieve the intangible goals. Specifically, they mentioned the objective of enabling the individual exchange persons to increase their technical skills, knowledge, and sophistication and the goal of hastening the economic and scientific development of developing countries.[16]

Citing the success of various IIE-administered technical exchange projects and the MIT Foreign Student Summer Project, Carl Spaeth of the Ford Foundation argued that pursuing the tangible goal of advancing technology and science throughout the world would contribute to the intangible purposes of promoting international friendship and improving foreign understanding of the United States. He expected that when tangible goals were adequately achieved, intangible ones would be fulfilled as well. Increased international understanding and friendship (the intangible goals) should be looked for as a byproduct rather than as the acknowledged purpose of each exchange. But behind the tangible goals should be the "unstated and equally important objectives of developing an appreciation of the basic values of the Western tradition" as represented by the United States.[17] Exchanges, therefore, should focus on tangible goals by bringing together persons of similar interests—and the Ford Foundation should give priority to tangible goals in its exchange programs.

This new approach to promoting and exporting American values through achieving tangible goals for exchange persons corresponded with the call of President Truman's Point Four, which emphasized technical assistance abroad, especially to developing countries. It seemed that two related issues were vital to making the exchange successful in terms of American Cold War foreign policy purposes. First, foreign exchange persons should be assured the opportunity to obtain useful knowledge and skills in exchange programs; and second, to make that happen, service facilities had to be strengthened to ensure effective placement and guidance for foreign students/exchange persons and to enhance their academic and social experiences in the United States.

## WORKING WITH THE STATE DEPARTMENT AND THE IIE

In designing and administering the exchange programs, the Ford Foundation developed a close working relationship with the State Department through constant consultation to make sure that the programs fit with government foreign policy objectives. The Cold War ideology and the flow of leadership personnel from the government to the Ford Foundation contributed to the close collaboration. The State Department made clear that the priority categories of exchange persons should be "developed on the principle of the interest of the United States in the global struggle in which we are now engaged."[18] William Johnstone, Jr., director of the State Department Educational Exchange Office, mentioned that in view of the Soviet tactic of propaganda via cultural activities, fine arts and other cultural activities should be of first priority for U.S. exchange programs, because "many people in foreign countries believe that the United States is devoid of culture," although they highly admired America's advanced technology.[19] In addition, leaders of socialist parties and those from socialist countries actually preferred to come on private grants for political reasons. As a private organization, the Ford Foundation was capable of playing a role that the government could not in facilitating this type of exchange. The Ford Foundation, therefore, developed programs that significantly supplemented those of the government, especially in the areas where political sensitivity could prevent potential candidates from coming to the United States on government grants. It was understood that the Ford Foundation's programs were to be conducted on a selective basis as far as "such supplementation promises to improve or strengthen" government programs.

The Ford Foundation was particularly interested in "the democratic evolution" of countries that were critical to "world peace." Its priority was to sponsor exchanges of groups and individuals who "could exercise the greatest influence on the formation of opinions and attitudes in their countries."[20] In combining its own interests and the needs of the government, the Ford Foundation sponsored various programs to help export American values. These programs included the Fulbright Supplementary Project that aimed to improve the selection and handling of Fulbright students and scholars; the African Scholarship Project for African students in the United States; the YMCA and YWCA Leadership Training Projects that trained community leaders in Asia, the Middle East, and Africa; and the International Farm Youth Exchange that targeted rural youth from developing countries who were "the most important potential leaders in the areas of [Ford] Foundation interest."[21] Moreover, the Ford Foundation provided travel grants to Fulbright scholars when government money was not available for such a purpose. Most officials at the Ford Foundation believed that the involvement would not only strengthen U.S. government programs, but also enhance the influence of the foundation's financial power. But some felt that the collaboration with the government would put the foundation at the disadvantage of being identified with government activities.[22] They questioned the advisability of being involved with government programs. Despite the doubt, the Ford Foundation continued the collaboration with government programs and adhered to the policy of conducting exchanges in consultation with the State Department.

Like the State Department, the Ford Foundation had neither the expertise nor the facilities to develop and implement exchange programs. Instead of spending lots of money to create a new unit or agency to handle the exchange, the Ford Foundation decided to use the IIE as its operating agency. The IIE was the only organization that was capable of providing a comprehensive service to all types of exchange clients—academic institutions, governments, foundations, businesses, and professional organizations. In providing the service to the Ford Foundation, the IIE was responsible "for overall operation in this activity, including initiation of non-academic exchange programs, review of projects from government and private agencies, supervision of funds and administration of all projects approved by the Ford Foundation, and evaluation of both the Foundation program and the individual projects."[23] Like other organizations that used IIE services, the Ford Foundation paid the IIE fees for administering the programs. Hence, the IIE served as an indispensable arm to both the Ford Foundation and the State Department in educational exchange.

But the IIE had to consult with the State Department on all the projects related to the Ford Foundation. The IIE would send the State Department basic information concerning each project, and the State Department would indicate its special preference, if any. "When a project is regarded favorably and of high priority, the [State] Department will return to IIE a *definite comment*; in the case of a project on which the Department takes no definite stand, the Department will indicate '*no comment*.'"[24] An IIE-State Department joint memo to the Ford Foundation emphasized that all projects were to be reviewed by the IIE Staff Review Committee and the National Board of Review before submission to the officers and trustees of the Ford Foundation for action. Given its special status as the major contractor for the government and its role in the entire educational exchange field, the IIE was in the best position to integrate the Ford Foundation's programs into the larger picture of U.S. worldwide cultural diplomacy of educational exchange.

The trio of the Ford Foundation, the State Department, and the IIE, in fact, gave shape to the entire educational exchange because each represented the financial power, the political leadership, and professional expertise, respectively. Within this triangle relationship, however, nothing was equal. The State Department expected a close cooperation from the IIE in the management of exchange programs because it was the implementation agency for both the State Department and the Ford Foundation. The State Department demanded that the "IIE must be willing to accept direction and advice from the State Department" as "our officers overseas supply information vital to the successfully handling of foreign visitors in the U.S." The IIE was expected to "never operate a competing program" but to "consider that one of its primary tasks from a public relations point of view is to hold and obtain greater support for the State Department's exchange program."[25] Officials of the State Department's Exchange of Persons Division believed that "unless the staff of the Institute [IIE] and the Board of Directors consider that they are engaged in a joint operation with the State Department, the program will not be effective." In short, the State Department cast the IIE in the role "of a private organization acting in effect as [an] agent for and on behalf of the State Department," although there were some IIE staff and "members of the Board of Directors who, very sincerely, desire to see the Institute remain free of too close connections with the State Department."[26] As long as the IIE remained the major contractor of the government, it had little choice but to comply with the State Department requirement.

The Ford Foundation also made clear its own stand about the State Department. It indicated that although its policy was to consult with the State Department on all exchange projects to ascertain their service to the government foreign policy objectives, it "cannot undertake to follow the advice of the State Department in all cases." Moreover, the Ford Foundation expressed its desire to consult with the Agriculture and Labor Departments on exchange projects in these areas.[27] The Ford Foundation obviously did not want to be controlled by the State Department, although consultation was the principle of cooperation.

The working relations between the IIE and the State Department did not go smoothly over the Ford Foundation's exchange projects, however. After a year of performance, complaints came from both the IIE and the State Department. Officers of the State Department criticized the IIE for not giving them sufficient information on projects for adequate consideration. They complained that the IIE never gave them enough time to review the projects and that the IIE sometimes passed their comments onto other governmental departments, causing confusion. They felt that in all cases they must be given adequate time if they were asked to review projects and that their opinions should be held confidential.[28] Likewise, the IIE questioned whether the State Department faithfully followed the review procedures upon which they had agreed. The State Department wished "to be considered as the major government channel and the sole source for government information on exchange projects," but the IIE doubted "that on the projects reviewed…by [the] State [Department] all government quarters had been checked." The IIE also "feels that [the] State [Department] has not cooperated in making available background information on its exchange planning." IIE officials complained "that in reviewing projects [the] State [Department] bases its judgment entirely upon its own limited objectives in relation to the *Campaign of Truth*, and that its comments, therefore, cannot necessarily serve as a final judgment on a Foundation-oriented project."[29]

The State Department felt that "present procedures were somewhat inhibiting in terms of their submission of program suggestions directly to the Foundation." Consequently, the Ford Foundation checked "directly with the State Department on Foundation-initiated projects...and on all other projects where it seemed to be necessary."[30] Meanwhile the Ford Foundation began to re-examine the IIE's handling of its exchange programs with external studies.[31] These studies eventually led to the questioning of whether it was realistic to "continue to delegate major responsibility for initiation and development of program and project review and supervision to any 'outside' agency." Officials at the Ford Foundation asked, "Is it sound for IIE—an operating agency—to be in the position of approving and supervising *all* Foundation sponsored projects of other private operating agencies?" Subsequently, the Ford Foundation decided that the foundation "will be responsible for developing the scope and content of its own exchange-of-persons program" while the "IIE will be recognized as the primary [operating] agency, but not necessarily the exclusive instrumentality, of the Foundation."[32]

## STRENGTHENING NATIONAL SERVICE CAPACITY FOR EDUCATIONAL EXCHANGE

The rapid increase of diverse exchange programs in the late 1940s gave rise to complicated educational and administrative challenges, which were further compounded by the ever-enlarging foreign student population of all races and cultures in the United States. Studies by the IIE and other organizations showed that institutional capabilities to handle "government and private exchanges were totally...inadequate." In many cases, foreign students and exchange persons were "poorly selected and badly placed." They were "not provided [with] opportunities adequately to explore their special fields or to meet American leaders in those fields; individuals at all levels were not given opportunities to meet Americans in their homes and to observe some of the most important aspects of our society."[33] There were increasing complaints from exchange persons, and exchange officers suspected that inadequacies in administrative facilities might very well have contributed to the exchange persons' misunderstanding, instead of understanding, of the United States.

The adequacy of national exchange service facilities directly impacted the "exchange program as a part of the conduct of American foreign policy" during the Cold War. Because the Ford Foundation and the State Department both relied on the expertise of the IIE to administer their exchange programs, they were aware of the severe inadequacy of service and were concerned with the possible negative impact on the efforts of creating favorable images of the United States among exchange persons. The State Department was anxious to get the service capacity strengthened and expanded, but it did not have the funds to do so. It then conveyed to the Ford Foundation the urgent financial need for strengthening national services and expanding the IIE. The State Department hoped that the Ford Foundation would provide the financial support for this purpose.[34]

The Ford Foundation indeed had an interest in strengthening the service for educational exchange. Its officials thought that educational exchange, if effectively directed and handled, could contribute to the increase of useful knowledge for the exchange persons and their understanding of the American society. But if exchange programs provided those people with "impractical and useless skills and knowledge" and "inadequate opportunities to establish a basis for understanding," it could "seriously jeopardize the foundations for peace" by confirming rather than dispelling stereotypes and prejudices of the United States.[35] In the Cold War, educational exchange became a vital instrument of cultural diplomacy and propaganda to enhance American national security interests and its international power politics. The Ford Foundation believed that if exchange persons were given adequate opportunities to observe "the processes and promise of a democratic society," "special administrative facilities and procedures had to be developed to handle the wide variety of problems that these different exchanges created."[36] Ford Foundation officials emphasized that they would concentrate the efforts to strengthen national exchange service facilities on a few key national organizations that were "in a position to have the widest possible impact" on the operations of educational exchange. These organizations included the IIE, NAFSA, and CFRFS, whose special roles and services not only covered the entire range of exchanges at the national level but also shaped the operation of exchange programs on individual campuses and in local communities.

The IIE, NAFSA, and CFRFS had intertwined working relations, and their services complemented each other in the work of international education. The IIE depended on the key members of NAFSA—foreign student advisors and Fulbright advisors—as representatives of higher educational institutions to deliver services to exchange persons. Similarly, NAFSA had close working relations with CFRFS when the general secretary of CFRFS, Benjamin Schmoker, served as secretary and president of NAFSA in the first half of the 1950s—integrating the leadership of the two organizations. Both NAFSA and CFRFS emphasized personal services to foreign students and scholars, and the sharing of leadership no doubt enabled NAFSA to benefit from the valuable experience of CFRFS that had been accumulated in the past decades of working with foreign students.

In 1951, the Ford Foundation gave one-year grants to these three organizations to strengthen and expand their operations ($16,575 to NAFSA,

$17,390 to CFRFS, and $500,000 to the IIE).[37] As the operating agency for the Ford Foundation, the IIE was asked to assist the foundation with disbursing the grants to NAFSA and CFRFS with the responsibility to supervise and evaluate their operations. Specifically, the grant to NAFSA aimed to strengthen its headquarters operation and improve the services of foreign student advisors on campuses throughout the United States. The grant was also to support the expansion of programs such as hospitality, orientation, job placement, and other services that NAFSA offered to foreign students.[38]

The grant to CFRFS aimed to enlarge the port-of-entry service by increasing the training of volunteers at smaller ports and to expand community hospitality activity by forming cooperative and inter-organizational community programs in the larger metropolitan areas. The port-of-entry service played a unique role in the national effort to improve the handling of exchanges and helped create a favorable impression of the United States among newcomers. The State Department and the IIE extensively utilized this service for their sponsored exchange persons. Moreover, CFRFS worked under contract for the Mutual Security Agency (formerly the Economic Cooperation Administration) to carry out government exchange programs.[39] When making grants to NAFSA and CFRFS, the Ford Foundation encouraged the continuation of the dual leadership of Benjamin Schmoker because "the interests of NAFSA and CFRFS [are] closely allied." It emphasized the advantage of continuing such an arrangement of leadership and suggested that NAFSA amend its constitution to allow the general secretary of CFRFS to be re-elected as the secretary of NAFSA. The Ford Foundation also suggested that the travel budget for Benjamin Schmoker and half of his salary should be paid by NAFSA and that Schmoker should travel in the interest of both NAFSA and CFRFS.[40]

The half-million grant to the IIE aimed to supplement the contributions made by 14 other philanthropic organizations.[41] It emphasized internal operations to improve administrative structure, establish regional offices, recruit professional personnel, expand the exchange programs of leaders and specialists, organize a research unit, and develop an alumni office with a central index of all exchange persons.[42] A separate grant of $40,000 was also made to help the IIE purchase the Vanderbilt House as its new headquarters in New York.

Satisfactory operations of the initial one-year grants convinced the Ford Foundation of the advisability of renewing the grants with increased sums for longer periods. Between 1951 and 1956, the Ford Foundation gave more than $2 million in grants to the IIE, NAFSA, and CFRFS to continue the efforts of strengthening national service facilities. The IIE received $1,910,000, which constituted 52 percent of its general non-contract operation budget; NAFSA received $118,200, which made up 80 percent of its total budget; and CFRFS was given $77,430, which contributed 12 percent of its budget.[43] The Ford Foundation's financial support significantly shaped the national operations of exchange services and the institutional development of the IIE and NAFSA.

## IMPACT OF THE GRANTS

With the grants from the Ford Foundation, CFRFS recruited and trained tens of thousands of volunteers in New York, Boston, Miami, New Orleans, Seattle, and San Francisco for the port-of-entry service. It also organized reception committees in smaller ports such as Norfolk and Montreal. The volunteers took their assignments to planes and ships, each wearing an armband with "Foreign Student Advisor" printed on it. The majority of the volunteers were women from local communities. During the peak travel time from June to November, CFRFS hired paid staff to stay at major airports in New York and San Francisco on day and night shifts to assist the newly arrived foreign students/visitors who were either on sponsored programs or coming on their own. CFRFS volunteers not only personally met thousands of incoming foreign students and trainees, but also helped them obtain temporary accommodations when they needed to stay overnight in the port city. They also contacted foreign student advisors or CFRFS community affiliates for receiving the incoming students. In the 1950s, CFRFS had about 40,000 community volunteers to work for the program. The IIE, government agencies, private organizations, and educational institutions all had used the port-of-entry service for their exchange persons. They acknowledged that "this service is of great importance in helping to give foreign students an initial favorable opinion of the United States" and that it helped soften the "cultural shock" of the tired and confused newcomers.

The Ford Foundation grants also enabled CFRFS to strengthen its community hospitality programs. CFRFS's field secretary traveled to campuses and communities all over the country to push for more community programs. As a result, new community hospitality committees formed in more than 100 cities by groups representing civic, social, industrial, and religious interests. Local committees utilized community resources to supplement the educational interests of foreign students and trainees in an effort to link campus life and community activity. Those committees were instrumental in creating contacts among foreign students, local businesses, and civic groups. In cooperation with local committees, CFRFS developed new projects such as the "Know America Program for International Students" (KAPIS) and "Ventures for International Students Interested in Travel" (VISIT). KAPIS was designed to systematically introduce foreign students and visitors to American society and institutions through visits to local American homes and institutions. VISIT offered a low-cost travel program for foreign students during their vacations.[44] CFRFS considered those personal services and programs "a long-term investment in peace." In an article entitled "Focus on Peace," CFRFS leaders expressed their belief that the presence of foreign students was "bound to make an impact on world history" and that the students were to return home "with definite ideas as to our sincerity and our acceptance of them as persons in whose problems and needs we are interested." CFRFS leaders asked the public to think about the effect "their memories of us will have on the possibility of world peace."[45] They hoped that CFRFS programs would make positive contributions to that end.

The IIE evaluation of CFRFS acknowledged the accomplishments of the services, but it pointed out that CFRFS needed to improve the coordination with the IIE and its regional offices and with other organizations in their shared activities concerning foreign students. The National Review Board of the IIE highly commended the port-of-entry service but questioned the operation of community hospitality programs. It pointed out that CFRFS had "some tendency to concentrate over-heavily on church and other religious groups in attempting to develop leadership" for community programs.[46]

As to NAFSA, the Ford Foundation grants greatly strengthened the general operation of the national headquarters and enabled it to create several new programs. First, NAFSA was able to set up its own small staff and headquarters in New York.[47] Second, it created a program called the "Foreign Student Advisor Field Service" to train newly appointed advisors through in-service internships, where the new ones worked as interns at institutions that had exemplary foreign student programs. The program also used a group of experienced advisors as consultants to help the new ones by visiting their campuses and holding workshops for them. Third, NAFSA organized foreign student advisors and teachers of English as a Second Language (ESL) on study tours abroad to gain a better understanding of other cultures and to improve the quality of their professional work. Various binational foundations and foreign governments, such as American Friends of the Middle East, the Asia Foundation, the Creole Foundation, the German government, and Scandinavian governments all provided NAFSA with travel grants for such purposes.[48] Moreover, NAFSA Secretary Benjamin Schmoker went on a tour to visit foreign student advisors and their programs across the country. His visits significantly improved the communication between NAFSA headquarters and foreign student advisors and university administrators on individual campuses. Finally, NAFSA increased its information service by publishing handbooks for foreign student advisors and books on foreign student orientation programs.[49] By 1955, NAFSA had more than 500 memberships with 1,200 foreign student advisors. As the sole financial sponsor of NAFSA, the Ford Foundation played a crucial role in shaping the institutional growth of NAFSA as a professional organization.

In assessing NAFSA operations, the IIE criticized NAFSA for the lack of coordination with the IIE and other organizations in the exchange field. The National Review Board of the IIE believed that many of NAFSA's problems arose from the fact that Benjamin Schmoker acted as both the secretary of

NAFSA and the secretary of CFRFS. Such a dual leadership was thought to have posed "too great a load" on Schmoker, with no one in either office to substitute for him in meeting with other organizations or making important decisions. The IIE indicated that although it was appropriate for NAFSA to have such a leadership arrangement with CFRFS in the early phase of its development, NAFSA "has now reached a stage where it needs a more professionalized staff operation." The IIE also advised that the appointment of a full-time secretary of NAFSA would not only reduce NAFSA's difficulty in inter-organizational coordination, but also would improve its internal administrative operations.[50] The IIE recommended that the Ford Foundation provide financial assistance to enable NAFSA to hire a full-time director.

The questions raised by the IIE prompted the Ford Foundation to investigate the NAFSA situation by holding discussions with people from NAFSA, the IIE, the State Department, and other individuals who were in a position to appraise NAFSA operations. The IIE explained that its evaluation was based on surveys of its staff opinions. IIE staff was not entirely convinced that NAFSA had extended its influence and expanded its activities to the degree expected under the Ford Foundation's grants. But the State Department commented that NAFSA had demonstrated growth and maturity as a professional organization and that it had done a great deal to advance the status of foreign student advisors. It also acknowledged that NAFSA "still has a long way to go but will not get there without help, and it is certainly in the interest of the [State] Department to endorse maximum help for it."[51]

In the end, all parties agreed that NAFSA was "performing a unique service with purpose, energy, and competence." NAFSA had been working with all interested groups on the immediate concerns of international educational exchange, namely immigration, income tax, selective service (drafting), credential evaluation, and activities of orientation and hospitality. Melvin Fox, a staff member of the Ford Foundation, commented that "there is no other group in the country that is so directly concerned with these problems" nor "any that is making a comparable effort to provide service to students on these many questions that affect their welfare in the United States."[52] The Ford Foundation consequently decided that NAFSA was doing an outstanding "front-line job" in serving foreign students' needs on a day-to-day basis and was improving the capacity and status of foreign student advisors through publications, headquarters services, conferences, and regional meetings.[53] It encouraged NAFSA to consult with the IIE and other organizations to avoid duplication of efforts in the field. NAFSA continued to have Benjamin Schmoker as secretary on a half-time basis and used part of the Ford Foundation grants to pay CFRFS to hire additional administrative assistance. At the same time, the Ford Foundation urged NAFSA to clarify its administrative and fiscal relationship with CFRFS so that NAFSA could establish an independent management at the earliest possible time.[54]

In the case of the IIE, the Ford Foundation grants proved vital to its institutional expansion and program development. Since the Fulbright Act and the Smith-Mundt Act, the IIE had been administering a wide range of academic and non-academic exchanges for the U.S. government. This new responsibility not only changed the IIE's traditional role of arranging student and scholar exchanges for colleges and universities, but also increased the volume and the complexity of its exchange operations. Interested parties such as the State Department and major philanthropic foundations were anxious to see the improvement of IIE management and its capability to meet the new challenge of postwar international educational exchange. For this purpose, two external studies of the IIE were sponsored jointly by the Ford Foundation, the Carnegie Corporation of New York, the Rockefeller Foundation, and the Commonwealth Fund in 1950–1952. One was a management survey conducted by a management consulting firm in New York in 1950–1951, and the other was a study undertaken by Ralph Tyler and his associates at the University of Chicago in 1952. The management survey concluded that the IIE's organizational structure needed to be strengthened especially at the top executive level and that the selection and placement of foreign students were inadequately planned. The survey recommended that the IIE strengthen the direction of programs by adding a third top executive and that the Development and Information Program of the IIE be separated, because each part of the program had different functions and audiences. Endorsing the IIE's plan to establish five regional offices within the United States, the survey also recommended the appointment of a field office director.

The Tyler study, which was a follow-up of the management survey, examined the functions of the IIE in the entire educational exchange field. The Tyler Report recommended, among other things, one major new function for the IIE; that is, "the establishment of a policy body to study and make pronouncements on questions" of major concerns in the exchange field. In view of the increasing services that the IIE provided to the exchange programs for specialists and leaders under the State Department contract and the Ford Foundation agreement, the Tyler Report called to attention that the IIE should recognize its basic clientele—the universities and colleges—and provide primary services to them. The IIE was advised to eliminate its role as the official reviewer for the Ford Foundation projects and was urged to serve as an information clearinghouse for all international education exchange programs.[55]

The Tyler Report was well received by the sponsoring foundations, primarily because it emphasized the need for the IIE to expand its services to academic clientele. The IIE agreed in general with the recommendation of emphasizing services to academic clientele but pointed out that "cooperative relations with government agencies, including administration of carefully selected government-financed educational exchange programs by IIE, is essential." The IIE argued that if it did not "serve as the major administrative agency for such exchange programs, either a new organization will need to be established by government, or government itself will expand its own operations."[56]

The Rockefeller Foundation had been critical of the IIE's diversion from service to academic institutions under the pressure of the Ford Foundation and others to develop non-academic exchange programs. It threatened to lower its financial support because the IIE "has been unwilling to set forth any firm policy on the relative extent to which IIE activities should be supported by service charges and by philanthropies." The Rockefeller Foundation also believed that the "IIE has been spreading itself too thin, watering down its talents, and undermining its unique long-range position in the exchange field."[57] The Ford Foundation hoped that the IIE's agreement to follow through with Tyler's recommendations and to increase its services to the "nuclear" academic clientele would restore the confidence of the Rockefeller Foundation in supporting the IIE again. Ford Foundation officials tried to impress upon the Rockefeller Foundation the importance of providing long-term support to the IIE. They also tried to enlist the Carnegie Corporation and other foundations to share the financial responsibility to support IIE regional offices. These efforts failed to materialize, however.

The restructuring of the IIE along the lines of the aforementioned two reports led to the major expansion of the IIE in the following seven areas: the creation of a vice-president position for program operations; the establishment of an administrative management staff and an office manager; the creation of an information and counseling division; the establishment of a new follow-up unit (central index project of all exchange persons); the establishment of a department of special projects; the creation of a research department; and the development of five regional offices in Washington, D.C., Houston, Chicago, Denver, and San Francisco, respectively.[58] In addition, a Standing Committee on Educational Interchange Policy was established as a result of the Tyler recommendation. The committee produced a series of studies of policy issues and concerns in the following decades, which addressed the relations of international educational exchange and American universities.[59]

In the first half of the 1950s, the IIE received grants from various philanthropic foundations—but the strongest financial support came from the Ford Foundation and the Carnegie Corporation, whose funds constituted more than 70 percent of the IIE's general operating expenses (see Table 6.1). It was obvious that the Ford Foundation had overtaken the Carnegie and Rockefeller philanthropies as the chief sponsor of the IIE. By 1956, the IIE staff had increased to 250 with a total operating budget of $1.5 million. The vastly increased operating budget enabled the IIE to expand and strengthen both its national headquarters and its regional office operations.

The Ford Foundation hoped that the IIE, NAFSA, and CFRFS would gradually be capable of raising funds from other sources to sustain their level of operations. But none of them except CFRFS was able to do so when the

**Table 6.1**

## Sources of IIE Income, 1951–1956 (in thousand dollars)

| General Support | 1951–1952 | 1952–1953 | 1953–1954 | 1954–1955 | 1955–1956 | Total | General % |
|---|---|---|---|---|---|---|---|
| Ford | 350* | 400 | 489 | 355 | 307 | 1901 | 51.1 |
| Carnegie | 150 | 150 | 150 | 150 | 150 | 750 | 20.5 |
| Rockefeller | 25 | 25 | 25 | 25 | 25 | 125 | 3.4 |
| Other foundations | 28 | 54 | 79 | 79 | 148 | 393 | 10.7 |
| Indiv./corps./ univs. | 24 | 43 | 48 | 85 | 132 | 332 | 9.1 |
| Others | 23 | 53 | 40 | 23 | 22 | 161 | 4.4 |
| General Total | 600 | 725 | 831 | 722 | 784 | 3662 | 100.0 |
| Contract fees | 550 | 621 | 624 | 673 | 647 | 3075 | |
| Total income | 1150 | 1346 | 1455 | 1355 | 1431 | 6737 | 100.0 |

Sources: Docket, Trustee meetings on IIE, June 18–19, 1956, 3, Ford Foundation Archives, PA540-064.

*This excludes grants of $75,000 toward mortgage and other expenses for IIE headquarters in a new building.

five-year grants came to an end in 1956. CFRFS received major financial support (more than 50 percent of its total budget) from church boards and the YMCA, whereas the IIE and NAFSA primarily relied on foundation grants and government contract fees. Although the IIE had received increased financial support from individuals, corporations, and universities, it still depended on philanthropic foundations for approximately two-thirds of its budget. NAFSA could not even raise funds for one-third of its operating budget, despite the fact that it had a substantial increase of institutional and individual memberships.

In 1956, each of the three organizations asked the Ford Foundation for a 10-year grant to enable them to realize long-term planning goals. Ford Foundation officials thought that the 10-year projection of operations by the IIE appeared to be a careful analysis of its potential to improve quality standards in the field of educational exchange. They believed that the IIE's centrality to the entire exchange required "our support of IIE at a level adequate for this purpose" and that the IIE must be sustained in both American national interest and the interest of developing privately sponsored educational exchanges. Subsequently, the Ford Foundation approved a 10-year grant to the IIE at the rate of $350,000 annually. This grant, however, decreased the Ford Foundation's contribution to the IIE's general operation budget from 52 percent to 44.3 percent, pushing the IIE to seek more funds from other sources. In cooperation with the Ford Foundation, the Carnegie Corporation appropriated a 10-year terminal capital grant of $1,500,000 to the IIE, and the Rockefeller Foundation doubled its previous support by providing it with a five-year grant of $250,000.60 NAFSA, in contrast, received a five-year grant from the Ford Foundation with $26,000 annually as a demonstration of the foundation's interest in maintaining NAFSA's current programs and encouraging its own fundraising. The Ford Foundation gave CFRFS a five-year terminal grant with $12,000 annually to sustain the operation of port-of-entry service and community hospitality programs.61 Those long-term grants of more than $3 million were earmarked as exchange strengthening grants to increase the quality of national services for educational exchange.62

In the early 1960s, CFRFS was integrated into the YMCA. Its hospitality programs were taken over by local groups of international friendship, although it continued the port-of-entry service. The work for foreign students' religious needs was taken over by the National Student Christian Federation, thus ending the long-time service of CFRFS to foreign students.63 NAFSA and the IIE thereafter became the two major organizations dominating professional services for educational exchanges and foreign students. There was no doubt that NAFSA benefited from the experiences of CFRFS in its professional transformation when Benjamin Schmoker served as secretary and president of NAFSA in the first seven years of its history. Moreover, both NAFSA and the IIE had made substantial progress in diversifying their sources of income. They began to receive funds from the State Department after Congress passed the Fulbright-Hays Act (Mutual Educational and Cultural Act) in 1961, although they continued to enjoy support from the Ford Foundation and other private sources.

In summary, the Ford Foundation provided the IIE and NAFSA with millions of dollars as efforts to strengthen the national service capacity for educational exchanges in the 1950s. The Ford Foundation's financial support helped transform both NAFSA and the IIE institutionally and fundamentally impacted the administration of exchange programs at both national and local levels. NAFSA grew into a dynamic national organization representing colleges and universities that enrolled four-fifths of the foreign nationals who were studying in the United States. Educational institutions increasingly relied on NAFSA for assistance and guidance in regard to their exchange programs and foreign student affairs. NAFSA had developed four indispensable services for American educational institutions: (1) providing admissions offices with concrete and detailed information about technical matters such as tax and immigration regulations that affected foreign students; (2) training individual foreign student advisors, English as a second language (ESL) specialists, and community leaders in the task of familiarizing foreign students with American culture and society; (3) serving as the liaison between academic institutions and the U.S. government; and (4) providing a forum for representatives from government, voluntary groups, professional associations, and educational institutions to examine foreign student matters of current importance and mutual interest.[64]

The IIE at the same time remained the largest service agency under contract with the State Department and other U.S. government agencies. The IIE failed to develop close ties with U.S. educational institutions, however, to respond effectively to their needs in international educational exchange. The proliferation of program operations had so stretched the IIE that it was not capable of clearly defining its purposes. Moreover, IIE activities revealed "costly obsolescence in operational procedures" and "serious weaknesses in leadership."[65] In contrast, NAFSA had developed dynamic relations with educational institutions. The number of memberships of foreign student advisors had increased to more than 1,000 by the end of the 1950s, and the English Language Section of NAFSA had designed special English courses for foreign students to help them adjust to American academic system and the society. NAFSA's constant contact with the INS officers helped improve the special procedures of immigration regulations concerning foreign students. NAFSA's success might very well have been built upon the weaknesses of the IIE in these areas. After all, it was the educational institutions that provided the day-to-day educational service to the exchange persons. Despite its inadequacies, the IIE was still the major American agency capable of providing a wide range of expertise in educational exchange. As one officer at the Ford Foundation mentioned, "The dollar volume of Ford Foundation projects for which IIE provides a wide variety of facilitating services has increased from an annual total of less than $500,000 in 1956 to close to $6 million currently [mid-1960s], involving a two-way flow of people related to Foundation's programs in all areas of the world."[66] In fact, the Ford Foundation had constantly increased its financial commitment to the IIE throughout the 1950s–1960s, even though by 1965 Ford Foundation grants constituted less than 25 percent of the IIE budget for core program operations and 11 percent of NAFSA's budget.[67] Given its vital position in the exchange field as the operating agency for both the U.S. government and the Ford Foundation, the IIE shaped the program direction of the entire field of international educational exchange while integrating the interests of the government, philanthropy, and professional organizations.

## NAFSA: WORKING WITH UNIVERSITIES AND DEFINING ITSELF

NAFSA made tremendous efforts at professionalizing foreign student advisors and establishing the international education office on American campuses. Foreign student advising was a field new to university administration and immature as a profession when NAFSA was founded in 1948, although a few universities had some sort of foreign student advisors or Faculty Committee on Foreign Student Affairs before that. For the majority of universities, the role of foreign student advisors was not clear when they were urged to appoint foreign student advisors to accommodate the needs of postwar expansion of foreign student programs. University administrators wanted to know what exactly those advisors were supposed to do, especially when services such as admissions, student affairs, and English language instruction were already available to foreign students through other offices on campus. They wanted NAFSA to define "what is to be done in setting up a foreign student advisory program and…ways in which it might be done." Fred H. Turner at the University of Illinois expressed the general feelings of university administrators when he pointed out that most universities would "appreciate being told how to do it." Howard Nostrand of the American Council on Education suggested that NAFSA make its mission known to university administrators through conferences and by sending a "traveling salesman" to campuses to set up and maintain standards for foreign student advising.[68]

In response to the demands of university administrators, NAFSA set out to standardize and professionalize foreign student advising. However, there were different views on how to professionalize the emerging occupation of foreign student advising. Some made ambitious suggestions that foreign student advisors should assume comprehensive responsibilities in both academic and administrative matters and that a centralized foreign student advisor office with close liaisons with other offices on campus should be established to make their work more effective; others made cautious warnings that foreign student advisors should have a focus of their job and not presume too much responsibility. Joe Neal, foreign student advisor at the University of Texas and an active NAFSA leader, represented the former view in pushing for standards to professionalize. He argued that foreign student advisors should be given complete responsibility to coordinate exchange programs and foreign student affairs. He reasoned that because many advisors had already been involved in the work of English instruction, admissions, and academic course evaluation, they should be given budgetary allocation, secretarial assistance, and office space. That was "the proper status and position of foreign student advisors we've been looking for," he exclaimed. He realized, however, that such a demand for the position of foreign student advisors would inevitably present a challenge to university administration because it was easier to add somebody onto an existing office than to create an entirely new one. He also suggested that foreign student advisors should be separate from Fulbright scholar advisors, with foreign student advisors responsible for all foreign students—"the largest and most tangible international activity on campus." He urged universities to accept as many foreign students as they could adequately train rather than having a suggested quota of 5 percent.[69]

Different from Joe Neal, Allen Blaisdell, director of International House Berkeley and vice-president of NAFSA, warned his colleagues, "Go slowly! Don't professionalize too much…We don't know where we are. We must feel our way." He was hesitant to institutionalize "an incipient profession" too quickly. Blaisdell believed that foreign students were just one element in the larger picture of internationalization of education. In his opinion, other offices on campus should accept some responsibility for "world education." He did not think it wise to professionalize foreign student advisors into a special group, because "they should be part of the whole university administration rather than a separate official function." He suggested that foreign student advisors might not be necessary in the end as educational institutions were internationalized.[70] Allen Blaisdell represented the old school of international education that developed in the interwar cultural internationalist movement, and his advice on and anticipation of postwar foreign student programs demonstrated the liberal concept of internationalizing American universities. In contrast, Neal represented those who regarded foreign students as a special component of American higher education, distinctly different in certain key aspects from American students.

Moreover, Blaisdell was concerned that NAFSA was trying to expand too fast. Immediately after NAFSA was founded, it established more than 20 committees to deal with almost any issue that came into educational exchange while its office was still housed in IIE headquarters with little staff support. Blaisdell urged NAFSA to confine its activities so as not to infringe upon other professional groups. Specifically, he wanted NAFSA to limit itself to non-academic services and have no part in foreign student admission, credit evaluation, course selection, academic advising, and special courses.

The issue of professionalization affected NAFSA's relationship with universities and other professional groups. There were concerns on "how far NAFSA could go in defining the position of foreign student advisors without meeting defensive opposition on the part of the university administration." There were also concerns that professional groups, such as the admission officers, teachers of English as a second language, and student affairs officers, might rightly feel that they had an equal or even superior competence to speak for the educational institutions in matters of foreign student education.[71] NAFSA was challenged both to spearhead the international education movement and to convince university administrators of the necessity of foreign student advisors. In order to better advise colleges and universities on foreign student programs, NAFSA requested several large universities that had long histories of educating foreign students to share their experience. Universities such as Berkeley, Wisconsin, Minnesota, Cornell, Kentucky, Washington, Michigan, Teachers College of Columbia University, and Harvard all responded with detailed reports of their foreign student programs, including the historical development of their programs, academic and non-academic activities, and problems encountered.[72] The U.S. Advisory Commission on Educational Exchange also used the information gathered by NAFSA to help the government formulate exchange policies.

NAFSA's competence as a professional organization was significantly tested by how foreign student advisors fared in the field of international education. In 1948 and 1952, NAFSA conducted surveys of the status of foreign student advisors in an effort to promote the profession. The findings indicated that although more foreign student advisors were appointed with the understanding that they "must serve as a coordinating agent . . . with service to the foreign student as the central core of his activity" and with responsibility "for the personal and educational welfare of the foreign student," the importance of their work was far from being acknowledged. Many foreign student advisors were faculty members who taught regular courses and carried out advising duties without a designated office or secretarial assistance. Their workload increased dramatically as more foreign students arrived on American campuses. Many were spread too thinly to provide proper counseling services, as well. NAFSA urged universities to offer additional compensation or a reduction of the teaching load for foreign student advisors and to establish a separate office for them. In defining the workload, NAFSA recommended that every 250–300 foreign students would require a full-time advisor and a full-time secretary for adequate counseling. Faculty members who served as foreign student advisors should have their teaching load reduced accordingly.[73]

In an effort to improve campus-wide administrative cooperation and coordination between campus and community programs, NAFSA requested universities and communities to "know and accept the function of the Adviser, and to establish and maintain satisfactory working relationship with the office of the Adviser." These requests and recommendations were then published in the booklet *The Office of the Foreign Student Advisor,* which the Advisory Commission on Educational Exchange of the State Department distributed to every educational institution in the United States and called the attention of university leaders to foreign student advising.

With the support of the State Department and the IIE, NAFSA was able to motivate universities to appoint more foreign student advisors. Before 1940, there were fewer than 50 foreign student advisors in the United States—but in 1950, there were about 400 officially appointed foreign student advisors, of whom 175 were also Fulbright advisors.[74] According to Homer Higbee's Report of 1961, the number of foreign student advisors rose steadily since the end of World War II (see Table 6.2), and by the mid-1960s more than 1,200 foreign student advisors were working in American colleges and universities. The increase of foreign student advisors indicated the growth of a new profession—international educators—and the professionalization of foreign student educational services.

**Table 6.2**

## Dates of Appointments of Interviewed Foreign Student Advisors

| Year of Appointment | Number | Percent |
|---|---|---|
| Pre-1940 | 16 | 2.4 |
| 1940–1945 | 25 | 3.7 |
| 1946–1950 | 127 | 18.7 |
| 1951–1952 | 59 | 8.7 |
| 1953–1954 | 64 | 9.4 |
| 1955–1956 | 107 | 15.7 |
| 1957 | 66 | 9.7 |
| 1958 | 81 | 11.9 |
| 1959 | 105 | 15.6 |
| 1960 | 6 | 0.8 |
| No answer | 23 | 3.4 |
| Total | 679 | 100 |

Sources: Homer Higbee, *The Status of Foreign Student Advising in the United States Universities and Colleges* (East Lansing, MI: Michigan State University, 1961), 3.

Patterns of foreign student advising varied from institution to institution. According to the Higbee Report, a multiple complex of offices served foreign students, and the foreign student advisor usually functioned as a coordinator in many universities. This setup fit well with the administrative structure of decentralization in big universities. Only a few universities had established central offices to provide complete services to foreign students. Of the 679 foreign student advisors interviewed by Higbee, 90 percent reported that they spent only one quarter or less time on foreign student affairs, whereas 50 percent of them were completely responsible for immigration and visa assistance to foreign students. They kept in contact most frequently with the INS and the IIE, and they also kept in regular touch with community organizations and service agencies to develop campus-community activities for foreign students (see Table 6.3 for services). An overwhelming majority of 90 percent of the interviewees mentioned that they did not seek the position but were requested by their universities to take the responsibility of foreign student advising. The ratio of men and women advisors was around 5:2. Those who served as foreign student advisors included regular professors, student deans, academic deans, admissions officers, department heads, vice-presidents, and presidents. More than half of foreign student advisors had no secretarial assistance, and 90 percent had no budget.

With the increase of international educational programs and foreign students in every state, NAFSA began to set up regional offices in the mid-1950s to coordinate educational exchange and foreign student services. Eleven (later 12) regions were established as follows:

1. West Coast—Washington, Oregon, North Idaho, California, Nevada, Arizona, Hawaii, and Alaska (subdivided into two regions later)

2. Rocky Mountain—Montana, Wyoming, South Idaho, Utah, Colorado, New Mexico, Kansas, and Nebraska

## Table 6.3
## Foreign Student Advisors' Services to Foreign Students

| Services | Complete duty | No duty | Shared duty | Not offered |
|---|---|---|---|---|
| Admissions | 20% | 18% | 53% | 1% |
| Registration | 22% | 19% | 48% | 3% |
| Immigration | 53% | 3% | 14% | 17% |
| Employment | 19% | 12% | 47% | 13% |
| Academic Advising | 26% | 13% | 49% | 3% |
| Social Activities | 34% | 8% | 33% | 18% |
| Program for Visitors | 19% | 11% | 32% | 26% |
| Housing | 17% | 22% | 40% | 11% |
| Scholarships | 21% | 16% | 40% | 14% |
| Loans | 16% | 15% | 40% | 19% |
| Discipline | 19% | 14% | 46% | 10% |
| Assist U.S. students | 25% | 16% | 20% | 29% |
| Community contacts | 45% | 6% | 26% | 14% |
| Personal counseling | 49% | 4% | 35% | 3% |
| Info. & correspondence | 54% | 4% | 22% | 10% |
| Orientation | 23% | 8% | 27% | 32% |

Sources: Homer Higbee, *The Status of Foreign Student Advising in the United States Universities and Colleges* (East Lansing, MI: Michigan State University, 1961), 11.

3. Southwestern—Texas, Oklahoma, Arkansas, Louisiana, and Mississippi

4. North Central—North Dakota, South Dakota, Minnesota, Iowa, and Missouri

5. Lake Michigan—Wisconsin, Illinois, and Michigan

6. Bluegrass—Indiana, Ohio, Kentucky, and West Virginia

7. Southeastern—Tennessee, Alabama, Florida, Georgia, North Carolina, South Carolina, and Puerto Rico

8. Capitol—District of Columbia, Virginia, Maryland, and Delaware

9. Pennsylvania—Pennsylvania and south New Jersey

10. Greater New York—New York, north New Jersey, and southeast Connecticut

11. New England—Maine, New Hampshire, Vermont, Massachusetts, Rhode Island, and northeast Connecticut

Regional offices were designed to increase the knowledge of and the sensitivity to the problems of foreign student programs across the country. Every regional office had a voluntary director who took care of regional planning for NAFSA. Regional workshops and conferences were also conducted to improve the communication among advisors. The network of the regions helped NAFSA work out policies at local, regional, and national levels. It also helped NAFSA better coordinate with IIE regional offices.[75]

## UNIVERSITIES AND FOREIGN STUDENT ADVISORS: THEIR RESPONSES TO FOREIGN STUDENT EDUCATION

In 1960, more than 50,000 foreign students were studying in the United States and more than 1,000 American institutions of higher learning had appointed foreign student advisors. How did American universities respond to their new role in world affairs? And how effective was the work of foreign student advising on American campuses? Two commissioned studies, the Higbee Report and the Morrill Report, aimed to find out the answers. In 1958, NAFSA proposed a thorough investigation of the status of foreign student advisors and their services after 10 years of "struggle to establish the administrative means to handle" the rapidly rising population of foreign students and scholars. With a grant from the Dean Langmuir Foundation, the study was carried out independently by the Institute of Research on Overseas Programs at Michigan State University, with Homer Higbee as the principal investigator. The findings, known as the Higbee Report, revealed that universities in general had been "superficially positive" in efforts to assist the U.S. government to achieve its Cold War foreign policy objectives through exchange programs. The Mutual Security Act had defined government objectives of exchange programs "to improve the level of technical and economic strength in developing countries so that they can effectively resist communism...Increase in world understanding is a by-product...Programs conducted by the Department of State...have as their broad objectives better understanding abroad of United States policies and institutions."[76] Higbee argued, "Governmental goals are well known to most universities and colleges, yet indecision about how and to what extent these goals are consonant with the [education] institutions' domestic goals has resulted in half-hearted, neutral, or negative measures. Such action is most frequently manifested in administrative form which tends to emphasize housekeeping services rather than programmatic concepts."[77] These attitudes fundamentally shaped universities' work toward educational exchange programs. Acceptance of foreign students appeared to be the only significant participation of most colleges and universities in the Cold War cultural diplomacy and propaganda to win the hearts and minds of "future world leaders."

American universities had different views of foreign student education. Some universities held dearly to the classical concept of cross-cultural education—the rounding out of the formal education of individuals, which Higbee interpreted as evidence of universities "suffering a 'cultural lag'"; other universities viewed their role "almost identical to that of the Department of State" in exchange programs. Although universities were encouraged to regard foreign student programs as contributions to the achievement of U.S. foreign policy during the Cold War and to the progress of developing countries, most educators thought that the primary objective of exchange programs should be educational. To them, "technical development, social and economic changes, better relations between nations are essentially by-products, although they represent legitimate and compelling goals in themselves."[78]

University presidents tended to view foreign student education in the context of broad academic goals of their own institutions. As American universities were highly individualistic, their own missions and educational tasks fundamentally shaped the educational objectives of each institution. The president of a state university with 90 percent of its graduates remaining in the state to earn a living would react quite differently than the president of a private university whose graduates dispersed all over the country or the world for their careers. One president of a state university frankly rejected foreign student education, believing that foreign students "do not fit in well here, and do not contribute to our educational objectives."[79] The attitudes of university officials were one of the important factors that determined the direction and vigor of foreign student programs. The Higbee Report demonstrated that the involvement of American universities in international education "did not take place quickly, evenly, or always with complete planning." Few universities had systematically considered their role in international education. University presidents seldom paid attention to the role of foreign student advisors in terms of the educational mission of the institutions. In fact, they worried about those foreign students who entered the universities without sufficient financial resources. They were also concerned about their lack of language proficiency, which they believed "created a burden for the institution" to provide language training and a burden for the professor and the student. Although faculty members usually showed little interest in the overall foreign student programs, they were sincerely interested in the academic well being of individual foreign students.[80]

Corresponding to the generally indecisive attitudes of university leaders toward foreign student programs and to the part-time nature of foreign student advising, quite a number of the foreign student advisors thought that the field had little or no career potential. They criticized NAFSA for setting up standards "too low from the intellectual point of view" and with "far too much emphasis on community relations and too little on academic interests." Some advisors thought that the foreign students' "program is shallow and of limited usefulness in developing and enriching the individual Foreign Student Adviser." In addition, "The Association [NAFSA] has been run too long by the original members of the organization, who have been unable to re-orient themselves to broader objectives commensurate with the expanded role foreign students play in the total involvement in international education."[81] There were positive comments about NAFSA, however, especially from foreign student advisors at small colleges who found NAFSA publications of Foreign Student Advisor Handbooks particularly useful in dealing with immigration and visa issues. Foreign student advisors also pointed out that the professional preparation of future advisors should be rooted in liberal arts curriculum, behavioral sciences, language training, and counseling training.[82]

In fact, the greater the involvement of an institution in international education, the clearer the role of foreign student advising was. Universities with a long history of educating foreign students usually had a clearly defined role for foreign student advisors. These were the well-known universities with emphasis on graduate studies and tended to be conservative on differentiating foreign students from American students. Most universities and colleges, however, lacked a clear understanding of whether foreign students should be treated differently from American students, and if differentiation was desirable, along what lines and why. But the tendency to view international education as an American contribution to the world had resulted in a patronizing attitude toward foreign students on many American campuses. Foreign students from developing countries emphatically pointed out this situation.

Concerned with the fact that foreign student advisors were not given high-level academic or administrative status on campuses, Higbee recommended—among other things—that foreign student advisors should be an integral part of the international activity team at their institutions. They should be kept advised of the total range of international educational activities in order to see the foreign student program in relation to other programs, such as international studies and area studies. He challenged NAFSA "to bring research findings to action stage and garner support from appropriate places to effect change." Although NAFSA had brought standards to the operations of foreign student programs, it was criticized for having narrowed its attention basically to foreign students and service-oriented activities and for failing to move into broader areas of international education and exchange.[83] In the 1950s, NAFSA professionalized the practice of foreign student advising based on the concepts of human service developed by the YMCA-affiliated CFRFS in the early decades of the century. But in the 1960s, NAFSA adopted the recommendations from foreign student advisors and emphasized professional training in administrative and academic qualifications.

The Ford Foundation, at the request of the State Department, sponsored in the late 1950s a study on the role of American universities in world affairs. An independent committee comprised of leaders of universities, foundations, businesses, and the U.S. government officials conducted the study. J.L. Morrill, former president of the University of Minnesota, chaired the committee. The study examined what American universities did to play their role in world affairs, especially in the efforts "to bring knowledge of other peoples into the mainstream of higher education for Americans, and to help educate the leaders and help strengthen the educational institutions of newly developing nations."[84] The findings of the study, published in the book *The University and World Affairs* (widely known as the Morrill Report),[85] showed that universities' responses to their role in international affairs were "largely sporadic and unplanned." International educational programs were not adequately integrated and coordinated.

One of the distinctions of the Morrill Report was its concern with how American higher education incorporated a knowledge of other societies in the mainstream curriculum. Since the Smith-Mundt Act, the government rhetoric of international exchange had been stressing the importance of other countries to understand and appreciate American culture and institutions. The IIE and NAFSA, functioning as the extensive cultural apparatus of the state machine, had been pushing universities in this direction with the major concern of creating a favorable image of America among foreign students and visitors. The Morrill Report demonstrated from a different perspective the desire of the private sector especially to emphasize as well the importance for Americans to learn about the world beyond the United States when the country was engaged in a worldwide cultural expansion.

The Morrill Report recommended that international studies and research programs be integrated as a permanent dimension of American higher education and that special educational programs be developed to meet the needs of foreign students and to provide assistance to foreign educational institutions. In terms of government and university relations in the field of international educational activities, the Morrill Report pointed out that "universities cannot be expected to serve as mere agents of government...They must be granted autonomy and long-term assurance of adequate financing."[86] The report also urged the improvement of cooperation and coordination among universities, national and state governments, foundations, and other private enterprises.

## ESTABLISHING INTERNATIONAL EDUCATION OFFICES

The Higbee and Morrill Reports had a far-reaching impact on international education and foreign student programs in the 1960s. Widely distributed to college and university libraries, educational leaders, foreign student advisors, and heads of interested organizations, the two reports pushed colleges and universities to re-examine their international programs, which stimulated new efforts to integrate campus international activities and to upgrade foreign student programs by strengthening the office of the foreign student advisor. It was acknowledged that foreign student advising should be supported with both staff and budget through the appropriation of institutional funds and matching grants from the federal government for counseling, orientation, language proficiency, and so on.[87]

The Ford Foundation provided NAFSA with another five-year grant of $150,000 in 1961 to support the expansion of the role of foreign student advisors and the research on international education. The Ford Foundation was particularly interested in the development of a centralized International Education Office (sometimes called the Office for Foreign Student Affairs) on individual campuses. In emphasizing the importance of a national movement to push for the establishment of International Education Offices, the Ford Foundation indicated that a substantial sum of the grant should be devoted to the encouragement of such an office. It also hoped that NAFSA would use a sizable portion of the grant to advance "certain crucial developmental areas such as regional conferences and workshops, professional training of foreign student advisers, publications, and research."[88]

IIE supported the Ford Foundation guideline and proposed a comprehensive service for both sponsored and non-sponsored foreign students, including overseas information, language training, orientation, counseling, employment, and follow-up programs after the students' return. The suggestion to include all foreign students for the same services was made at a time when the Soviet Union increased its competition with the United States in educating foreign students to extend its influence on the future leaders of other countries. Integrating all foreign students in American educational and social services, hence, was directly linked with the service of American national interest in the Cold War.

International education received a boost with new laws and presidential initiatives during the Kennedy administration. The Fulbright-Hays Act of 1961 authorized broader exchange programs and "restored international educational and cultural exchange programs as a recognized area of our official foreign relations, parallel with overseas information programs, technical assistance, and other programs."[89] The new law further encouraged the developments of international education and foreign student advising on American campuses. Congress increased appropriations for international educational and cultural exchanges. The State Department began to provide NAFSA with grants for the Field Service Program, which primarily focused on issues of foreign student advising. Thus, a new national effort to establish the Office of International Education was set in motion on American campuses in the early 1960s. NAFSA, the IIE, and the State Department urged universities to consolidate campus international activities and strengthen the organization of international educational services. In the new enthusiasm to integrate international education and foreign student programs, the Office of Foreign Student Advisors was gradually changed to the Office of International Education.

## EVALUATING EDUCATIONAL EXCHANGE

Various assessment surveys of educational exchange were conducted in the 1950s under the auspices of both public and private agencies to estimate the "benefits" of foreign student education. The studies aimed "to test the impact of our system upon these visitors" and to assess the effectiveness of exchange programs in meeting their stated objectives. The surveys focused on the impact of American professional training on foreign students and the impact of those students on American classrooms and American society.

In 1951, the Fund for Adult Education sponsored a study of the returned students of Western Europe to evaluate the students' experiences in the United States under the premise that the students were "potential advocates of [the] American way of life." To the surprise of the sponsor, student responses challenged the premise. Many returnees pointed out that American society had strong isolationist sentiments and that Americans did not pay much attention to their various ethnic groups "who could be so useful for the United States to know any foreign country they came from." They also indicated that their experiences in the United States were short and limited, with much of the one-year exchange spent on campuses. Particularly, they were disappointed with the International Houses they lived in because the nationality cliques in these residential centers hindered the development of international friendships. They suggested that more dining rooms and social halls be built and that foreign students be located in student dormitories so that they had more opportunities to mingle with Americans.[90] Although the findings of the survey indicated serious problems in many areas, the student criticism nevertheless provided useful insight for the improvement of programs.

Another survey was conducted by the U.S. Advisory Commission on Educational Exchange of the Department of State in March 1953 on the various aspects of the International Educational Exchange Service (IES). Two hundred and seventeen academic institutions, along with 107 other institutions and business organizations, responded. Ninety percent of the respondents felt that the program was worthwhile and that it did an effective job in creating international understanding and friendship for the United States. But many respondents called for the improvement of coordination between the government and private agencies. Educational institutions in particular wanted the government to clearly define the goals of educational exchange. They pointed out that unclear objectives of the exchange programs had resulted in a movement without much achievement of purpose. They emphasized that exchange programs should be made flexible enough to enable students to complete their educational objectives, as in the case of Fulbright scholars who wished to continue their study for a degree after their tenure of Fulbright scholarship expired. In support of these suggestions, NAFSA recommended that Fulbright scholars should be allowed to secure an exchange alien visa and be permitted to transfer from the State Department to university sponsorship. NAFSA emphasized that the student's interest was in the university and that "the controls set up by IIE [the administering agency for Fulbright programs] are to him [the student] an irrelevant and annoying intrusion." NAFSA argued that such controls encouraged disputes between the exchange student and the campus advisor. If such a transfer was permitted, all requests for an extension of stay should come from the local campus, which should "relieve IIE of annoying and time-consuming decisions." This change would make the foreign student advisor the key person responsible for the exchange programs and not a mere advocate for the IIE and the State Department. The aim of NAFSA's suggestions was to simplify the procedure and to make foreign student programs efficient.[91]

At the same time, foreign student advisors also made evaluations of the exchange programs and the change of foreign students' attitudes toward the United States between their arrival in and their departure from this country. The evaluations indicated that students' experiences varied from campus to campus, although many foreign students faced similar problems. Small colleges and big universities handled administrative services and programs differently. Faculty members at small colleges tended to be more involved in foreign student programs than those in big universities. Large universities additionally had internal communication problems, which made the advising of foreign students easily fall into a bureaucratic routine. Foreign students at smaller colleges tended to have a more positive experience of the American education system and society than those at big universities.[92]

Foreign student advisors and university officials generally believed that "foreign students contribute to the broad educational objectives of universities through creating a cosmopolitan atmosphere by offering American students a cross-cultural experience, and advancing better relations and understanding between Americans and foreigners." These assumptions, however, contrasted with "the feelings of foreign students that, on the whole, American students have a limited interest in learning about foreign countries and cultures."[93] For instance, the majority of foreign students (90 percent) were willing to teach American colleagues about their home countries, but half of them found that American students showed little or no interest in their countries. There were variations, though, regarding different cultures. Students from Europe and Asia found American students interested in their countries and cultures, but those from Latin America, the Middle East, and Africa found Americans least interested in their cultures. University officials admitted that international understanding did not automatically occur and that not much cross-cultural contact was taking place among foreign and American students.[94]

In addition to program evaluations, scholarly research was undertaken to examine the role of universities in international affairs and foreign student education. The Carnegie Endowment for International Peace, for example, initiated in 1950 a series on Studies in Universities and World Affairs, which resulted in several books ranging from socio-anthropological studies to political science and policy analysis.[95] Those studies demonstrated that international education and foreign students had become a prominent subject of research, where psychological and cultural analyses were broadly applied in order to produce "a scientific approach" to educating foreign students. One of the influential works was Cora Du Bois's *Foreign Students and Higher Education in the United States* (1956). Du Bois drew upon the data collected by the Social Science Research Council and analyzed foreign student experiences in America with the insights of anthropology and psychology. She addressed foreign students as social-psychological entities, and her analysis of their cross-cultural experiences resulted in the finding of the U-curve phenomenon. That is, foreign students often went through a process of favorable-unfavorable-favorable experience toward the United States, depending on the length of their stay. Her findings paralleled with that of CFRFS's surveys, in which foreign students mentioned that their first three to four months were the most difficult adjustment. They felt lonely and did not receive much help. Sometimes their loneliness continued for the whole year of the exchange. The U-curve theory was supposed to help international educators improve their services and programs, but few follow-up studies seemed to indicate any major changes. In fact, foreign student advisors pointed out that research on educational exchange had limited usefulness for two reasons: 1) "it is too general to offer much assistance on case by case problems," and 2) "it is often written in technical terms that it is unintelligible to the non-social science trained person."[96]

Another major study of the cross-cultural experiences of foreign students was reported in *Attitudes and Social Relations of Foreign Students in the United States* by Claire Selltiz and her associates under the auspices of the Social Science Research Council. The State Department showed support and encouragement for the project while big foundations such as the Carnegie Corporation, the Ford Foundation, and the Rockefeller Foundation provided the grants. This study relied heavily on personal interviews and questionnaires. Using the concept of inter-group relations, the study sought to provide a comprehensive examination of the effects of cross-cultural experience of foreign students and to give policy guidance for the improvement of exchange programs. After years of collecting and analyzing data, the investigators presented their findings with no definite conclusions. The data were full of contradictions and inconsistencies, which failed to generate convincing argument and adequate policy recommendations.

One critic pointed out that the concept of inter-group relations taken from traditional social science research was not appropriate for studying the experiences of foreign students, whose norms and expectations were defined by their own cultures.[97] Equally problematic was the lack of a serious analysis of how racial discrimination in American society had shaped the experience of foreign students. The survey asked foreign students about their opinion on race relations in America but failed to examine how foreign students' lives were directly affected by racial prejudices. In contrast, the CFRFS' surveys from the 1910s through the 1950s had demonstrated that "racial discrimination has shocked them [foreign students] deeply," and they personally experienced racial discrimination in American society. In the 1952–1953 surveys, CFRFS indicated that in postwar America the racial problem was still as much a barrier to true understanding between Americans and non-white foreign students as it had been before the war. A student from the Bahamas said, "My most embarrassing moment was when I was refused a hair-cut at a barber shop." An Indian student observed with deep pessimism: "I am from India, and I believe there is no possibility to promote understanding between Asians and Americans for reasons too unpleasant for discussion. I have been led to this belief during my stay in this country through personal experiences." A Norwegian student wrote: "I have no unpleasant experiences as a foreigner in the U.S., but my colored and Indian friends have had their trouble due to racial prejudice...It is bad these students get unfavorable impressions of the United States." Some students commented that "American people have a sort of curtain, though invisible. They are friendly, but not real friends."[98]

But foreign students unanimously endorsed services such as immigration and visa facilitation, port-of-entry reception, housing, loans, and employment. They considered these services vital for their survival in America. Some students even recommended that academic advising should be part of the adjustment to university life and that a special introductory orientation course should be established. Students from Latin America, Asia, and Africa thought that universities should actively help them establish contact with Americans and create programs to facilitate social contact. European students generally found it easy to have social contacts on American campuses while students from Latin America, Asia, and Africa encountered much difficulty in this effort.[99]

In conclusion, the Ford Foundation's support to the national organizations of the IIE, NAFSA, and CFRFS not only strengthened their operations and the quality of exchange services, but also relieved the U.S. government of the financial and administrative pressures in the expansion of educational exchange. Without the Ford Foundation grants, the IIE could not have improved its programs and services to government-sponsored exchanges, nor could NAFSA have carried out programs aimed at standardizing the professional criteria of foreign student advisors. In cooperation with the IIE and the State Department, NAFSA pushed for the nationwide movement of establishing International Education Offices on individual campuses in the 1960s. These developments shaped the national practices and programs of educational exchange and helped build a national bureaucratic structure of international exchange administration. By strengthening the IIE and NAFSA, the Ford Foundation helped build a more effective national apparatus to handle the exchange and foreign student affairs. The accomplishments of these organizations, in return, contributed to the achievement of the goals of the Ford Foundation's international exchange programs.

The financial power of the Ford Foundation was crucial to the strengthening of educational exchange services and the development of the new profession of international education. The Cold War had a direct impact on shaping the scope and size of the foundation's exchange programs. The Ford Foundation made it clear that it did not support exchange programs merely "to exhibit good will to other countries or to stimulate good will for this country abroad" but to achieve certain goals of world peace interpreted from the foundation's standpoint.[100] In light of this policy, the Ford Foundation defined the needs of other countries and attempted to impose its own agenda on those countries with which it had developed exchange programs. The special relationship that the Ford Foundation developed with the State Department and the IIE enabled it to play a unique role in the Cold War cultural diplomacy. An emphasis on the unilateral approach of exporting American cultural and political values was formulated and implemented through educational exchange in the Cold War propaganda competition with the Soviet Union. This unilateral emphasis not only undermined the true meaning of international understanding, but also institutionalized the practice of expecting others to appreciate American values and ways of life while ignoring the equally important element of understanding others, although most educators attempted to bring the latter back in the full spectrum of educational exchange. Moreover, the disconnection between educational exchange and international/area studies testified this divergent contention within the field of international education. Much effort was made to strengthen national exchange services only for the purpose of effectively creating a more favorable impression of the United States among the foreign exchange scholars, students, and trainees. In order to achieve the utmost effect of shaping a pro-American public opinion in other countries, "scientific methods" were sought in selecting candidates for exchange. Educational exchange was used as a sales pitch to project the American system. "International understanding" remained a watchword for the rhetoric of educational exchange, but the implications had changed in the Cold War. Educational exchange became a venue in the dynamic cultural expansion of America.

The institutional growth of NAFSA as the leading professional organization of international educators demonstrated the maturity of a new profession in postwar America. In cooperating with the government to expand educational exchange and foreign student programs, NAFSA made frequent recommendations to help shape government policies and procedures regarding foreign students and scholars. Although program evaluations indicated that the political investment in these cultural programs—educational exchanges—did not generate as high returns as expected, a fundamental change, indeed, had occurred with the construction of a national administrative infrastructure for international education.

In the national movement of expanding international education, American universities responded in very different manners to the "top-down" efforts at "professionalizing" services of educational exchange and foreign student programs. In the 1950s, some universities appointed full-time advisors to handle foreign student affairs, but most others had an appointee ex officio spending only a quarter of his or her time on foreign students. The major problem with this "half-hearted" attitude of university administrators toward foreign student programs lay in the disconnection between the institution's educational mission and the objectives of foreign student programs. The foreign policy objectives of exchange programs appeared to have little value to the domestically oriented university education. Furthermore, foreign student education, which could contribute to international and areas studies that were developing on many campuses in the 1950s and 1960s, was not integrated with these programs. Therefore, foreign students appeared to be of little asset to American educational institutions.

## NOTES

1. Those universities included Columbia, Harvard, Yale, Princeton, Vanderbilt, Johns Hopkins, Tulane, Pennsylvania, North Carolina, Michigan, Minnesota, Texas, Wisconsin, Northwestern, and Washington. See Robert A. McCaughey, *International Studies and Academic Enterprise: A Chapter in the Enclosure of American Learning* (New York: Columbia University Press, 1984).

2. International Education is a term used broadly to include any educational activity with an international dimension, especially educational exchange, foreign student education, and international studies and areas studies.

3. *The Ford Foundation Annual Report for 1951* (New York: The Ford Foundation, 1951).

4. "Scope and Content Note," The Office of the President Papers of H. Rowan Gaither, n.d., Ford Foundation Archives.

5. Memo to Carl Spaeth from Dyke Brown, "The Foundation's Exchange of Persons Program and the Institute of International Education," 6 March 1952, 2, Ford Foundation Archives, Report #003325.

6. Waldemar A. Nielsen, *The Big Foundations* (New York: Columbia University Press, 1972), 81; Eric Thomas Chester, *Covert Network* (Armonk, NY: M. E. Sharpe, 1995), 43–44.

7. *The Ford Foundation Annual Report for 1951*.

8. Volker R. Berghahn, *America and the Intellectual Cold Wars in Europe* (Princeton, NJ: Princeton University Press, 2001), 144.

9. Memo to Carl Spaeth from Dyke Brown, "The Foundation's Exchange of Persons Program," 6 March 1952, 7–9; Melvin Fox, *Oral History,* 17, Ford Foundation Archives.

10. Memo to Carl Spaeth from Dyke Brown, "The Foundation's Exchange of Persons Program," 6 March 1952, 9.

11. Memo to Programs Officers from Clarence Faust, "Exchange of Persons," 17 January 1961, 1, Henry Herald Papers, box 3, folder 42, Ford Foundation Archives.

12. Memo to Carl Spaeth from Dyke Brown, "The Foundation's Exchange of Persons Program," 6 March 1952, 3–4; memo to Stanley T. Gordon from Melvin J. Fox, "Meeting with State Department on September 24," 26 September 1951, 1, Ford Foundation Archives, PA51–29.

13. Minutes of the Social Science Research Council conference on "Evaluation of International Student Exchange," October 6, 1951, Ford Foundation Archives, Report #003325.

14. Memo to Carl Spaeth from Dyke Brown, "The Foundation's Exchange of Persons Program," 6 March 1952, 5.

15. Ibid.

16. Minutes of the Social Science Research Council Conference on "Evolution of International Student Exchanges," 6 October 1951, Ford Foundation Archives, Report #003325.

17. Memo to Carl Spaeth from Dyke Brown, "The Foundation's Exchange of Persons Program," 6 March 1952, 4–7.

18. Letter to Chester Davis, from William C. Johnstone, Jr., 27 July 1951, Ford Foundation Archives, PA51–29.

19. Ibid.

20. The Ford Foundation to the IIE, "Relationships and Procedures Governing Ford Foundation Exchange of Persons Activities," 27 February 1951, 3, Ford Foundation Archives, PA51–29.

21. Chester Davis, "Exchange of Persons," April 1953, 12, Ford Foundation Archives, Report #010590.

22. Ibid., 15.

23. The Ford Foundation to the IIE, "Relationships and Procedures Governing Ford Foundation Exchange of Persons Activities," 27 February 1951, 2, Ford Foundation Archives, PA51–29.

24. Memo to Chester Davis from Kenneth Holland, "General Procedures for Review of Projects in International Exchange of Persons for the Ford Foundation," 5 November 1951, 2, Ford Foundation Archives, PA51–29.

25. Memo to Chester Davis from William C. Johnstone, 27 February 1951, 5–6, Ford Foundation Archives, PA51–29.

26. Ibid.

27. The Ford Foundation to the IIE, "Relationships and Procedures Governing Ford Foundation Exchange of Persons Activities," 27 February 1951, 9, Ford Foundation Archives, PA51–29.

28. Memo to Chester Davis from Bernard Gladieux, "State Department Comments on Present Review Procedures," 18 January 1952, Ford Foundation Archives, PA51–29.

29. Memo to Bernard Gladieux from Melvin Fox, "IIE Exchange Persons Activities," 6 March 1952, 4, Ford Foundation Archives, PA51–29.

30. Ibid., 5.

31. See the Tyler Report and the management study report discussed later in this chapter.

32. The Ford Foundation to the IIE, "Relationships and Procedures Governing Ford Foundation Exchange of Person Activities," 27 February 1951, 3–9.

33. Chester Davis, "Exchange of Persons," April 1953, 6.

34. Memo to Chester Davis from William C. Johnstone, 27 February 1951, 4–5.

35. Chester Davis, "Exchange of Persons," April 1953, 4–6.

36. Ibid., 5.

37. In 1951, the Ford Foundation appropriated a total of $857,447 for the exchange of persons projects, of which $459,565 (54 percent) was earmarked as grants to the IIE, NAFSA, and CFRFS to strengthen national service facilities. See Chester Davis, "Exchange of Persons," April 1953, 8.

38. "Excerpt," 4 February 1952, Ford Foundation Archives, PA51–293.

39. Memo to Chester Davis from William Johnstone, 27 February 1951, 3–4, Ford Foundation Archives, PA51–29.

40. Memo to A. S. Anderson from Benjamin Schmoker, 14 April 1952, folder titled "Reports 1942–54," CFRFS #12, YMCA Archives. Schmoker served as NAFSA secretary from 1950–1955 until he became NAFSA president in 1955 and held that position for two years.

41. The foundations included the Marion R. Ascoli Fund, the Max Ascoli Fund, the Carnegie Corporation of New York, the Carnegie Endowment for International Peace, the Columbia Foundation, the Commonwealth Fund, the Cleveland H. Dodge Foundation, the Grant Foundation, Independent Aid, the Henry Janssen Foundation, the Phelps-Stokes Fund, the Reader's Digest Foundation, the Rockefeller Foundation, the Felix M. and Frieda Shiff Warburg Foundation, and the Wyomissing Foundation. See "IIE Thirty-First Annual Report" December 1950, 63.

42. Memo to B. L. Gladieux from Chester Davis, "Institute of International Education," 27 April 1951, Ford Foundation Archives, R-0411, PA51–29; memo to R. Hutchins from the IIE, "Draft for Annual Report," 17 December 1951, Ford Foundation Archives, PA51–29.

43. International Programs, International Training and Research, "Grant Summary: Appropriation for Exchange Strengthening," 1956, 2, Ford Foundation Archives, PA54–63; Docket, "Background Materials Regarding Committee on Friendly Relations among Foreign Students," trustee meeting, 18–19 June 1956, Ford Foundation Archives, PA54–63.

44. "Background Materials Regarding Committee on Friendly Relations," 18–19 June 1956, Ford Foundation Archives, PA54–63.

45. *The Unofficial Ambassadors*, annual report of the Committee on Friendly Relations Among Foreign Students (1953), 3–4.

46. Melvin Fox, "Summary Reports on Exchange of Persons Projects Supported by the Ford Foundation," 18 February 1953, 8–8b, Ford Foundation Archives, Report #001272.

47. NAFSA moved out of the IIE building into the headquarters of CFRFS at 291 Broadway, New York, in 1952 and then established its office at New York University in 1954 and in International House New York in 1958. Finally, as its work with the U.S. government increased dramatically, NAFSA moved its headquarters to Washington, D.C. in 1966.

48. NAFSA Executive Committee Minutes, 4–6 June 1952, folder titled "Reports 1942–1954," CFRFS box #12, YMCA Archives.

49. Memo to Carl Spaeth from Melvin Fox, "Background Notes on Exchange Recommendations in June Docket," 23 June 1953, 1, Ford Foundation archives, PA53–130.

50. Ibid., 2.

51. Memo to Carl Spaeth from Melvin Fox, 13 August 1952, 3, Ford Foundation Archives, PA52–177.

52. Memo to Bernard Gladieux from Melvin Fox, 30 April 1952, 1, Ford Foundation Archives, PA51–293.

53. Memo to Carl Spaeth from Melvin Fox, 13 August 1952, 5.

54. Memo, New York Inter-Office, n.d., Ford Foundation Archives, PA52–177.

55. Melvin Fox, "Report on Exchange of Persons Activities of the Ford Foundation," January 1953, 3, and Carl Spaeth, "Proposed Study of Exchange of Persons Activities and the Role of the Institute of International Education," 12 June 1952, 3–4, Appendix A, Ford Foundation Archives, Report #001567.

56. "A Preliminary Memorandum to Foundations from the Institute of International Education on the Proposed Implementation of the Recommendations of the Tyler Report," 5 December 1952, 2–6, Ford Foundation Archives, R-0411, PA51–29.

57. Memo to Paul Hoffman from Melvin Fox, "Carnegie Corporation Foundation Meeting on January 22," 21 January 1953, Ford Foundation Archives, R-0411, PA52–103.

58. In the Tyler Report, it was suggested that the regional offices should reorient their services as demonstration centers and regional clearinghouses rather than reception centers for government programs.

59. The series included *Orientation of Foreign Students: Signposts for the Cultural Maze* (1956); *Expanding University Enrollments and the Foreign Student* (1957); *African Students in the United States* (1960); *College and University Programs of Academic Exchange* (1960); and *Foreign Professors and Research Scholars at U.S. Colleges and Universities* (1963).

60. Docket, "Institute of International Education," trustee meeting, 18–19 June 1956, 5–6, Ford Foundation Archives, PA54–63; Docket, "Appropriation for Exchange Strengthening," 19 June 1956, 3–4, Ford Foundation Archives, PA54–63.

61. "Appropriation for Exchange Strengthening," 19 June 1956, 4–5, Ford Foundation Archives, PA54–63.

62. In 1956, the Ford Foundation gave more than $46 million in grants to cover all areas of its programs. More than $7 million of the appropriations were earmarked for fellowship programs and international exchanges of persons. The 10-year grant to the IIE and the five-year grants to NAFSA and CFRFS came out of the $7 million.

63. Memo to the Administrative Board of CFRFS from Benjamin Schmoker, CFRFS box #13, 15 August 1962, 5, folder titled "Reports, 1956–63," YMCA Archives.

64. Memo to McGeorge Bundy et al. from David Bell, "Grant Request—International Division," 17 July 1967, 2, Ford Foundation Archives, PA67–191.

65. Memo to Henry Heald from Clarence Faust, 2 November 1965, 3, Ford Foundation Archives, PA54–64.

66. Ibid., 1–2.

67. A. Noyes, "Note on General Support for the IIE, Grant Series 540-0064," 12 March 1968, Ford Foundation Archives, PA 54–64; memo to McGeorge Bundy et al. from David Bell, "Grant Request—International Division," 17 July 1967, Ford Foundation Archives, PA67–191.

68. Robert L. Blair, "Status of the Foreign Student Adviser," n.d., box 10, file 15, NAFSA Archives; excerpt of NAFSA files, 19–22 June 1949, box 10, file 9, NAFSA Archives.

69. Joe W. Neal to Clarence Linton, 27 June 1949, box 10, file 11, NAFSA Archives.

70. Allen Blaisdell to Clarence Linton, 12 August 1949, box 10, file 11, NAFSA Archives.

71. Blair, "Status of the Foreign Student Adviser."

72. Letters and reports from those universities in NAFSA Association file 1:A, pre-1950 period, NAFSA Archives.

73. *Report of the Conference on International Educational Exchanges* (Denver, CO: April 11–14, 1951).

74. Clarence Linton to Joe Neal, 27 February 1950, NAFSA Association file 1:A, NAFSA Archives.

75. "Regional Plan," NAFSA 1:13; *NAFSA Newsletter* (August 15, 1954), 7; NAFSA proposal to The Dean Langmuir Foundation, 28 July 1958, 1, folder titled "Development Committee, 1958–60: The NAFSA Study," NAFSA Association, files, box #14, NAFSA Archives.

76. Homer Higbee, *The Status of Foreign Student Advising in the United States Universities and Colleges* (East Lansing, MI: Michigan State University, 1961), xii–xiii.

77. Ibid., xii.

78. *Education for One World* (New York: IIE, 1953–1954), 17.

79. Higbee, *The Status of Foreign Student Advising*, 40.

80. Ibid., 42–44.

81. Ibid., 39.

82. Ibid., 40.

83. NAFSA set forth four objectives in its 1948 constitution: 1) to promote the professional preparation, appointment, effectiveness, recognition, and association of foreign student advisors, teachers of ESL, advisers on studying abroad, and others who were concerned with international education; 2) to serve the interests and needs of exchange students, faculty, and visitors; 3) to initiate and execute systematic studies, conferences, and so on; and 4) to aid educational institutions in developing exchange programs and to facilitate communication between these institutions and the national and international agencies involved.

84. *The University and World Affairs* (New York: The Ford Foundation, 1960), 2.

85. There was a follow-up study of the role of colleges in world affairs to supplement the Morrill Report called *The College and World Affairs* (New York: The Ford Foundation, 1964).

86. *The University and World Affairs*, 3–5.

87. Higbee, *The Status of Foreign Student Advising*, vii–viii.

88. *NAFSA Newsletter* (February 1961), 1.

89. J. Manuel Espinosa, *Landmarks in the History of the Cultural Relations Program of the Department of State 1938–1936*, 1976, 10, CU Collections, Department of Special Collections, University of Arkansas Libraries.

90. "Programs Evaluation," NAFSA Association file box #2, NAFSA Archives.

91. Board of Directors Minutes, 13–14 November 1953, exhibit 1, letter to Donald Cook, chief of Youth Activities Division, International Educational Exchange Service, State Department, NAFSA 1:12, NAFSA Archives.

92. *Report of the Conference on International Educational Exchanges* (Congress Hotel, Chicago, IL: March 22–25, 1950), 39; *Report of the Conference on International Educational Exchanges* (Denver, CO: April 11–14, 1951), 60; *Report of the Conference on International Educational Exchanges* (East Lansing, MI: Michigan State College, April 23–26, 1952), 41–42.

93. Higbee, *The Status of Foreign Student Advising*, 30.

94. Ibid., 41–42.

95. The books include *American College Life as Education in World Outlook* (Howard Wilson, 1956); *Foreign Students and Higher Education in the United States* (Cora Du Bois, 1956); *The University, the Citizen, and World Affairs* (Cyril Houle and Charles Nelson, 1956); *Training of Specialists in International Relations* (C. Dale Fuller, 1957); *International Relations in Institutions of Higher Education in the South* (Fred Cole, 1958); *University Research on International Affairs* (John Gange, 1958); *World Affairs and the College Curriculum* (Richard N. Swift, 1959); and *American Higher Education and World Affairs* (Howard Wilson and Florence Wilson, 1963).

96. Higbee, *The Status of Foreign Student Advising*, 40.

97. Jeanne Watson, *American Journal of Sociology* 70 (July–May 1964–1965), 259.

98. 1952–1953 survey, "Everett Stowe folder," CFRFS box #3; "This Is What They Say," *The Unofficial Ambassadors*; "Foreign Students Look at the Campus," summary of a brief opinion survey made in May 1945, folder titled "Reports, 1942–54," CFRFS box #12, YMCA Archives.

99. Higbee, *The Status of Foreign Student Advising*, 25–29.

100. Memo to Carl Spaeth from Dyke Brown, "The Foundation's Exchange of Persons Program," 6 March 1952.

# Chapter 7

## Educational Exchange and National Interest: The Role of the State

Educational exchange and international programs of various studies expanded substantially under the auspices of the U.S. government and private foundations in the 1950s and 1960s. In the course of developing educational, technical, and cultural exchanges, many policy questions arose that generated heated debate within the government and among interested groups of the general public. Congress, governmental departments and agencies, and the White House all showed keen interest in the exchange programs. Laws were passed to support cultural and educational exchanges, but different attitudes toward and contrasting views of exchange activities existed throughout this period. Tensions within the government revealed the clash between isolationist and internationalist views over the function of educational exchange in American foreign relations.

Different beliefs in the usefulness of educational exchange led Congress to fight over the control of federal budgetary allocations for exchange programs. The 1950s witnessed frequent frustration over getting governmental funds to support educational exchange. McCarthyism found educational exchange an easy target of attack in the early 1950s. Moreover, Congressman John J. Rooney, chairman of the House Subcommittee on Appropriations, and Secretary of State John Foster Dulles were not keen on educational exchanges, either. But in the 1960s, new government policies emerged under the leadership of Presidents John F. Kennedy and Lyndon Johnson, which pushed the international education movement to a new height. In 1961, the Fulbright-Hays Act was enacted to consolidate previous educational and cultural exchange legislation and to authorize broader educational and cultural exchange programs. Under this law, Congress appropriated annual funds to support educational exchange and international/area studies. The passage of the International Education Act in 1966 further raised the prospect that the government was about to provide substantial financial support for the expansion of international educational programs. Anticipating funding from the government, American universities and colleges mobilized to expand and consolidate their programs of international education with unprecedented enthusiasm in the mid-1960s. The failure of Congress to appropriate funds in the end, however, brought a discouraging anti-climax to the international education movement in the United States. This chapter concentrates on the role of the state in international education during the 1950s–1960s.

## CONGRESSIONAL BATTLES OVER THE INTERNATIONAL EDUCATION BUDGET IN THE 1950s

In the early 1950s, as part of the "Campaign of Truth," the U.S. government emphasized political propaganda in international educational exchange as a means of combating the new "Communist aggression" seen particularly in the Korean War. Support for aggressive political propaganda came from the operations of Senator Joseph McCarthy's investigating committee, which proclaimed that the overriding threat of Communism "called for the concentration of all efforts and the use of the entire arsenal of psychological weapons against this menace."[1] But the long-term educational and cultural activities that might contribute indirectly to the immediate objectives of the propaganda battle against Communism were accorded little importance. Communism was apprehended in dual dimensions in American politics: the Cold War without and Communist subversion within. For a small group of Americans, this fear had become paranoia—as personified by Joseph McCarthy. They were afraid of cultural exchange with Communist countries. Furthermore, they aggressively attacked educational exchange programs. McCarthy was absolutely against cultural exchange, and he accused the Fulbright Program of bringing Communists and foreign spies into the United States by sponsoring exchanges of professors, teachers, and students. He also charged that the overseas libraries of the United States Information Service were full of books by Communists.[2] Secretary of State John Foster Dulles, showing his ardent anticommunist colors, "ordered books authored by Communists, fellow travelers, et cetera" to be removed from the libraries of American overseas information centers.[3] Bureaucrats gave the broadest interpretation of "et cetera" and tossed out any books considered to be too liberal/leftist—many of which were by well-known journalists and scholars who were not Communists at all. But Senator Fulbright defended educational exchange as "a field in which we have a monopoly because the Iron Curtain nations can't stand examination by outsiders as this country can."[4] At a hearing before the Senate Appropriations Committee, McCarthy and Fulbright thumped tables and yelled at each other, clashing over the budget of student exchange programs.⁵ Although McCarthy and Fulbright held opposite positions on the issue of educational exchange, they both were fighting against Communism—only their approaches were different. McCarthy represented the tradition of isolationism, reinforced by his paranoia of communist subversion in the country, whereas Fulbright represented the tradition of internationalism—confident in the final triumph of American democracy over Communism through international outreach.

The debate over government support for educational exchanges did not end with the McCarthy episode, however. In Congress, there were sharply contrasting views on how much money the government should appropriate for educational exchange. Educational exchange programs were subject to constant budgetary cuts in Congress throughout the 1950s, despite the fact that the program enjoyed widespread public support.⁶ For instance, the National Opinion Research Center showed in a 1951 survey that seven out of 10 Americans knew something about the exchange program and approved the use of government funds to support it.⁷ But the House voted to cut the requested $15 million down to $9 million for educational exchanges in 1954. When the cut was reported, many individuals and organizations protested. Walter Lippmann called the vote of Congress "wanton carelessness." The cut, he said, would "virtually destroy the Smith-Mundt program and will seriously cripple the Fulbright program." He argued that the exchange program was important because it enabled peoples to have direct personal contact across national boundaries, which would "dissolve the effect of the indoctrination of the Iron Curtain."⁸ Favorable testimony and expressions to restore the original amount were also presented by universities and colleges as well as by a wide range of national educational organizations, religious groups, women's organizations, labor organizations, Veterans Committees, Chambers of Commerce, and the National Farmer Union. In addition, Senators Homer E. Capehart, J. William Fulbright, Karl E. Mundt, Edward J. Thye, and Congressman Walter Judd (many were ardent cold warriors) urged the Senate to restore the cut. Moreover, Vice President Richard Nixon, who had made his reputation by fighting Communism, took an unusual action by personally appearing before the Senate to express his support for the continuation of exchange programs. Under such public pressure, the Senate Appropriations Committee approved the full budget of $15 million for fiscal year 1955. This amount, in fact, was approximately the same as that for the 1954 exchange programs.⁹

The next year, the House came back with a more vigorous reduction of the educational exchange budget by cutting down the requested $22 million to $12 million. This reduction of funds meant the elimination of exchanges with 31 countries. Widespread criticism arose of the House's action of limiting the budgetary allocation for educational exchange. Petitions to the Senate were circulated on campuses protesting the House's slash of educational exchanges. Delegates at the NAFSA annual conference on

International Educational Exchanges unanimously voted for the full restoration of the $22 million for exchange programs while reaffirming the strategic importance of educational exchange as a unique instrument of American foreign policy.[10]

The decision of the House of Representatives to reduce the funding for educational exchange was attributed primarily to Congressman John J. Rooney, chairman of the House Subcommittee on Appropriations, and to some of his colleagues, who saw little importance of educational exchange to American foreign policy. Although 16 Congressmen of both parties spoke against the cut and only one defended it on the floor, a motion to restore the original budget failed to muster the necessary majority.[11] This behavior clearly reflected the general dubious attitude of Congress toward educational exchange programs. As chairman of the House Appropriations Subcommittee, Rooney was certainly instrumental and powerful in slashing the budget for exchange programs. Senator Fulbright and other Congressmen attempted on several occasions to talk Rooney into seeing the value of educational exchange for foreign policy purposes, but their efforts had little success. Finally, Fulbright decided to go to Eleanor Roosevelt, who had kept a keen interest in international education, and hoped that she would change Rooney's views. Mrs. Roosevelt wrote Rooney personal letters to emphasize the importance of educational exchanges. But Rooney was not to be persuaded. Disappointed and upset, Mrs. Roosevelt took the issue to the public and openly criticized Rooney in national newspapers for his role in reducing the federal budgetary support for educational exchange.[12]

The State Department, under the leadership of Secretary of State John Foster Dulles, did not fight for the increase of funding for educational exchange, either. On the contrary, the State Department even suggested the reduction of the recommended budget. For instance, in 1956 the Advisory Commission on Educational Exchange recommended $31 million to extend exchange programs in areas of Latin America and Asia, but the State Department presented Congress with a request of only $20 million. The House cut the $20 million down to $18.5 million. Fulbright was very disappointed with the State Department. He wrote Dulles that the budget for the International Cooperation Administration and Information Program had been substantially increased, while in contrast the budget for educational exchange had significantly decreased. Fulbright made clear that he was not happy with the State Department's evaluation of the exchange program and pointed out that the State Department was placing emphasis in the wrong place.[13]

Dulles was not interested in supporting educational exchange, even though the State Department was the authorized government agency to administer the exchange program. When McCarthy attacked educational exchange, Dulles did not take any action to defend the program. Dulles even wanted the entire International Information and Educational Program to be removed from the Department of State. J. L. Morrill, chairman of the U.S. Advisory Commission on Educational Exchange, complained about the "uninterested and reluctant or even hostile State Department" in handling educational exchange and doubted whether the location of the exchange program in the State Department could make it successful.[14] Although Dulles was not supportive of educational exchange, he was shielded from criticism by certain leaders of the Senate Foreign Relations Committee. Meanwhile, there was a disjunction between the public rhetoric and the behind-the-scene politics. While NAFSA, the IIE, and the Ford Foundation were worked up by the State Department to push for a rapid growth of educational exchange in the 1950s, the State Department only submitted a request of $20.8 million for 1959 educational exchange programs. Senators Fulbright and Lyndon B. Johnson strongly recommended an additional increase of $10 million to the requested sum. However, their efforts only resulted in a slight addition with the final amount agreed upon by both Houses at $22.8 million.

## INFORMATION MANAGEMENT AND EDUCATIONAL EXCHANGE IN THE 1950s

The budgetary debate in the 1950s clearly demonstrated that the government had a greater interest in political propaganda than in educational exchange. Such emphasis led to structural changes in the administration of information and educational exchange. In January 1952, the State Department integrated information and educational exchange into one office called International Information Administration (IIA) while eliminating the "Office of Educational Exchange." As the name of the new office suggested, educational exchange disappeared in the administration of information management—or at least was subordinated to information management. This change led to unpopular reactions among educational groups, however, and caused enormous confusion in the entire field of international educational exchange. The U.S. Advisory Commission on Educational Exchange criticized the elimination of educational exchange and recommended that the title of the IIA should be broadened to include the word "education."[15] The issue became so controversial that President Eisenhower had to intervene. In June 1953, President Eisenhower sent Congress a "Reorganization Plan No. 8," which aimed to establish a separate information organization called the United States Information Agency (USIA).[16] The plan separated information (overt propaganda) from education by designating the State Department as the agency responsible for cultural relations and educational exchange and the USIA as the agency responsible for cultural and political information dissemination and propaganda.

The President's decision on the establishment of a new information agency and the retention of educational exchange within the State Department was

influenced by the arguments of different groups. Both Secretary of State
Dulles and the Advisory Commission on Information favored the removal of
the IIA from the State Department. But the question was whether educational exchange should go with information in this transfer. Robert L.
Johnson, head of the IIA, believed that the exchange of persons program was
essential to the entire information operation, and he would like to keep educational exchange with the IIA. Many educators, however, were opposed to
such integration. They found Senator Fulbright their powerful spokesman
when he argued for the separation of educational exchange from information. Fulbright maintained that educational exchange would suffer the risk
of being interpreted as propaganda if closely linked with information activities. He urged that educational exchange should stay within the State
Department, because a permanent government department would provide
the program with continuous and stable support. Fulbright's argument won
the support of a group of senators, including Karl E. Mundt, H. Alexander
Smith, and Bourke B. Hickenlooper. This group sent President Eisenhower
a recommendation in May 1953, urging the separation of educational
exchange from information and keeping educational exchange within the
State Department. In the meantime, the Advisory Commission on
Educational Exchange also advocated the separation of educational exchange
from information.[17]

The President's Reorganization Plan became effective on August 1, 1953
after the approval of Congress. The purpose of establishing separate offices to
manage information and educational exchanges was to achieve the maximum effectiveness of propaganda and educational exchange, respectively.
But in reality, the distinction between educational exchange and information
management did not have any real significant meaning as far as American
foreign policy was concerned, because the cultural/educational officers of the
Foreign Service were made responsible to the USIA by the State Department
and so were the information officers in American embassies.

Despite these setbacks, several developments contributed to the expansion
of educational exchange nonetheless. First, government emphasis on technical assistance abroad gave rise to the multitude of development of educational exchange programs. The International Cooperation Administration
(ICA), which evolved from the Foreign Operations Administration, emphasized the training of foreign technical personnel. The ICA's technical and
defense aid programs involved the sending of American technical personnel
abroad and the training of foreign nationals in the United States. The ICA
relied on American universities to operate these programs. It contracted the
universities to train foreign technical personnel and to send faculty members
abroad as technical specialists. In 1956, the ICA spent $136 million on
training activities and on the exchange of thousands of technical and defense
personnel. Moreover, there was a correlation between foreign student enrollment and participation in foreign aid at American universities. The top 33

universities in foreign student enrollment (42 percent of the total foreign student population) were also most heavily involved in ICA university contracts for foreign aid.[18]

Second, the International Educational Exchange Service (IES) of the State Department also carried out large-scale technical training programs via educational exchange. Almost 80 percent of the foreign students under the IES programs received technical training. Foreign technical trainees were usually older than traditional students. They lacked English proficiency and tended to live in isolation from campus and community life. Given these problems, they obviously needed greater help in order to adjust to their living and studying environments in America. The ICA and the IES worked with NAFSA to improve the cooperation of American universities in providing adequate services to their sponsored exchange students. NAFSA recommended that campus foreign student advisors should be used as coordinators for the ICA and IES programs. It also urged that universities should be flexible "in instruction or curricula for ICA students and trainees without a lowering of academic standards."[19] In addition, NAFSA suggested that a central office should be established to coordinate international exchange and training programs, because many university faculty members were sent abroad as specialists.

In an effort to provide central direction to technical and educational exchanges, a Special Assistant Secretary for Educational and Cultural Relations was appointed in 1958 in the State Department, who was to serve as an "action center" for all concerned governmental agencies and for developing cooperation with the private sector. Educational institutions welcomed the creation of the position of the Special Assistant Secretary. For years, professional organizations such as the American Council on Education, the IIE, and NAFSA had urged the State Department to establish a position that might carry "considerable weight in international relations and with Congress." They expected that the new assistant secretary would provide a means to help achieve a more effective and unified operation of national programs of educational exchange. Also in 1958, the State Department established the Bureau of International Cultural Relations, which was later renamed the Bureau of Educational and Cultural Affairs, to centralize the cultural activities. The creation of the bureau also indicated an increased recognition on the part of the executive branch and Congress of the importance of international cultural and educational exchanges.

Third, various American presidents had shown a strong interest in educational exchange programs, which constituted another important component that contributed to the expansion of educational exchange. During his presidential campaign, Dwight D. Eisenhower had expressed his support for educational exchange: "I firmly believe that educational exchange programs are an important step toward world peace." He added, "It is my personal hope that this activity...will continue to expand in the coming years."[20]

After taking office, President Eisenhower played an active part in promoting international educational exchange and the extension of American educational influence abroad. In 1956, he suggested that U.S. educational leaders should establish "institutions of modern techniques and sciences" in the less developed areas of the world. He also called for more sympathetic understanding among peoples of the world and urged "a voluntary effort in people-to-people partnership" to expand what the government was doing. His instruction to the USIA in 1953 to work toward "the correlation between United States policies and the legitimate aspirations of other peoples of the world" demonstrated the President's emphasis on finding common connections between the United States and other countries. He pointed out, "The purpose of the United States Information Agency shall be to submit evidence to peoples of other nations…that the objectives and policies of the United States are in harmony with" their aspirations for freedom, progress, and peace.[21] More importantly, this emphasis, which no doubt was the precursor of his call for people-to-people partnership, indicated the first major attempt to depart from the unilateral approach of the Smith-Mundt Act that emphasized the understanding of the United States by other countries. In October 1957, a group of foreign students was invited to the President's office to observe "Foreign Student Day." Futhermore, both President Eisenhower and Vice President Nixon participated in the IIE's Conference on the Exchange of Persons in January 1959 in Washington, D.C. "to promote world progress through educational exchange."[22]

In 1956, a People-to-People Program was launched with President Eisenhower's initiative. The program aimed to create mutual understanding between different peoples through the direct communications of local groups across national boundaries. After the President made a speech at Baylor University in May 1956, calling for a people-to-people exchange, he invited to the White House in September that year scores of American business leaders, artists, writers, journalists, educators, sports stars, and entertainers to set forth a people-to-people international program. Literally, people of all walks of life in America were encouraged to create channels of international communications and friendship. Towns and cities were urged to establish sisterhood relations with their counterparts in other parts of the world, and individual Americans were asked to write letters to individuals in foreign countries and to offer home and community hospitality to visiting foreigners in the United States. Even Americans traveling abroad were given pamphlets that told them to make a friend on this trip.[23] This mass movement of international outreach to popularize America abroad, however, appeared to be a short-lived fanfare because of limited funding and a lack of organizational mechanisms. Still, the program continued with steady, if slow, growth. In 1961, the program changed into People to People International and since then it has developed hundreds of chapters in local communities across the globe to bring international relations to community action for world peace and understanding.[24]

Cultural and educational exchanges with the Soviet Union and Eastern European countries were also started in the spirit of people's diplomacy. In 1957, a group of scholars of the Comparative Education Society, "eager to promote international understanding through comparative studies of education and to thaw the Cold War at governmental and local levels," started a non-governmental exchange with the Soviet Union.[25] Private efforts eventually led to the signing of government agreements on cultural exchange between the United States and the Soviet Union. At the same time, a group of universities—in order to increase knowledge about the Soviet Union— formed the Inter-University Committee on Travel Grants to facilitate scholarly activities with the Soviet Union.[26] The Inter-University Committee, which received financial support from sources such as philanthropic foundations, the government, and university funds, dealt directly with the Soviet Ministry of Higher Education for exchanges of scholars and students. The opening of US-USSR educational exchange also led to the U.S. educational exchange with Eastern Europe. The United States developed educational exchanges with Romania, Czechoslovakia, and other Soviet Bloc countries after exchange agreements were signed in the same fashion as that of the US-USSR agreement.[27]

## DEMANDS FOR NEW POLICIES OF INTERNATIONAL EDUCATION

Since the late 1950s, the newly independent countries of Asia and Africa began to emerge as a "power bloc" in the United Nations. Less developed as they were in an economic sense, these largely non-Western, non-Christian, and non-Caucasian societies nonetheless shifted the political maneuver on the world stage. Their increasing demand for educational assistance and economic development provided a new opportunity for the superpowers to compete against each other to extend their spheres of influence, thus dramatically changing the international scene of educational exchange.[28]

The Soviet Union expanded educational exchanges in the late 1950s, especially with the newly independent countries in Asia and Africa. In their efforts at nation building, the developing countries emphasized education as a key to achieving economic, political, and social advancement in the modern world. Both the United States and the Soviet Union were eager to offer the newly independent nations educational resources and political ideologies to expand their respective dominance in the Cold War world. In 1958, Albert Sims, vice president of the IIE, traveled to Southeast Asia and reported: "Southeast Asia in general was exposed to a great abundance of scholarship offerings, mostly from Red China and the Soviet Union, where one could practically write his own ticket." He noted that many Asian countries forbade their nationals from accepting foreign scholarships without the authorization of their own governments. As a counter-attraction to communist educational exchange in that area, the International Cooperation Administration offered 7,000 student scholarships for secondary and higher educational exchanges. The IIE also set up more programs in Taiwan and Hong Kong to strengthen the U.S. influence in the Far East.[29] In the ideological battle against the Communist bloc, American universities were called upon to play a prominent and creative role in helping the government meet the challenge. In this context, educational exchanges were emphasized as vital arteries of the international activity of the American academic community. In addition to Asia, many American educators were sent to Africa to help build local communities. Their participation in local peoples' lives was so extensive in converting Africans from a traditional lifestyle to a modern American lifestyle that they began to call themselves "educationaries" as compared to "missionaries" in the earlier decades.

Interestingly, the competition between the Soviet Union and the United States in international educational exchanges enhanced the bargaining power of the newly independent nations in seeking educational aid from the superpowers. Moreover, two-thirds of the foreign students in the United States came from developing countries. The majority of them did not come on government exchange programs, however. Those students, because of their non-sponsored status, did not enjoy many of the services available to the sponsored students in American society and the American academic system. They were nonetheless future leaders in many professions in their own countries. How these students fared in the United States would have a significant impact on U.S. international relations. In response to these challenges, the U.S. government began to make important changes in international education policies.

## THE KENNEDY ADMINISTRATION—NEW DIRECTIONS OF INTERNATIONAL EDUCATION

In 1960, the young and resourceful John F. Kennedy was elected President of the United States. Kennedy continued the White House tradition of supporting educational exchange, only with greater enthusiasm and more action. During his presidency, the U.S. government made major policy changes in the field of international educational exchange.

### Presidential Initiatives

John F. Kennedy organized a Task Force on International Educational Exchanges even before he moved into the Oval Office. In the fall of 1960, Kennedy's staff asked NAFSA to set up a task force on international education with James Davis, NAFSA president, as chairman. "We were given a broad assignment to explore the entire subject of the international exchange of persons and to recommend needed changes which could be accomplished by regulations and by legislation. We had to complete the job in about seven weeks, prior to the January 20 inaugural," said Davis.[30]

The task force received no funding from the government, and Davis had to search many places for financial support. After several fruitless efforts, he finally secured a small grant from the Creole Foundation, which enabled the task force to start operating. Shortly afterwards, when Davis was attending an IIE conference in San Francisco, he found himself suddenly surrounded by officials of various key organizations and agencies, such as the Bureau of Educational and Cultural Affairs of the State Department, the International Cooperation Administration (later the Administration of International Development, or AID), the Pan American Union, and the IIE. They had learned about his mission as head of the Task Force for the President. Anticipating that the task force would effect new administrative and legislative proposals regarding international educational exchange programs, these groups asked Davis to emphasize their services in the forthcoming report of the task force.[31] When Davis came back to Washington, all doors were open to him and his team. The new enthusiasm demonstrated by governmental and non-governmental agencies was overwhelming. "Never has the carpet been so red," Davis happily recalled. Whenever the task force made requests, cooperation came promptly from those foundations and governmental agencies that conducted educational exchange programs.[32]

The task force convened in both New York and Washington, D.C. In the report it submitted to President Kennedy, it emphasized that "a unified and purposeful effort in educational, cultural, technical, scientific, and international cooperation programs is essential to our foreign policy objective of the achievement of peace through the extension of knowledge and understanding in the world."[33] The task force stated that a strong presidential leadership was required to create a national effort with a purpose and thrust for international educational exchange. Specifically, the task force recommended that the President of the United States should provide leadership in four directions: (1) keeping this part of foreign relations uppermost in the minds of the American people; (2) securing legislative appropriations from Congress; (3) insisting upon more coordinated and effective work within the Executive Branch; and (4) assuring other nations of the United States' continuing and unequivocal engagement with them in worldwide educational, cultural, scientific, and technical development.

The task force also suggested, among other things, the following changes: (1) the creation of an undersecretary or deputy undersecretary of state for educational and cultural affairs; (2) the provision of grants to universities and colleges for counseling, orientation to American life, English language training, and other assistance to foreign students; (3) improvement of visa regulations to place the spouse and minor children of a foreign scholar/student on the same type of visa and the extension of employment privileges of foreign students; and (4) an increase of U.S. exchange programs with the Communist-bloc European countries and an initiation of exchanges with the People's Republic of China. Kennedy was happy with all the suggestions except the one regarding China. He did not think that contact with Communist China was politically feasible at the time. Kennedy asked that the task force report be distributed to Congress and to administrative officers of the government.[34]

In addition, Kennedy sought further advice on this matter from individuals, organizations, and committees involved in exchange programs and services. He appealed personally to educational institutions, private foundations, and professional organizations for more efforts to promote educational and cultural contacts between Americans and peoples of other countries. To increase American educational influence abroad, he announced the establishment of the Peace Corps to help developing countries. Peace Corps volunteers undertook the mission of assisting the needy of foreign lands and thereby brought American influence to the masses of the developing world.[35]

The theme of the Fourth IIE Conference on Exchange of Persons held in late 1960 was "Educational Exchange for the Mutual Development of Nations." Kenneth Holland, president of the IIE, made a report to President Kennedy on the major concerns of educational exchange at the conference. Holland pointed out that participants emphasized education as a crucial means to develop human resources. Education was viewed as a keystone of economic growth and political development in all nations. Conference attendants argued that education should be given the highest priority in U.S. foreign aid programs and that it should be planned and budgeted carefully with a long-term perspective. They recommended that international and domestic non-governmental organizations should be utilized to administer the programs and "neutralize" the public and private funds. They also suggested that emphasis should be placed on building and strengthening educational institutions in the recipient nations and on the training of teachers. All of these factors, they emphasized, required the strengthening of two-way exchanges.[36]

President Kennedy's involvement in international educational exchanges gave rise to speculations that new directions in educational exchange would soon develop. The reshaping of both government and private exchange programs immediately became a popular topic in Washington. Those who were involved in international educational exchanges looked at the President's leadership in coordinating the activity as a stimulating sign. They expected that the President's interest would soon be reflected in new legislation and administrative actions with a possible increase of governmental funding. There were also growing convictions that a clear national policy was needed for international educational, technical, and cultural operations and that some major changes were needed in the agencies "that are primarily responsible for government's role in international cultural, informational and foreign aid relationships."[37]

## The Fulbright-Hays Act: A New Turning Point in International Education

President Kennedy's efforts to push for more government commitment to international educational exchange met a supportive Congress. In the late 1950s, there were major changes of leadership within congressional foreign relations committees, which helped create an encouraging environment for supporting international educational exchange. In 1959, Senator Fulbright became the chairman of the Senate Foreign Relations Committee with a group of younger Democratic senators sitting on the committee, including Michael Mansfield, Hubert Humphrey, Wayne Morse, John Kennedy, and John Sparkman. Those younger Democrats believed that "a spur should be placed under the State Department to make it move faster."[38] The change in the Foreign Relations Committee, which was regarded as a point of departure in shaping American foreign policy, brought about increased legislative support for international educational and cultural exchange activities.

In March 1961, Senator Fulbright introduced a comprehensive bill that aimed at consolidating and extending most of the previous legislation on educational and cultural exchanges. In August that year, Representative Hays introduced a companion bill in the House. The final Fulbright-Hays Act was passed by Congress on September 16, 1961 with overwhelming support, especially from the House (Senate 79–53; House 378–32), and President Kennedy signed it into law a week afterward.[39] The significance of the new legislation lay in the shift from emphasis on promoting "a better understanding of the United States in other countries" (the Smith-Mundt Act) to the new stress on increasing "mutual understanding between the people of the United States and the people of other countries." The Fulbright-Hays Act, known as the Mutual Educational and Cultural Act, had drawn on the long-term recommendations made by the President's Task Force on International Educational Exchange. The task force had worked in close collaboration with the Senate Foreign Relations Committee and testified before the House and Senate Foreign Relations Committees in support of the new legislation.[40] To a considerable extent, NAFSA contributed to the formation of this national policy on international educational and cultural exchange, because key members of the task force came from NAFSA. With the passage of the Fulbright-Hays Act, educational and political objectives of educational exchange were further integrated, because the ultimate purpose of the new legislation was "to assist in the development of friendly, sympathetic and peaceful relations between the United States and the other countries of the world" via promoting "international cooperation for educational and cultural advancement."[41]

The Fulbright-Hays Act also had a significant implication for the treatment of all foreign students in the United States, as well. The new law specifically stated that the U.S. government had interests in all foreign students, including those who were not sponsored by the United States or their own governments. According to the Fulbright-Hays Act, the American President "may make suitable arrangements, by contract or otherwise, for the establishment and maintenance at colleges and universities in the United States attended by foreign students of an adequate counseling service."[42] The law further stated that funds available for programs under the act could be used to provide for orientation courses, language training, or other appropriate services and materials and to provide or continue services to increase the effectiveness of such programs.[43]

That the U.S. government would make no distinction between government-sponsored and non-government-sponsored foreign students was a major change of policy. In the 1950s, the federal government and its agencies focused their attention only on government-sponsored students, providing them with various kinds of assistance and services that were not available to the non-government-sponsored students. And yet, the government-sponsored students constituted only about 10 percent of the total foreign student population in 1961. Moreover, more than 7,600 foreign doctors and nurses were studying and serving as staff members in more than 800 American hospitals in the early 1960s. The government's recognition of the necessity to provide the same services to the remaining 90 percent of foreign students who did not come under government sponsorship thus tremendously affected the life and education of foreign students as a whole in the United States.

Moreover, the new law indicated that the federal government not only recognized the importance of foreign student advising to the successful operation of educational exchange but also pronounced its support for services for all foreign students at American educational institutions. Hence, the Field Service Program of NAFSA began to receive funds from the government under the Fulbright-Hays Act. The Field Service Program aimed to increase the quality of foreign student advising and counseling at colleges and universities through consultations, workshops, in-service training of advisors, and other programs.[44] NAFSA was invited to provide the government with consultation and recommendations on how to expand government services to non-government-sponsored foreign students. NAFSA was also asked to work with the government on the new student visa (I-20 Form) and the improvement of visa implementation.[45]

As the largest membership organization representing American educational institutions in international education, NAFSA had conducted extensive surveys of campus services for foreign students. It also held seminars to promote research on intercultural programs and sent foreign student advisors abroad on study tours. When the government acknowledged foreign student advising as crucial in the entire endeavor to improve international educational exchange, NAFSA began to assume a new role in calling upon universities to establish offices for international education and foreign student affairs. This movement to establish an international education office, as discussed in a previous chapter, institutionalized foreign student education in the administrative structure of American higher education. Furthermore, the new government policy helped NAFSA rationalize campus participation in the new thrust of international education and prepare universities more effectively for carrying out the "mission they are being assigned in support of the national interest." As a result, NAFSA's working relations with the government increased. In keeping up with the interest and concerns of the government, NAFSA moved its headquarters from New York to Washington, D.C. in 1966.

In this new campaign of international education, what could American education contribute to shaping foreign students' pro-American attitudes? Direct indoctrination of American ideology did not seem feasible in the eyes of foreign student advisors. Experience in educating foreign students during the past several decades had demonstrated that American education impacted the students in a very personal way. Educational exchange officers believed that if the students had the freedom and the opportunity to develop themselves in this country, they would reject any system that denied the free and full development of their potentials. "He will judge in terms of what he has learned and his judgment will rise above both ideologies...His choice will be based upon what has happened to himself."[46] Because foreign student advisors played an important part in the lives of the students, the success of foreign student programs in contributing to the achievement of American national interests would be determined in large part by the individual skills of foreign student advisors and the collective effectiveness of foreign student counseling. The importance of foreign student advisors to international educational exchange and American interest in the Cold War was therefore self-evident.

The change in government policy also further integrated international education into the service of American foreign relations in the 1960s. In the public sector, the Departments of State, Defense, Health, Education, and Welfare, the United States Information Agency, and the International Cooperation Administration expanded their exchange programs with new momentum. These departments had been operating various technical, educational, and cultural exchange programs, but now their educational programs were extended to foreign diplomats. In the early 1960s, young diplomats mainly from African and Asian countries were brought to Colonial Williamsburg, Virginia to attend seminars to study mass communication, the formation of United States foreign policy, and American thought and philosophy.[47]

In the private sector, international educators spoke with great enthusiasm about the new directions in international education. NAFSA leaders reiterated the old idea that international education shaped people's attitudes and beliefs, which in turn played an important part in determining the future of a country. American universities and colleges were explicitly recruited in the effort to promote "national interest" in international affairs. The responsibilities of American colleges and universities in screening, selecting, accepting, and guiding foreign students were defined with four main objectives: (1) the strengthening of Cold War cultural diplomacy, (2) the education of future world leaders, (3) the United States' responsibility to assist developing countries, and (4) cultural interaction of American students with foreign students, particularly at the undergraduate level.[48] Colleges and universities were urged to move into the "new frontier," where they could discover additional opportunities to enhance national interest in international relations. They were also advised to apply new approaches to their new responsibility in international activities.

Funding was the major problem for universities, however. Local campuses needed money to strengthen and consolidate their educational exchange and foreign student programs. NAFSA president James Davis pointed out, "The most urgent need is for funds to strengthen the private operations at the cutting edge: in individual universities and colleges, local visitor programming agencies, and other operational agencies. Universities need matching grants to provide improved counseling, orientation, English language instruction, and emergency assistance for foreign students."[49] International education organizations such as NAFSA and the IIE had been helping campuses upgrade their services for educational exchange and foreign student affairs, but they had little leverage in providing financial resources to individual universities and colleges. All they could do was call attention to the need. NAFSA, acting as the spokesperson for colleges and universities, appealed to private foundations and to the government for financial support for this endeavor.

The government, with the mandate of the Fulbright-Hays Act, began to provide funding in the early 1960s to improve and enlarge international education programs—namely, Language and Area Studies, Comparative and Topical Studies, Professional Studies (including international programs in law, business, economics, communications, public administration, and so on), and General Education (including world history, Asian civilizations, and so on). But only a minimal amount of funds had actually been appropriated for programs related to foreign students. For instance, the first annual allocation (fiscal year 1963) under the authority of the Fulbright-

Hays Act was only $750,000 to support activities related to foreign student education. In the next two years, government support in this area declined even further to $394,000 and $395,000 in 1964 and 1965, respectively. Although the funds were so limited, they were supposed to improve a wide range of services to foreign student programs, such as the improvement of selection, placement, and overseas counseling; orientation and language instruction; the strengthening of campus programs; summer work and study programs; financial assistance for foreign students in the United States; and the strengthening of community programs.[50] Obviously, these programs suffered from the inadequate funding. International educators were torn between the encouraging governmental rhetoric and new legislation on one hand and the meager financial support that the government actually offered to help implement the programs on the other hand.

## EXTENDING THE "GREAT SOCIETY" TO THE WORLD

In the international expansion of educational and cultural exchanges, the United States had established the most productive educational relations with Western European countries. Although exchanges were conducted with countries in Latin America, Asia, and Africa, programs in these regions were relatively weak. In the 1960s, the U.S. government increased efforts in promoting educational exchanges with countries in these developing areas. Educational exchange programs were even extended to the Communist-bloc countries on a reciprocal basis.

President Lyndon Johnson continued the international educational exchange policy of the Kennedy administration with new innovations. On February 2, 1966, President Johnson sent a special message to Congress proposing to strengthen the United States' capacity for international educational cooperation. He articulated that education "must be at the heart of our international relations," because it gave every nation hope and purpose. Citing the founding fathers as passionate believers in the revolutionary power of ideas, he stressed the importance of ideas in the contemporary world: "Ideas, not armaments, will shape our lasting prospects for peace."[51] He reminded Congress and the public that "International education cannot be the work of one country. It is the responsibility and promise of all nations. It calls for free exchange and full collaboration."[52]

Specifically, President Johnson proposed four major points for his new international education plan. First, in strengthening U.S. capacity for international education cooperation through the administrative directions of the Secretary of Health, Education, and Welfare, new programs of international studies should be established in elementary and secondary schools, and competent international research and training at universities must be carried out. Second, in stimulating the exchange of students and teachers with other countries, school-to-school partnerships should be increased and educational exchange Peace Corps and American education placement services abroad should also be established. Third, in assisting the progress of education in developing nations, AID programs should be enlarged and bi-national educational foundations should be established. Fourth, in building new bridges of international understanding, international conferences of leaders and experts and a flow of books and other educational material should be increased, the quality of U.S. schools and colleges abroad should be improved, and special programs for future leaders studying in the United States should be created.[53]

The President's proposal for international education was part of a new educational initiative from the White House. President Johnson, whose other major career besides serving in Congress was as a public school teacher, had a great passion and belief in education as a means to a better human society. Since he took office as President, dozens of educational laws were enacted and federal education programs increased from about 20 to more than 100, including landmarks such as the Elementary and Secondary Education Act, the Higher Education Act, the National Endowments for the Arts and Humanities, Teachers Corps, Project Head Start, and Follow Through, in addition to college work-study programs, school breakfast, bilingual education, and so on.[54] Federal aid to schools and colleges surged from about $2 billion to more than $12 billion annually from the Kennedy administration to Johnson's.[55]

President Johnson had certainly established himself as an education President by the time he introduced the International Education Proposal. But the work of the details came from a powerful group of distinguished government officials and academicians who served as a task force for the President. Among those who played a key role in shaping the development of the International Education Act (IEA) of 1966 were Douglass Cater, a Harvard-educated journalist who worked for the President as a special assistant; Charles Frankel, a philosophy professor at Columbia University who was appointed by the President as an Assistant Secretary of State for Education and Cultural Affairs in 1965; William W. Marvel, president of Education and World Affairs—a New York-based research center for international education that offered policy recommendations to both the government and the academic communities; John W. Gardner, president of the Carnegie Corporation before joining the Johnson administration as Secretary of Health, Education, and Welfare in 1965; and Congressman John Brademas (D-IN), who had previously played a vital role in shaping such Acts such as Head Start, the Higher Education Act, and the Elementary and Secondary Education Act. This group mostly consisted of East Coast intellectuals who not only provided the ideas and worked on the specific items of the IEA but also maneuvered through the intricate political inner workings of Capitol Hill to secure the passage of the IEA.

Congress passed the International Education Act on October 21, 1966, and President Johnson signed it into law on October 29 when he was still on an official visit to Thailand. As if it were a coincidence, Johnson received an honorary degree of Doctor of Political Science from Chulalongkorn University in Bangkok on that same day. The new law began with a clear emphasis on the importance of understanding other countries as a foundation for world peace:

The Congress hereby finds and declares that a knowledge of other countries is of the utmost importance in promoting mutual understanding and cooperation between nations; that strong American educational resources are a necessary base for strengthening our relations with other countries...it is therefore both necessary and appropriate for the Federal Government to assist in the development of resources for international study and research, to assist in the development of resources and trained personnel in academic and professional fields, and to coordinate the existing and future programs of the Federal Government in international education, to meet the requirements of world leadership.[56]

The International Education Act came as one of the major commitments of the Johnson administration to transform the world into a "Great Society" through education. It intended to bring "the world into U.S. education and U.S. education into the world." At home, President Johnson had already launched a campaign to create a Great Society in America. This effort, as demonstrated through a series of new laws and government programs and funds, was mainly carried out through educational reform. In initiating the international education plan, President Johnson strongly emphasized the development of cooperative relations among educational institutions that had the capacity to implement the proposed programs. "The anticipated widespread effects of international education are enormous, and never in the recent history of international relations in education are expectations so high among those who are involved already in the fields of international, comparative, and developmental education."[57] Educators were immensely encouraged by the President's leadership in international education and the passage of the IEA by Congress.

The International Education Act authorized, among other things, grant programs for advanced and undergraduate international studies. Grants under Title I of the law "may be used to cover part or all of the cost of establishing, strengthening, equipping, and operating research and training" centers of advanced international studies. The grants could also be used to pay stipends to individuals undergoing training in such centers and the cost of visiting scholars and faculty. For the undergraduate programs in international studies, the federal government would provide institutions of higher learning with grants to plan, develop, and carry out specific activities to improve undergraduate instruction in international studies. The International Educational Act authorized Congress to appropriate $40 million for the fiscal year 1967 and $90 million for 1968 for the implementation of the provisions of international studies.[58]

With strong political support and financial promises from the federal government, universities and colleges across the country began to re-examine their existing programs and design new ones to enlarge their international studies programs. As educational leaders and international educators anticipated the arrival of increased federal funds for international programs, many universities established new international education programs beyond their academic resources and administrative abilities in order to get government money. In regions where institutions of higher learning were limited, universities formed regional consortia within a state or within a region across states to develop stronger programs than they could individually offer.[59] Universities and colleges, which had scarce external funding for international education programs, eagerly looked forward to the funds from the federal government.

## CONGRESS'S FAILURE TO APPROPRIATE THE FUNDS

No appropriations of funds from Congress were forthcoming, however. The International Education Act, ironically, was renewed for two more years despite the fact that no money was ever appropriated. It was all lip service. Several reasons were cited for the failure of Congress to appropriate the funds for international studies programs that apparently embodied worthy educational as well as national political objectives. On the part of Congress, there was confusion concerning the purposes of the 1966 International Education Act. Some thought that the act would primarily benefit foreign trainees through technical assistance, although the large purpose of the act was to increase the international dimension of American education. To justify their inaction to provide financial support for international education, some Congressmen publicly condemned the act as a foreign aid gimmick.[60] Critics contended that the increase of international education programs would be made at the expense of drastic cuts in domestic educational programs and that "children of servicemen and Negroes...would suffer seriously reduced educational opportunities...while considerably increased educational benefits would be made available to foreign students."[61]

Second, President Johnson did not pursue the world version of the "Great Society" with persistence, either. After his brilliant success in initiating the program, the President "became so distracted" by the Vietnam War. According to Paul Miller, former Assistant Secretary of Education, "the IEA just could not remain very centered in their [the President and his staff's] interest."[62] Congressional leaders refused to fund any new educational programs or agencies in the face of heavy military involvement in Vietnam. U.S. ground troops deployed in Vietnam during the time that the act was under consideration increased dramatically from 70,000 to 427,000. The Vietnam War appeared the dominant factor that shaped U.S. government policy and Congressional appropriation priorities. Moreover, the fact that Johnson was outraged at the criticism of his war policy from the academic community might also have contributed to his decreased enthusiasm in pushing Congress to fund the act. Had he done so, he would probably have had a hard time convincing Congress to go his way, because "[t]he mounting expense of the war and fears of inflation made it increasingly difficult for President Johnson to bargain on Capitol Hill."[63] The Vietnam War not only alienated the President from the public but also split the country, causing a growing crisis in presidential credibility. Additionally, the Congress that was to make the appropriations of the funds was different from the one that passed the act. In the 1966 Congressional election, more Republicans gained seats in both the House and the Senate. Even among the democrats of the Congress, more members turned against Lyndon Johnson as the Vietnam War escalated along with the surge of inflation and anti-war protests. In short, the President was facing an increasingly resistant Congress about his programs of international studies.

From another perspective, the lack of strong political clout by the academic community contributed to the failure of Congressional appropriation as the third factor. As one scholar pointed out, the majority of university presidents did nothing to convince Congress except a few who worked enthusiastically on behalf of the act. The underlying concept of the act—the expansion of international understanding among American college students—never caught the imagination of the many leaders of higher educational institutions, although most research universities with extensive international educational exchanges and centers of international studies did present a united front in support of the act. Furthermore, turf battles and competition for the limited funding from the government divided the academic community of existing international education programs. Worse than that, many colleges and universities had set up international education programs and offices only in anticipation of the promised funds of the act. These new international programs were not mature enough to develop a strong political persuasion on campus. University administrators and faculty in general basically sat there and waited for the money to come.[64] In this context, it was no wonder that Congressional leaders accused college presidents of not giving high enough priority to international studies when testifying to their needs.[65] The lack of wide support from educational leaders of higher learning guaranteed no enthusiastic lobbying from the academic community. In spite of these various factors, the fundamental problem, nonetheless, remained with many Congressmen who doubted the political value of such an educational investment.

## *FROM INTERNATIONAL TO DOMESTIC*

In the 1960s, the federal government had become the primary external sponsor of university international programs. One survey showed that in 1967, the government provided 55 percent of all financial support for international education while private foundations supplied 42 percent.[66] Historically, foundations had been the major financial source for international education in the United States, but the government—from the Eisenhower administration through Kennedy's—brought a major change in this enterprise of international education by assuming an increasing role in financial sponsorship, especially for international programs related to national security. Government funds to universities came mainly through the State Department, the Agency of International Development, and the Office of Education under the authority of the National Defense Education Act and the Fulbright-Hays Act. Universities used part of the funds as fellowships and teaching and research assistantships for foreign and American students alike, which further integrated foreign students into university research and teaching and enhanced the institutionalization of foreign students in American higher education.

But by the mid-1960s, many domestic problems—in addition to the Vietnam War—caught the attention of the government and the general public. Problems such as equal educational opportunities for the poor and minorities began to preoccupy the American public's conscience. Colleges and universities faced an increasingly heavy demand for the admission of domestic students, especially "the socially disadvantaged." In the campaign to build a Great Society, foundations and other private agencies that had been active supporters of international exchanges and international studies began to shift their attention to "urgent domestic needs." As interests and policy priorities changed, private funds for international education shrank drastically. There was a general feeling among private foundations that the federal government had a great stake in international education and that it should assume a larger role in supporting international programs. With the enactment of the 1966 International Education Act, foundations now had firm grounds to believe that the federal government would soon fund international education programs.

The failure of the Congress to appropriate the promised funds, coupled with the withdrawal of private funds, created an anti-climax in international education. Those who were involved in international education worried about the shift of interest in both the public and private sectors as "everyone with money [was] giving it to domestic problems." The disillusion was even expressed by a foundation officer: "The Very Rich (whether vieux or nouveau…) are a fickle lot. Internationalism has lost its juice."[67] Despite great efforts made by international educational organizations such as NAFSA and the IIE to reiterate the importance of continued sponsorship for international education programs, little financial support came. Universities were left to cope with their international education with limited resources, resulting in a dismal environment for international education in the United States.[68]

In conclusion, the government was vitally important to promoting international education. It mobilized the entire country for worldwide cultural and educational exchanges with political rhetoric and legislative measures in the Cold War. Effective Presidential leadership and persistent pursuit contributed to the successful implementation of new policies in the field of international education in the 1950s–1960s. Both John F. Kennedy and Lyndon B. Johnson played an active role in initiating new international education policies and programs. The Kennedy administration substantially increased federal funding for international programs. The Johnson administration attempted to extend the "Great Society" to the world by initiating sweeping educational reform policies and international studies programs. But when it came to financial support, the government was less committed. International education, important as it was for U.S. national interest in the broadest sense, had a hard time convincing Congress of its values. There were serious doubts about the usefulness of international education, and Congress would not put money in a cause unless short-term political values were evident. The constant attempts to reduce the budget for educational exchange in the 1950s and the failure of the appropriation of the IEA in the 1960s well illustrated this attitude. International educational programs often got funded only when national interest was clearly at stake and the government needed a quick fix. Federal funding for international education programs was primarily used to address practical and strategic concerns such as national defense and intelligence. International education as a long-term educational and cultural concern was a hard sell to Congress.

## NOTES

1. Charles Thomson and Walter C. H. Laves, *Cultural Relations and U.S. Foreign Policy* (Bloomington, IN: Indiana University Press, 1963), 97.

2. *Times-Herald* (Washington, D.C., October 30, 1953), second accession, State Department, series 2, educational and cultural exchange, box 14-b, Fulbright Papers.

3. Thomas G. Paterson, J. Garry Clifford, and Kenneth J. Hagan, *American Foreign Relations: A History Since 1895* (Lexington, MA: D.C. Heath and Company, 1995), 333.

4. *Gazette* (Little Rock, AR: July 25, 1953), second accession, State Department, series 2, educational and cultural exchange, box 14-b, Fulbright Papers.

5. Ibid.

6. In the 1950s, private money was the major source for exchange programs. J. Manuel Espinosa, *Landmarks in the History of the Cultural Relations Programs of the Department of State 1938–1976* (Washington, D.C.: State Department, 1976), 6.

7. Fulbright Papers, BCN 58:1.

8. "Today or Tomorrow," *The Washington Post* (May 27, 1954), second accession, State Department, series 2, educational and cultural exchange, box 14-b, Fulbright Papers.

9. Letter to the public from Style Bridges, chairman of the Senate Appropriations Committee, 9 June1954, NAFSA Association files, box 7, NAFSA Archives; Thomson and Laves, *Cultural Relations and U.S. Foreign Policy*, 118.

10. NAFSA Board of Directors Minutes, NAFSA 1:14, 25 April 1955, NAFSA Archives.

11. *Congressional Record* 101, 14 April 1955, 4,460–4,499. The Department of State, "Effects of House Cut: International Education Exchange for 1956," BCN 90:13, 16 April 1955, Fulbright Papers; Thomson and Laves, *Cultural Relations and U.S. Foreign Policy*, 118–119.

12. Mrs. Franklin Roosevelt to John Rooney, 30 April 1958, BCN 86:48, Fulbright Papers, newspaper clippings from *The Washington News,* 26 March 1958, and other newspapers (not identified).

13. Fulbright to Foster Dulles, 12 January 1956, BCN 84:27, Fulbright Papers.

14. J. L. Morrill to Fulbright, 12 May1953, BCN 90:4, Fulbright Papers.

15. Thomson and Laves, *Cultural Relations and U.S. Foreign Policy,* 105.

16. The USIA took over the information and library activities of the State Department and the information functions of the Mutual Security Agency.

17. Thomson and Laves, *Cultural Relations and U.S. Foreign Policy,* 105.

18. "Third Report of the ICA Inter-Agency Working Group on University Relationships, April 14, 1960," NAFSA Association files, box 14, NAFSA Archives; Melvin Fox, "Why Foreign Students: Need for New Look at Educational Exchange," 15 September 1961, 7, Ford Foundation Archives, Report #003166 .

19. "Report on the First & Second Meetings of the Working Group on University Relationships, June 24–July 1, 1959," NAFSA Association files, box 14, NAFSA Archives.

20. Dwight D. Eisenhower to Kenneth Holland, 16 October 1952, BCN 1:20, Fulbright Papers.

21. "Mission of USIA Defined," White House press release, statement by the President, *The U.S. Department of State Bulletin* 29 (October 28, 1953), 756.

22. *NAFSA Newsletter* (August 1956), 4; *NAFSA Newsletter* (April 1958), 20; *NAFSA Newsletter* (January 1959), 1.

23. Thomson and Laves, *Cultural Relations and U.S. Foreign Policy,* 132–133.

24. For more information on "People to People International," check http://www.ptpi.org.

25. The Comparative Education Society was founded in the fall of 1956. It became the *Comparative and International Education Society* (CIES) in September 1969 when international education was added to the society. CIES Archives, Kent State University Libraries.

26. There were 35 universities involved, including the University of California, California Institute of Technology, Case Institute of Technology, University of Chicago, University of Colorado, Columbia University, Cornell University, Harvard University, University of Illinois, Indiana University, Iowa State University, Massachusetts Institute of Technology, University of Michigan, University of Minnesota, Notre Dame University, University of Pennsylvania, Princeton University, Stanford University, Syracuse University, University of Washington, University of Wisconsin, and Yale University.

27. Second accession, series 2, BCN 14:6, Fulbright Papers.

28. Melvin Fox, "Why Foreign Students: Need for New Look at Educational Exchange," 15 September 1961, 2, Ford Foundation Archives, Report #003166.

29. "Minutes of Meeting of the NAFSA-IIE Liaison Committee, March 17–18, 1958," NAFSA Association files, box 11, 1–2.

30. Lee Zeigler, *NAFSA: Forty Years* (Washington, D.C.: National Association for Foreign Student Affairs, 1988), 11.

31. Ibid.

32. *NAFSA Newsletter* (April 1961), 2.

33. Lee Zeigler, *NAFSA: Forty Years,* 11.

34. Ibid., 11–13.

35. Many of the Peace Corps volunteers also learned a great deal from the people they came to educate. See Timothy Light, "Erasing Borders: the Changing Role of American Higher Education in the World," *European Journal of Education* 28, no. 3 (1993), 253–271.

36. Kenneth Holland to President John F. Kennedy, 25 January 1961, "Report on the 4th IIE Conference on Exchange of Persons," second accession, series 2, BCN 14:6, Fulbright Papers.

37. *NAFSA Newsletter* (January 1961), 4.

38. Letter to J. William Fulbright from J. Lash, 5 February 1959, and J. Lash, "Point of Departure" *The New York Post*, Tuesday, February 3, 1959, BCN 135:24, Fulbright Papers.

39. Public Law 256, approved on September 21, 1961, "to provide for improvement and strengthening of international relations of the United States by promoting better mutual understanding among peoples of the world through educational and cultural exchanges," *Monthly Catalog of the United States Public Documents* (November 1961), 36.

40. "NAFSA Report to the Ford Foundation for the Year Ending June 30, 1961," 1–2, Ford Foundation Archives, PA52–177.

41. *Monthly Catalog of the United States Public Documents*, 36.

42. Fulbright-Hays Mutual Educational and Cultural Exchange Act of 1961, sec. 104(e)(3), quoted in the *NAFSA Newsletter* (October 1961), 1.

43. Fulbright-Hays Mutual Educational and Cultural Exchange Act of 1961, sec. 104(e)(2), quoted in the *NAFSA Newsletter* October 1961, 1.

44. "Board Minutes November 2–3, 1962," NAFSA box 1, file 21, NAFSA Archives.

45. "Report to the Ford Foundation from the National Association for Foreign Student Affairs, July 1, 1961–June 30, 1962," Ford Foundation Archives, PA52–177.

46. *NAFSA Newsletter* (May 1961), 1–2.

47. *NAFSA Newsletter* (February 1961), 7.

48. "The Foreign Student: Whom Shall We Welcome?" memo from Maurice Harari of the Education and World Affairs to the Ford Foundation, Ford Foundation Archives, Report #003166 (1964). See also, "The Foreign Student: Whom Shall We Welcome?" The Report of the EWA Study Committee on Foreign Student Affairs (New York: Education and World Affairs, 1964) 4–5.

49. *NAFSA Newsletter* (May 1961), 2.

50. "The Foreign Student: Whom Shall We Welcome?" (1964), 9.

51. Lyndon B. Johnson, "Remarks at the Smithson Bicentennial Celebration, September 16, 1966," in Theodore M. Vestal, *International Education: Its History and Promise for Today* (Westport, CT: Praeger, 1994), Appendix I, 184.

52. Lyndon B. Johnson, "Special Message to the Congress Proposing International Education and Health Programs, February 2, 1966," in Vestal, *International Education*, 188.

53. Ibid., 188–194.

54. Vestal, *International Education*, 31.

55. Hugh Davis Graham, *The Uncertain Triumph: Federal Education Policy in the Kennedy and Johnson Years* (Chapel Hill, NC: University of North Carolina Press, 1984), xix.

56. Sec. 2, International Education Act of 1966, Public Law 89–698, Vestal, *International Education*, Appendix II, page 198.

57. Stewart E. Fraser, "Some Aspects of University Cooperation in International Education," *Educational Imperatives in a Changing Culture*, ed. William Brickman (Philadelphia, PA: University of Pennsylvania Press, 1967), 187.

58. Sec. 101, Sec. 102, and Sec. 105, International Education Act of 1966, Vestal, *International Education*, Appendix II, 199–201.

59. Irwin T. Sanders et al., *Bridges to Understanding* (New York: McGraw-Hill, 1970), 7.

60. Ibid., 7–8. Vestal, *International Education*, 102–104.

61. Robert Allen and Paul Scott, "Exporting of Great Society Would Curtail Educational Aid," *The State Journal* III, no. 296, (Lansing, MI, February 17, 1966), A-10. See also William Brickman, ed., *Educational Imperatives in a Changing Culture,* 187–188.

62. Vestal, *International Education,* 107.

63. Ibid., *International Education,* 102, 107–108.

64. Ibid., 119–120.

65. Sanders et al., *Bridges to Understanding,* 8.

66. *A Crisis of Dollars: The Funding Threat to International Affairs in U.S. Higher Education,* report of a survey conducted by Irwin T. Sanders (New York: Education and World Affairs, 1968), 45. The survey was conducted among 36 universities that had major international studies programs.

67. Memo to Sutton from Robert Edwards, n. d., Ford Foundation Archives, PA67–191.

68. Foreign students did not stop coming to the United States, however. After a few years of flat flow, the number of foreign students began to increase significantly again from 1975, due to several factors. One of them was the rapid economic growth in several student-sending regions such as the Middle East, Japan, Southeast Asia, and Latin America. The new global economic structure emerging in the 1970s made it possible for more individuals from developing countries to come to the United States by themselves. Because the new global economy relied heavily on high technology and modern science, there was an increasing demand for high tech personnel in the fast developing nations. Human capital became vital to national development. The U.S. position of leadership in world technology and sciences made American higher education extremely attactive to many potential students.

At the same time, Amercian domestic cohort for college enrollment was declining. A considerable number of American higher educational institutions needed foreign students to fill in their student bodies and maintain academic competitiveness, which led them to more serious recruiting of foreign students. Educational institutions increasingly handled their international education issues, such as educational exchange and foreign students, on their own with little promotion from such external forces as the government and foundations.

# Appendix

## Foreign Students in the United States, 1921–1980

**Table A.1**

**Foreign Students in the United States, 1921–1945**

| Year | 1921–1922 | 1922–1923 | 1923–1924 | 1924–1925 | 1925–1926 | 1926–1927 | 1927–1928 | 1928–1929 | 1929–1930 |
|---|---|---|---|---|---|---|---|---|---|
| Students | 6488 | 7494 | 6988 | 7518 | 6961 | 7541 | 8955 | 9685 | 10,033 |
| Year | 1930–1931 | 1931–1932 | 1932–1933 | 1933–1934 | 1934–1935 | 1935–1936 | 1936–1937 | 1937–1938 | 1938–1939 |
| Students | 9961 | 8688 | 6849 | 5805 | 5887 | 5641 | 7342 | 7253 | 6004 |
| Year | 1939–1940 | 1940–1941 | 1941–1942 | 1942–1943 | 1943–1944 | 1944–1945 | | | |
| Students | 6630 | 7152 | 7500 | 8056 | 7244 | 7542 | | | |

Sources: *Annual Report of the Director of the Institute of International Education*, 1928, 1929, 1930, 1936, 1941, 1943, and 1945. IIE reprinted the annual surveys of foreign students by the Committee on Friendly Relations among Foreign Students.

**Figure A.1**
**Foreign Students in the United States, 1921–1945**

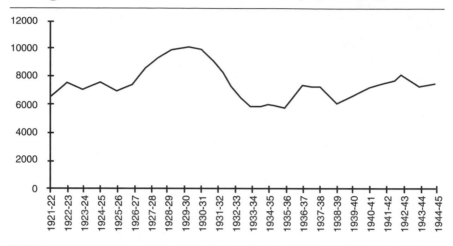

Sources: Compiled from *Annual Report of the Director of the Institute of International Education*, 1928, 1929, 1930, 1936, 1941, 1943, and 1945.

**Table A.2**
**Foreign Students in the United States, 1945–1980**

| Year | 1944–1945 | 1946–1947 | 1947–1948 | 1948–1949 | 1950–1951 | 1951–1952 | 1952–1953 | 1953–1954 | 1954–1955 |
|---|---|---|---|---|---|---|---|---|---|
| Students | 6,954 | 14,942 | 17,218 | 26,759 | 29,813 | 31,100 | 33,675 | 33,833 | 34,232 |

| Year | 1955–1956 | 1956–1957 | 1957–1958 | 1958–1959 | 1959–1960 | 1960–1961 | 1961–1962 | 1962–1963 | 1963–1964 |
|---|---|---|---|---|---|---|---|---|---|
| Students | 36,494 | 40,666 | 43,391 | 47,245 | 48,486 | 53,107 | 58,081 | 64,705 | 74,814 |

| Year | 1964–1965 | 1965–1966 | 1966–1967 | 1967–1968 | 1968–1969 | 1969–1970 | 1970–1971 | 1971–1972 |
|---|---|---|---|---|---|---|---|---|
| Students | 82,045 | 82,709 | 100,262 | 110,315 | 121,362 | 134,959 | 144,708 | 140,126 |

| Year | 1972–1973 | 1973–1974 | 1974–1975 | 1975–1976 | 1976–1977 | 1977–1978 | 1978–1979 | 1979–1980 |
|---|---|---|---|---|---|---|---|---|
| Students | 146,097 | 151,066 | 154,580 | 179,340 | 203,070 | 235,510 | 263,940 | 286,340 |

Sources: Data prior to 1954 came from *Education for One World* (New York: IIE, 1952–1954); data after 1954 came from *Open Doors* (New York: IIE, 1989), 17. Please note the number for 1945 in this table did not match that of Table 0.1 because they came from different sources.

**Figure A.2**
## Foreign Students in the United States, 1945–1980

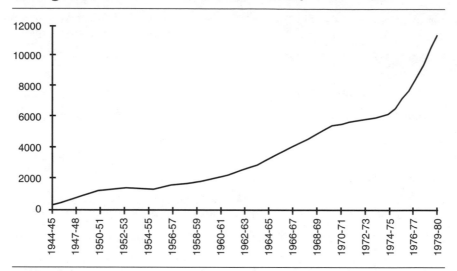

Sources: Data prior to 1954 came from *Education for One World* (New York: IIE, 1952–1954); data after 1954 came from *Open Doors* (New York: IIE, 1989), 17.

# Selected Bibliography

## ARCHIVAL SOURCES

Annual Conference Files, 1942–1979, NAFSA Archives, Special Collections of University of Arkansas Libraries, Fayetteville, AR. (NAFSA Archives were not completely processed yet in 1993 when I did research there, but they are processed now.)

Anson Phelps Stokes Family Papers, RG #299, Manuscripts, the Sterling Memorial Library, Yale University Archives, New Haven, CT.

Archives of the World Student Christian Federation, RG #46, Yale Divinity School Library Special Collections, New Haven, CT.

Associational Files, 1949–1980, NAFSA Archives, Special Collections of University of Arkansas Libraries, Fayetteville, AR.

Benjamin Schmoker Oral History, YMCA Archives, University of Minnesota Libraries, St. Paul, MN.

Charles Hurrey Papers, YMCA Archives, University of Minnesota Libraries, St. Paul, MN.

Collection of Archives of the Chinese Student Christian Association in North America, YMCA Archives, University of Minnesota Libraries, St. Paul, MN.

Collections of Archives of the Committee on Friendly Relations among Foreign Students, YMCA Archives, University of Minnesota Libraries, St. Paul, MN. (The collections were not finally processed when I did research there in 1993. A special arrangement was made with archivist Dagmer Getz.)

Collection of the Chinese Student Christian Association in North America, RG #13, Yale Divinity School Library Special Collections, New Haven, CT.

CU Collections: Archives of the Bureau of the Educational and Cultural Affairs of the Department of State. (The CU Collections were not completely processed when I did the research in 1993.) Special Collections of University of Arkansas Libraries, Fayetteville, AR.

East-West Exchange, YMCA Archives, University of Minnesota Libraries, St. Paul, MN.

Foreign Student Advisor, RG #25, Special Collections of Teachers College, Columbia University, New York.

Foreign Student and Intercultural Activities, University of Pittsburgh Archives, University Libraries Special Collections, Pittsburgh, PA.

Fulbright Papers, Special Collections of University of Arkansas Libraries, Fayetteville, AR.

General Education Board Collection, series 1, Rockefeller Archive Center, North Tarrytown, NY.

Grants to the IIE, Ford Foundation Archives, New York.

Grants to NAFSA, Ford Foundation Archives, New York.

Grants to YMCA—the Committee on Friendly Relations among Foreign Students, Ford Foundation Archives, New York.

Herald Papers, Ford Foundation Archives, New York.

International Education Board Collection, series 1, Rockefeller Archive Center, North Tarrytown, NY.

International House Chicago Archives, Chicago. (The archives were not processed, and I did the research through a special arrangement.)

International House New York Archives, New York. (The archives were not processed, and I did the research through a special arrangement.)

John R. Mott Papers, RG #45, Yale Divinity School Library Special Collections, New Haven, CT.

Laura Spelman Rockefeller Memorial Collection, series 3, Rockefeller Archive Center, North Tarrytown, NY.

Melvin Fox Oral History, Ford Foundation Archives, New York.

*NAFSA Newsletters* 1952–1979, NAFSA Headquarters, Washington, D.C.

NAFSA: Association of International Educators Records, Manuscript Collection 715, NAFSA Archives, Special Collections of University of Arkansas Libraries, Fayetteville, AR.

Official Records (including minutes, bylaws, reports, and guidelines) 1948–1979, NAFSA Archives, Special Collections of University of Arkansas Libraries, Fayetteville, AR.

Paul Monroe Papers, RG #28, Special Collections of Teachers College, Columbia University, New York.

President's Reports, Columbia University, 1910–1948, Columbiana, Columbia University Archives, New York.

Registra's Reports, Columbia University, 1948–1974, Columbiana, Columbia University Archives, New York.

Rockefeller Family Archives, Record Group 2 (omr), educational interests series. Rockefeller Archive Center, North Tarrytown, NY. (Rockefeller Family Archives on International Houses were not processed when I did the research at RAC in 1993. I was able to examine the archives with the special permission and assistance of the archivist, Mr. Thomas Rosenbaum.)

Ruth Crawford Mitchell Papers, University of Pittsburgh Archives, University Libraries Special Collections, Pittsburgh.

*The Unofficial Ambassadors* (Annual Report of the Committee on Friendly Relations among Foreign Students) 1929–1953, YMCA Archives, University of Minnesota Libraries, St. Paul, MN.

William F. Russell Papers, RG #6, Special Collections of Teachers College, Columbia University, New York.

## REPORTS AND YEARBOOKS

*Annual Report of the Ford Foundation,* 1950–1970.
*Annual Report of the Rockefeller Foundation,* 1918–1950.

*Carnegie Endowment for International Peace Yearbook.* Washington, D.C.: CEIP, 1919–1925.

*Conference on International Student Exchanges.* Ann Arbor, MI, May 10–12, 1948.

*Dean's Report,* Teachers College Bulletin, 1923–1938, Special Collections of Teachers College, Columbia University, New York.

*Education for One World.* New York: IIE, 1950–1954.

*Open Doors.* New York: IIE, 1952–1994.

*Report of the Conference of Foreign Student Advisers.* Cleveland, April 28–30, 1942.

*Report of the Conference on International Educational Exchanges.* Congress Hotel, Chicago, March 22–25, 1950.

*Report of the Conference on International Educational Exchanges.* Denver, April 11–14, 1951.

*Special Report: The National Association of Foreign Student Advisers Annual Meeting.* Wade Park Manor, Cleveland, March 28–30, 1949.

*The Annual Report of the Director of the Institute of International Education,* 1920–1950.

*The Unofficial Ambassadors.* Annual Report of the Committee on Friendly Relations among Foreign Students, 1924–1956.

*Yearbook of International House New York,* 1926–1934.

## SECONDARY SOURCES

Arnove, Robert F. *Philanthropy and Cultural Imperialism: The Foundations at Home and Abroad.* Bloomington, IN: Indiana University Press, 1982.

*The Autobiography of Fukuzawa Yukichi.* Translated by Eiichi Kiyooka. Tokyo: Hokuseido Press, 1960.

Bailey, Thomas. *A Diplomatic History of the American People.* New York: Appleton-Century Crofts, 1964.

Bereday, George Z. F. *Comparative Method in Education.* New York: Holt, Rinehart and Winston, 1964.

Berghahn, Volker R. *America and the Intellectual Cold Wars in Europe.* Princeton, NJ: Princeton University Press, 2001.

Bjork, Richard Emil. "The Changing Roles of American Universities in International Relations: A Study of Certain Perceptions of Universities' International Activities and the Impacts of Such Activities on Universities' Participation in International Relations." Ph.D. dissertation, Michigan State University, 1961.

*Blueprint for Understanding: A Thirty Year Review.* New York: Institute of International Education, 1949.

Bok, Derek. *Higher Learning.* Cambridge, MA: Harvard University Press, 1986.

———. *Universities and the Future of America.* Durham, NC: Duke University Press, 1990.

Booth, Ken, ed. *Statecraft and Security: The Cold War and Beyond.* New York: Cambridge University Press, 1998.

Brademas, John. *The Politics of Education: Conflict and Consensus on Capitol Hill.* Norman, OK: University of Oklahoma Press, 1987.

Brickman, William W. *Introduction to the History of International Relations in Higher Education.* New York: New York University, 1960.

———, ed. *Educational Imperatives in a Changing Culture.* Philadelphia: University of Pennsylvania Press, 1967.

Brink-Gabler, Gisela, ed. *Encountering the Other(s): Studies in Literature, History, and Culture.* Albany, NY: State University of New York Press, 1995.

Bronfenbrenner, Martin. *Academic Encounter: The American University in Japan and Korea.* New York: Free Press of Glencoe, 1961.

Burn, Barbara B. *Expanding the International Dimension.* San Francisco: Jossey-Bass, 1980.

Butler, Nicholas M. *The International Mind: An Argument for the Judicial Settlement of International Disputes.* New York: Charles Scribner's Sons, 1912.

Capen, Samuel Paul. *Opportunities for Foreign Students at Colleges and Universities in the United States.* United States Bureau of Education, Bulletin no. 27, Washington, D.C.: Government Printing Office, 1915.

Chatfield, Charles. *For Peace and Justice, Pacifism in America, 1914-1941.* Knoxville, TN: The University of Tennessee Press, 1971.

Cherrington, Ben M. "Ten Years After," *Association of American Colleges Bulletin* 34, no. 4 (December, 1948).

Chester, Eric Thomas. *Covert Network: Progressives, the International Rescue Committee, and the CIA.* Armonk, NY: M. E. Sharpe, 1995.

Chomsky, Noam, et al., eds. *The Cold War and the University: Toward an Intellectual History of the Postwar Years.* New York: New Press, 1997.

———. *Objectivity and Liberal Scholarship.* Detroit: Black and Red, 1997.

Cieslak, Edward Charwood. *The Foreign Student in American Colleges: A Survey and Evaluation of Administrative Problems and Practice.* Detroit: Wayne University Press, 1955.

Close, Kathryn. "That Brotherhood May Prevail," *The International House Quarterly* (Autumn, 1944).

Cole, Fred. *International Relations in Institutions of Higher Education in the South.* Washington, D.C.: American Council on Education, 1958.

*The College and World Affairs.* New York: The Ford Foundation, 1964.

Colligan, Francis J. "Twenty Years After: Two Decades of Government-Sponsored Cultural Relations," *The U.S. Department of State Bulletin* 39 (1958).

Committee on Educational Interchange Policy. *African Students in the United States.* New York: IIE, 1960.

———. *College and University Programs of Academic Exchange.* New York: IIE, 1960.

———. *Expanding University Enrollments and the Foreign Student.* New York: IIE, 1957.

———. *Foreign Professors and Research Scholars at U. S. Colleges and Universities.* New York: IIE, 1963.

———. *Orientation of Foreign Students: Signposts for the Cultural Maze.* New York: IIE, 1956.

Coombs, Philip. *The Fourth Dimension of Foreign Policy: Educational and Cultural Affairs.* New York: Harper and Row, 1964.

Cremin, Lawrence, et al. *A History of Teachers College, Columbia University.* New York: Columbia University Press, 1954.

*A Crisis of Dollars: The Funding Threat to International Affairs in U.S. Higher Education.* New York: Education and World Affairs, 1968.

Curti, Merle. *American Philanthropy Abroad.* New Brunswick, NJ: Transaction Books, 1963.

———. *Peace or War: The American Struggle, 1636–1936.* Boston: J. S. Canner, 1959.

Daniels, Roger. *Coming to America.* New York: HarperCollins, 1990.

Davis, Jerome Dean. *A Maker of New Japan, Rev. Joseph Hardy Neesima.* New York: Fleming H. Revell Company, 1894.

Divine, Robert A. *Eisenhower and the Cold War.* New York: Oxford University Press, 1981.

Du Bois, Cora. *Foreign Students and Higher Education in the United States.* Washington, D.C.: American Council on Education, 1956.

Duggan, Stephen. *A Professor at Large.* New York: Macmillan, 1943.

Epstein, E. H. "Comparative and International Education: Overview and Historical Development," *The International Encyclopedia of Education* vol. 2, 2nd ed. Edited by Husén, Torsten, and T. Neville Postlethwaite. New York: Pergamon, 1994.

————. *Landmarks in the History of the Cultural Relations Programs of the Department of State, 1938–1976.* Washington, D.C.: State Department, 1976.

Espinosa, J. Manuel. *The Inter-American Beginnings of U.S. Cultural Diplomacy, 1936–1948.* Washington, D.C.: State Department, Bureau of Educational and Cultural Affairs, History Studies, Government Printing Office, 1976.

*Excerpts from the Memoirs of Harry Edmonds.* New York: International House, 1983.

Finn, Chester E. *Scholars, Dollars, and Bureaucrats.* Washington, D.C.: Brookings Institution, 1978.

Fisher, Edgar J. *Counseling the Foreign Student.* IIE Pamphlet series, no. 5. New York: IIE, March 1943.

Fonte, John, and Andre Ryserson. *Education for America's Role in World Affairs.* Lanham, MD: University Press of America, 1994.

*The Foreign Student: Whom Shall We Welcome?* New York: Education and World Affairs, 1964.

*Forty Years of Educational Exchange, 1919–1959.* 39th Annual Report of IIE, 1959.

————. *John D. Rockefeller, Jr.: A Portrait.* New York: Harper and Brothers, 1956.

Fosdick, Raymond Blaine. *The Story of the Rockefeller Foundation.* New York: Harper, 1952.

Foucault, Michel. *Power/Knowledge: Select Interviews and Other Writings, 1972–1977,* ed. Colin Gordon, trans. Colin Gordon et al. Brighton, Sussex: Havester Press, 1980.

Fraser, Stewart E., and William W. Brickman, eds. *A History of International and Comparative Education.* Glenview, IL: Scott, Foresman and Company, 1968.

Fraser, Stewart, ed. *Governmental Policy and International Education.* New York: John Wiley and Sons, 1965.

*The Fulbright Experience and Academic Exchanges.* Newbury Park, CA: Sage Publications, 1987.

Fuller, C. Dale. *Training of Specialists in International Relations.* Washington, D.C.: American Council on Education, 1957.

Gange, John. *University Research on International Affairs.* Washington, D.C.: American Council on Education, 1958.

Gardner, John. *Aid and the Universities.* New York: Education and World Affairs, 1964.

Geiger, Roger. *To Advance Knowledge: The Growth of American Research Universities, 1900–1940.* New York: Oxford University Press, 1986.

Geyelin, Philip. *Lyndon B. Johnson and the World.* New York: Praeger, 1966.

————. "Shame on US? Academics, Cultural Transfer, and the Cold War—A Critical Review," *Diplomatic History* 24, no. 3, (Summer 2000).

Gienow-Hecht, Jesicca C. E. *Transmission Impossible: American Journalism as Cultural Diplomacy in Postwar Germany, 1945–1955.* Baton Rouge, LA: Lousiana State University, 1999.

Glad, Betty. *Charles Evans Hughes and the Illusions of Innocence.* Urbana, IL: University of Illinois Press, 1966.

Gladieux, Lawrence E., and Thomas R. Wolanin. *Congress and the Colleges.* Lexington, MA: Lexington Books, 1976.

Gordon, Lynn. *Gender and Higher Education in the Progressive Era.* New Haven, CT: Yale University Press, 1990.

Graham, Hugh Davis. *The Uncertain Triumph: Federal Education Policy in the Kennedy and Johnson Years.* Chapel Hill, NC: University of North Carolina Press, 1984.

Grassmuck, George. *Sectional Biases in Congress on Foreign Policy.* The Johns Hopkins University Studies in Historical and Political Science, LXVIII. Baltimore: The Johns Hopkins University Press, 1950.

Gray, George W. *Education on an International Scale.* New York: Harcourt, Brace and Company, 1941.

Groennings, Sven, and Davis S. Wiley, eds. *Group Portrait: Internationalizing the Disciplines.* New York: The American Forum, 1990.

Gruber, Carol. *Mars and Minerva: World War I and the Uses of the Higher Learning in America.* Baton Rouge, LA: Louisiana State University Press, 1975.

Gumperz, Ellen. *Internationalizing American Higher Education: Innovations and Structural Change.* Berkeley, CA: University of California, Center for Research and Development in Higher Education, 1970.

Gutek, Gerald L. *American Education in a Global Society: Internationalizing Teacher Education.* White Plains, NY: Longman, 1993.

Hahn, Emily. *The Soong Sisters.* New York: Doubleday, 1944.

Hallam, Elizabeth, and Brian V. Street, eds. *Cultural Encounters: Representing "Otherness."* London and New York: Routledge, 2000.

Halpern, Stephen Mark. "The Institute of International Education: A History." Ph.D. dissertation, Columbia University, 1969.

Harr, John E., and Peter Johnson. *The Rockefeller Century.* New York: Scribner's, 1988.

Hawley, Ellis Wayne. *The Great War and the Search for a Modern Order.* Prospect Heights, IL: Waveland Press, 1997.

Hewlett, Theodosia. *A Decade of International Fellowships.* New York: IIE, 1930.

Higbee, Homer D. *The Status of Foreign Student Advising in the United States Universities and Colleges.* East Lansing, MI: Institute of Research on Overseas Programs, Michigan State University, 1961.

Hixson, Walter L. *Parting the Curtain: Propaganda, Culture, and the Cold War, 1945–1961.* New York: St. Martin's Griffin, 1997.

Hogan, Michael J. "Corporatism: A Positive Appraisal," *Diplomatic History* 10 (Fall 1986).

———, ed. *America in the World: The Historiography of American Foreign Policy since 1941.* New York: Cambridge University Press, 1995.

———. *The Ambiguous Legacy: U.S. Foreign Relations in the "American Century."* Cambridge [Eng.]; New York: Cambridge University Press, 1999.

Hoh, Yam Tong. "The Boxer Indemnity Remissions and Education in China." Ph.D. dissertation, Teachers College, Columbia University, 1933.

Hopkins, C. Howard. *20th Century Ecumenical Statesman: John R. Mott, 1865–1955, A Biography.* Grand Rapids, MI: William B. Eerdmans Publishing Company, 1979.

Houle, Cyril, and Charles Nelson. *The University, the Citizen, and World Affairs.* Washington, D.C.: American Council on Education, 1956.

Hu Shi, "John Dewey in China," *Philosophy and Culture—East and West: Philosophy in Practical Perspective.* Honolulu, HI: University of Hawaii Press 1958.

Humphrey, Richard A., ed. *Universities and Development Assistance Abroad.* Washington, D.C.: The American Council on Education, 1967.

Hunter, Allen, ed. *Rethinking the Cold War.* Philadelphia: Temple University Press, 1998.

Hurrey, Charles. "Foreign Students in the United States," *International Law and Relations* VI, no. 9, 1937.

Immerman, Richard H., ed. *John Foster Dulles and the Diplomacy of the Cold War.* Princeton, NJ: Princeton University Press, 1990.

*Institute of International Education: Its Origin, Organization and Activities.* New York: IIE Bulletin no. 1, Ninth series, March 1, 1928.

*International House Berkeley: An Informal History.* Berkeley, CA: International House Berkeley, 1990.

Iriye, Akira. "Culture and Power: International Relations and Intercultural Relations," *Diplomatic History* 10 (Spring 1979).

———. *Cultural Internationalism and World Order*. Baltimore: The Johns Hopkins University Press, 1997.

———. *The Cambridge History of American Foreign Relations* III, Cambridge University Press, 1993.

Jenkins, Hugh M., et al. *Educating Students from Other Nations: American Colleges and Universities in International Interchange*. San Francisco: Jossey-Bass Publishers, 1983.

Johnson, Walter, and Francis J. Colligan. *The Fulbright Program: A History*. Chicago: The University of Chicago Press, 1965.

———. *The Impact of the War upon American Education*. Chapel Hill, NC: University of North Carolina, 1948.

Kandel, Issac L. *United States Activities in International Cultural Relations*. Washington, D.C.: American Council on Education, 1945.

Kearns, Doris. *Lyndon Johnson and the American Dream*. New York: Harper and Row, 1976.

Keenan, Barry. *The Dewey Experiment in China*. Cambridge: MA: Harvard University Press, 1977.

Kiang, Wen-Han. *The Chinese Student Movement*. New York: King's Crown Press, 1948.

Kramer, Hilton. *The Twilight of the Intellectuals: Culture and Politics in the Era of the Cold War*. Chicago: I. R. Dee, 1999.

Kraske, Gary E. *Missionaries of the Book: The American Library Profession and the Origins of United States Cultural Diplomacy*. Westport, CT: Greenwood Press, 1985.

Kroes, R., et al. *Cultural Transmissions and Receptions*. Amsterdam, Netherlands: VU University Press, 1993.

Lagemann, Ellen Condliffe. *The Politics of Knowledge: The Carnegie Corporation, Philanthropy, and Public Policy*. Middletown, CT: Wesleyan University Press, 1989.

Latourette, Kenneth S. *World Service: A History of the Foreign Work and World Service of the Young Men's Christian Associations of the United States and Canada*. New York: Association Press, 1957.

Lemons, J. Stanley. *The Woman Citizen: Social Feminism in the 1920's*. Urbana, IL: University of Illinois Press, 1973.

Lowen, Rebecca S. *Creating the Cold War University: The Transformation of Stanford*. Berkeley, CA: University of California Press, 1997.

Mason, Edward S. *Foreign Aid and Foreign Policy*. New York: Harper and Row, 1964.

Mathews, Basil. *John R. Mott, World Citizen*. New York: Harper and Brothers, 1934.

May, Ernest R. *Anxiety and Affluence: 1945–1965*. New York: McGraw-Hill Book Company, 1966.

———. *Imperial Democracy: the Emergence of America as a Great Power*. New York: Harcourt, Brace and World, 1961.

McCaughey, Robert. *International Studies and Academic Enterprise: A Chapter in the Enclosure of American Learning*. New York: Columbia University Press, 1984.

McMurry, Ruth E., and Muna Lee. *The Cultural Approach—Another Way in International Relations*. Chapel Hill, NC: University of North Carolina Press, 1947.

Metraux, Guy S. *Exchange of Persons: The Evolution of Cross-Cultural Education*. New York: Social Science Research Council, 1952.

Michie, Allan A. *The University Looks Abroad*. New York: Walker and Co., 1965.

Monroe, Paul. "'The Cross-Fertilization of Culture:' The Function of International Education." *News Bulletin,* Institute of Pacific Relations, Honolulu, HI (February 1928).

Neave, Guy, ed. *The Universities' Responsibilities to Society: International Perspectives.* New York: Pergamon, 2000.

Ninkovich, Frank, and Liping Bu. *The Cultural Turn: Essays in the History of U.S. Foreign Relations.* Chicago: Imprint Publications, 2001

Ninkovich, Frank A. *The Wilsonian Century: U.S. Foreign Policy Since 1900.* Chicago: University of Chicago Press, 1999.

————. *U.S. Information Policy and Cultural Diplomacy.* New York: Foreign Policy Organization, 1996.

————. *The Diplomacy of Ideas.* Cambridge [Eng.]; New York: Cambridge University Press, 1981.

Nye, Joseph S. *Bound to Lead: The Changing Nature of American Power.* New York: Basic Books, 1990.

Ou, T. C. "Dewey's Influence on China's Efforts for Modernization." Jamaica, NY: Center of Asian Studies at St. John's University, 1978.

Paterson, Thomas G., J. Garry Clifford, and Kenneth J. Hagan. *American Foreign Relations, A History Since 1895.* Lexington, MA: D. C. Heath and Company, 1995.

Pells, Richard H. *Not Like Us.* New York: Basic Books, 1997.

————. *The Liberal Mind in a Conservative Age.* New York: Harper and Row, 1985.

Pierson, Harry H. "Are We Ready for the Postwar Foreign Students?" *The Educational Record,* Washington, D.C.: The American Council on Education (April 1945).

Prevots, Naima. *Dance for Export: Cultural Diplomacy and the Cold War.* Middletown, CT: Wesleyan University Press, 1998.

*The Record: International Exchange* 6, no. 5. Washington, D.C.: The Department of State, September–October 1950.

*Report of the United States Commissioner of Education for the Year 1904* 2, Washington, D.C.: Government Printing Office, 1906.

Robertson, David. "International Relations of the United States." *Educational Record* 6 (1925).

Robin, Ron Theodore. *The Making of the Cold War Enemy: Culture and Politics in the Military-Intellectual Complex.* Princeton, NJ: Princeton University Press, 2001.

Rosenberg, Emily S. *Spreading the American Dream.* New York: Hill and Wang, 1982.

Ryan, Alan. *John Dewey and the High Tide of American Liberalism.* New York: W. W. Norton, 1995.

Sanders, Irwin T., et al. *Bridges to Understanding.* New York: McGraw-Hill, 1970.

Saunders, Frances Stoner. *The Cultural Cold War: The CIA and the World of Arts and Letters.* New York: New Press, 1999.

Schantes, Robert S. *Japanese and Americans: A Century of Cultural Relations.* New York: Harper, 1955.

Selltiz, Claire, et al. *Attitudes and Social Relations of Foreign Students in the United States.* Minneapolis: University of Minnesota Press, 1963.

Simpson, Christopher, ed. *Universities and Empire: Money and Politics in the Social Sciences During the Cold War.* New York: W.W. Norton, 1998.

Slater, David, and Peter J. Taylor, eds. *The American Century: Consensus and Coercion in the Projection of American Power.* Malden, MA: Blackwell, 1999.

Smith, Douglas. "An Impact Analysis of John Dewey and His China Experience." Paper presented at the 1995 Shanghai International Symposium on "Important Issues in Sino-American People's Friendly Exchanges Since the 19th Century." Shanghai, 1995.

Smith, Tony. *Foreign Attachments: The Power of Ethnic Groups in the Making of American Foreign Policy.* Cambridge, MA: Harvard University Press, 2000.

Speakman, Cummins. *International Exchange in Education.* New York: The Center for Applied Research in Education, 1966.

Spence, Jonathan D. *The Search for Modern China.* New York: W. W. Norton, 1999.

Spencer, Cornelia. *Three Sisters: The Story of the Soong Family of China.* New York: John Day Co., 1939.

Stephanson, Anders. *Manifest Destiny: American Expansionism and the Empire of Right.* New York: Hill and Wang, 1995.

Stone, I. F. *The Truman Era 1945–1952.* Boston: Little, Brown, 1972.

Swift, Richard N. *World Affairs and the College Curriculum.* Washington, D.C.: American Council on Education, 1959.

Taft, John. *American Power: The Rise and Decline of U.S. Globalism, 1918–1988.* New York: Harper and Row, 1989.

Tchen, John Kuo Wei. *New York before Chinatown: Orientalism and the Shaping of American Culture, 1776–1882.* Baltimore and London: The Johns Hopkins University Press, 1999.

Thompson, Mary A., ed. *Unofficial Ambassadors: The Story of International Student Service.* New York: International Student Service, 1979.

Thomson, Charles, and Walter H. C. Laves. *Cultural Relations and U.S. Foreign Policy.* Bloomington, IN: Indiana University Press, 1963.

*Twenty Years of the Foreign Policy Association.* New York: The Foreign Policy Association, 1939.

Tyack, David. *The One Best System.* Cambridge, MA: Harvard University Press, 1974.

*The University and World Affairs.* New York: The Ford Foundation, 1960.

Vestal, Theodore M. *International Education: Its History and Promise for Today.* Westport, CT: Praeger, 1994.

Veysey, Laurence. *The Emergence of the American University.* Chicago: University of Chicago Press, 1965.

Wagnleitner, Reinhold. *Coca-Colonization and the Cold War.* Chapel Hill, NC: University of North Carolina Press, 1994.

Wala, Michael. *The Council on Foreign Relations and American Foreign Policy in the Early Cold War.* Providence, RI: Berghahn Books, 1994.

Warrick, W. Sheridan. "International Houses and Centers," *The International Encyclopedia of Higher Education* 4. Edited by Asa S. Knowles, San Francisco: Jossey-Bass, 1977.

Weidner, Edward W. *The World Role of Universities.* New York: McGraw-Hill, 1962.

Wheeler, William Reginald, Henry Hall King, and Alexander Barkolow Davidson, eds. *The Foreign Student in America.* New York: Association Press, 1925.

Williams, William Appleman. *The Tragedy of American Diplomacy.* New York: W.W. Norton, 1972.

Wilson, Howard, and Florence Wilson. *American Higher Education and World Affairs.* Washington, D.C.: American Council on Education, 1963.

Wilson, Howard. *American College life as Education in World Outlook.* Washington, D.C.: American Council on Education, 1956.

Wing, Yung. *My Life in China and America.* New York: Henry Holt and Company, 1909.

Wood, Richard H. *U.S. Universities: Their Role in AID-Financed Technical Assistance Overseas.* New York: Education and World Affairs, 1968.

Zeigler, Lee. *NAFSA: Forty Years.* Washington, D.C.: National Association for Foreign Student Affairs, 1988.

# Index

**About the Author**

LIPING BU is Associate Professor of History at Alma College. She is co-editor of *The Cultural Turn: Essays in the History of U.S. Foreign Relations.*

## DATE DUE